P9-CEY-334

REFERENCE

American Revolution Biographies

Volume 2: K–Z

American Revolution Biographies

Linda Schmittroth
and
Mary Kay Rosteck
Stacy A. McConnell, Editor

AN IMPRINT OF THE GALE GROUP
DETROIT · SAN FRANCISCO · LONDON
BOSTON · WOODBRIDGE, CT

Linda Schmittroth and Mary Kay Rosteck

Staff

Stacy McConnell, *U•X•L Editor*
Judy Galens, *U•X•L Contributing Editor*
Carol DeKane Nagel, *U•X•L Managing Editor*
Thomas L. Romig, *U•X•L Publisher*

Margaret Chamberlain, *Permissions Specialist (Pictures)*

Rita Wimberley, *Senior Buyer*
Evi Seoud, *Assistant Production Manager*
Dorothy Maki, *Manufacturing Manager*

Tracey Rowens, *Senior Art Director*

LM Design, *Typesetting*

Library of Congress Cataloging-in-Publication Data

Schmittroth, Linda

American Revolution : biographies / Linda Schmittroth and Mary Kay Rosteck ; edited by Stacy McConnell.

p. cm.

Includes bibliographical references and index.

Summary: Profiles sixty men and women who were key players on the British or American side of the American Revolution.

ISBN 0-7876-3792-0 (set) — ISBN 0-7876-3793-9 (v. 1). — ISBN 0-7876-3794-7 (v. 2)

1. United States—History—Revolution, 1775-1783—Biography—Juvenile literature. [1. United States—History—Revolution, 1775-1783—Biography.] I. Rosteck, Mary Kay. II. McConnell, Stacy A. III. Title.

E206 .S36 2000

973.3'092'2—dc21 99-046941

CIP

Front cover photographs (top to bottom): Crispus Attucks reproduced courtesy of the Library of Congress; Patrick Henry reproduced courtesy of the Library of Congress.

Back cover photograph: Mount Vernon reproduced by permission of the Detroit Photographic Company.

Printed in the United States of America

10 9 8 7 6 5 4 3 2 1

Contents

Volume 1: A-J

Volume 2: K-Z

Advisory Board

Special thanks are due for the invaluable comments and suggestions provided by U•X•L's American Revolution Reference Library advisors:

- Mary Alice Anderson, Media Specialist, Winona Middle School, Winona, Minnesota.
- Jonathan Betz-Zall, Children's Librarian, Sno-Isle Regional Library System, Edmonds, Washington.
- Frances Bryant Bradburn, Section Chief, Information Technology Evaluation Services, Public Schools of North Carolina, Raleigh, North Carolina.
- Sara K. Brooke, Director of Libraries, Ellis School, Pittsburgh, Pennsylvania.
- Peter Butts, Media Specialist, East Middle School, Holland, Michigan.

Reader's Guide

American Revolution: Biographies presents biographies of sixty men and women who took part in, influenced, or were in some way affected by the American Revolution. Among the people profiled in each of the two volumes are American patriots and presidents; colonists who remained loyal to England; Native Americans, royalty, politicians, scoundrels, and military officers from foreign nations who helped or hindered the American fight for freedom; writers, poets, and publishers; and heroic colonial women who wrote, took up arms, acted as spies, or raised funds for American independence.

American Revolution: Biographies not only includes the biographies of such famous patriots as George Washington, Benjamin Franklin, John Adams, Samuel Adams, Thomas Paine, and Thomas Jefferson, it also features the life stories of less celebrated people such as Phillis Wheatley, renowned poet and former slave; Frenchman Pierre Charles L'Enfant, who designed the city of Washington, D.C.; Deborah Sampson, a woman who donned a military uniform and served as an army soldier; and Frederika von Riedesel, a German who chronicled the Revolution while traveling throughout the colonies with her young family as her husband fought for the British.

Other features

American Revolution: Biographies also highlights interesting people with ties to the main biography subjects, and adds details that help round out events of the Revolutionary period. Each entry contains cross-references to other individuals profiled in the two-volume set, and each offers a list of sources—including web sites—for further information about the individual profiled. A timeline and glossary introduce each volume and a cumulative subject index concludes each volume.

American Revolution: Biographies has two companion volumes: *American Revolution: Almanac,* which describes in narrative form the events leading up to the war and the major events of the war; and *American Revolution: Primary Sources,* which contains excerpts from more than thirty Revolutionary-era documents.

Acknowledgments

The authors wish to thank Mary Reilly McCall, who contributed encouragement, enthusiasm, and several biographies to this set.

Comments and suggestions

We welcome your comments on this work as well as your suggestions for topics to be featured in future editions of *American Revolution: Biographies*. Please write: Editors, *American Revolution: Biographies,* U•X•L, 27500 Drake Rd., Farmington Hills, MI 48331-3535; call toll-free: 1-800-877-4253; fax: 248-414-5043; or send e-mail via www.galegroup.com.

Timeline of Events in Revolutionary America

1754 Start of the French and Indian War, pitting the French and their Indian allies against the British for control of North America.

1760 **George III** becomes King of England.

1762 James Otis Jr., brother of **Mercy Otis Warren**, publishes a pamphlet arguing for a limitation on Parliament's right to interfere with colonial affairs.

1763 French and Indian War ends with a British victory. To appease Native Americans, King **George III** forbids colonial settlement west of the Appalachian Mountains.

1765 In March, King **George III** approves the Stamp Act, which taxes the American colonies to pay for the French and Indian War. **Horace Walpole**, British Member of Parliament, opposes the Stamp Act before Parliament and speaks out for the rights of American colonists.

In July, Boston patriots ("Sons of Liberty") unite in opposition to the Stamp Act. In August, a mob destroys the house of Massachusetts Lieutenant Governor Thomas Hutchinson to protest the act.

In September, **Deborah Read Franklin** defends her property when an angry mob outside her home protests that her husband, **Benjamin Franklin**, has not fought vigorously enough against the Stamp Act.

In October, delegates at a Stamp Act Congress adopt **John Dickinson**'s Declaration of Rights and Grievances, protesting the Stamp Act.

1766 The British government repeals the Stamp Act and replaces it with the Declaratory Act, asserting England's right to make laws that colonists must obey.

British politician **William Pitt** makes a famous speech in Parliament, declaring his opinion that Britain "has no right to lay a tax upon" the American colonies.

1767 In June, British politician **Charles Townshend** pushes through Parliament the Townshend Acts, imposing new taxes on American colonists.

In December, **John Dickinson**'s "Letters from a Farmer in Pennsylvania" appear in colonial newspapers, protesting Parliament's power to tax the colonies.

1768 In February, **Samuel Adams** writes a letter opposing taxation without representation and calls for the colonists to unite against British oppression.

In May, British troops arrive in Boston to enforce the Townshend Acts.

In June, tax collectors seize **John Hancock**'s ship the *Liberty* and sell its cargo.

1769 **George Mason**'s *Virginia Resolves,* which opposes British taxation and other policies, is presented to Virginia lawmakers.

1770 **Benjamin Rush** publishes the first American chemistry textbook.

Hector St. John de Crèvecoeur begins writing the pieces that are later published as *Letters from an American Farmer.*

In March, during the Boston Massacre, five colonists are killed by British soldiers, including a black man named **Crispus Attucks.**

In April, most of the Townshend Acts are repealed by Parliament, except the tax on tea.

In October, **John Adams** and Josiah Quincy successfully defend British soldiers on trial for firing shots during the Boston Massacre.

In November, at the urging of **Samuel Adams,** a committee of correspondence is formed in Boston; it issues a declaration of rights and a list of complaints against British authorities.

1772 **Mercy Otis Warren**'s patriotic play *The Adulateur* is published.

1773 **Phillis Wheatley**'s *Poems on Various Subjects, Religious and Moral* is published in London and sold in Boston.

In May, the Tea Act, a new tea tax, takes effect.

In December, patriots protest the Tea Act by throwing crates of tea into Boston Harbor (the Boston Tea Party).

1774 In March, Parliament passes the Intolerable Acts to punish Boston for the Boston Tea Party.

In May, British General **Thomas Gage** replaces Thomas Hutchinson as Royal Governor of Massachusetts.

In September, the First Continental Congress meets in Philadelphia to discuss the tense situation with Great Britain.

In October, Massachusetts lawmakers, including **John Hancock**, begin war preparations.

1775 In March, British politician **Edmund Burke** gives his speech "On Conciliation" before Parliament, urging the British government to settle differences with colonists. **Patrick Henry** gives a famous speech to Virginia lawmakers explaining why Virginia must arm a citizen army to confront the British.

In April, Massachusetts governor **Thomas Gage** is told to put down the "open rebellion" of the colonists using all necessary force. **Paul Revere** rides to Concord and Lexington to warn the patriots that British soldiers are on the way. The first shots of the Revolutionary War are fired between Minutemen and British soldiers at Concord. The British retreat to Boston. British politician **John Wilkes** presents a petition to King **George III** protesting his treatment of the colonies.

In May, Governor **Thomas Gage** imposes martial law in Massachusetts. The Green Mountain Boys, led by **Benedict Arnold** and **Ethan Allen,** capture Fort Ticonderoga in New York. The Second Continental Congress meets in Philadelphia and appoints **John Hancock** its president. **Mary Katherine Goddard** becomes publisher of *Maryland Journal* and keeps colonists informed about events in the fight for independence.

In June, **George Washington** is appointed commander-in-chief of a new Continental army. Before he arrives in Boston, patriots are defeated by British at the Battle of Bunker Hill.

In July, **George Washington** takes command of Continental army outside Boston. The Continental Congress approves **John Dickinson**'s Olive Branch Petition calling for King **George III** to prevent further hostile actions against the colonists until a reconciliation can be worked out. **Benjamin Franklin** is appointed first American Postmaster General.

In August, King **George III** declares the colonies in open rebellion against Great Britain.

In November, **James Rivington**'s print shop is burned to the ground because patriots are upset that his newspaper publishes articles presenting both sides of the quarrel between England and America.

In December, Continental army soldiers under **Benedict Arnold** fail in an attempt to capture Quebec, Canada.

King **George III** proclaims the closing of American colonies to all trade effective March 1776.

1776 In January, **Thomas Paine**'s *Common Sense* is published, in which he urges independence from England.

In March, British general **William Howe** and his troops abandon Boston for Canada; patriots reclaim Boston. **Abigail Adams** writes her famous "Remember the Ladies" letter to **John Adams.**

In May, the Continental Congress tells each of the thirteen colonies to form a new provincial (local) government.

In June, **George Mason** proposes a plan for a state government to Virginia lawmakers. **Betsy Ross** of Philadelphia is believed to design the first American stars and stripes flag.

In July, Congress adopts the Declaration of Independence. A massive British force lands in New York City to crush colonial rebellion.

In August, General **William Howe** defeats **George Washington** at the Battle of Long Island, New York. In the fighting, **Margaret Cochran Corbin** steps in and takes over firing a cannon when her soldier husband is killed by enemy fire.

In September, **Benjamin Franklin** is one of three men appointed by Congress to go to Paris to seek French assistance in the war. **Nathan Hale** is executed by the British for spying.

In October, the American navy is defeated at Battle of Valcour in Canada, in which **Benedict Arnold** commands a fleet of American ships.

In December, **George Washington**'s troops flee to Pennsylvania; fearing attack, the Continental Congress abandons Philadelphia for Baltimore. The Continental army defeats Great Britain's hired German soldiers in a surprise attack at Trenton, New Jersey.

1777 Loyalist **Flora Macdonald** refuses to take an oath of allegiance to America and loses her plantation.

In June, British general **John Burgoyne**'s troops capture Fort Ticonderoga from the Americans. **George Washington** loses at Brandywine and Germantown near Philadelphia; the British seize Philadelphia.

In July, France's **Marquis de Lafayette** is appointed major general of the Continental army. **Jane McCrea** is killed by Indians scouting for the British. Polish war hero **Casimir Pulaski** arrives to help the American cause.

In August, Mohawk Indian **Mary "Molly" Brant** reports American troop movements to the British, who then beat the Americans at the Battle of Oriskany, New York.

In September, German general Friederich von Riedesel helps the British win the first Battle of Saratoga at Freeman's Farm, New York.

In October, Polish soldier **Thaddeus Kosciuszko** helps Americans defeat General **John Burgoyne** at Saratoga, New York. Baroness **Frederika von Riedesel** and her family are captured by the Americans.

In November, the Continental Congress adopts the Articles of Confederation, America's first constitution.

In December, **George Washington**'s troops set up winter quarters at Valley Forge, Pennsylvania. France's King **Louis XVI** recognizes American independence, paving the way to openly assist the war effort.

1778 In February, France and the United States sign treaties of trade and alliance. German Baron von Steuben joins the Continental army as Inspector General and begins to train troops.

In March, the British fail at an attempt to make peace with the Americans. Frontiersman **Simon Girty** goes over to the British side.

In June, General Sir Henry Clinton (who replaced **William Howe**) abandons Philadelphia and heads for New York. On the way, he is attacked by Americans at the Battle of Monmouth, New Jersey. **Mary McCauley** ("Molly Pitcher") participates in the battle.

In July, France declares war on Great Britain.

1779 Essays and poems by **Jonathan Odell** are printed in newspapers; they encourage the Loyalists and criticize the Continental Congress.

Spain declares war on Great Britain. **Bernardo de Gálvez**, the Spanish governor of Louisiana, begins to openly aid the American cause.

1780 In May, Charleston, South Carolina, falls to British troops.

In June, Massachusetts's constitution asserts that "all men are born free and equal"; this includes black slaves. In *Sentiments of an American Woman,* **Esther De Berdt Reed** calls on colonial women to sacrifice luxuries and instead give money to the American army.

In September, **Benedict Arnold** openly goes over to the British side.

1781 In March, the Articles of Confederation are ratified by all the states.

In August, **Elizabeth Freeman**, a slave living in Massachusetts, sues and wins her freedom under the new Massachusetts constitution.

In October, British general Charles Cornwallis surrenders his troops at Yorktown, Virginia; Great Britain loses all hope of winning the Revolutionary War.

1782 **Benjamin Franklin, John Adams, John Jay**, and Henry Laurens go to France to draw up a peace treaty.

Deborah Sampson, disguised as a man, enlists in the Fourth Massachusetts Regiment and fights against the Tories and Native Americans.

1783 Mohawk Chief **Joseph Brant** and the Iroquois Confederacy begin blocking American westward expansion.

In April, Congress declares the Revolutionary War officially ended; Loyalists and British soldiers pack up their headquarters in New York City and depart for Canada or England.

In May, the Society of Cincinnati is formed by former Continental army officers. Among its early members are **George Washington**, **Alexander Hamilton**, and **Thaddeus Kosciuszko.**

In November, **George Washington** delivers a farewell speech to his army; he resigns his military commission.

1784 In January, the Treaty of Paris is ratified by Congress, bringing the Revolutionary War to an official end.

In March, **Thomas Jefferson**'s plan for dividing the western territories is adopted by Congress.

1785 In January, Congress relocates to New York City.

In February, **John Adams** becomes the first U.S. ambassador to England.

1786 In January, **Thomas Jefferson**'s Virginia Statute for Religious Freedom is passed by the Virginia legislature.

In August, **Daniel Shays** masterminds Shays's Rebellion to protest what he calls unfair taxation.

In September, the Annapolis Convention meets; **Alexander Hamilton** proposes and Congress approves his plan for a 1787 convention to replace the Articles of Confederation with a Constitution.

1787 In May, convention delegates meet in Philadelphia to rewrite the Articles of Confederation.

In July, Congress adopts the Northwest Ordinance (order), based on one written earlier by **Thomas Jefferson,** that prohibits slavery in U.S. territories and provides a method for new states to enter the union.

In October, **Alexander Hamilton, James Madison,** and **John Jay** publish the *Federalist* in defense of the new American Constitution.

1788 In February, in Massachusetts, **Samuel Adams** and **John Hancock** agree to support the new Constitution, but only if amendments will be added that guarantee civil liberties.

In June, in Virginia, **James Madison** and his followers succeed in getting ratification of the Constitution despite opposition by **Patrick Henry** and **George Mason.** The U.S. Constitution is adopted by all of the states. Congress is granted land for a new federal capital.

In July, Congress formally announces that the Constitution of the United States has been ratified and is in effect.

In September, New York City is named the temporary seat of the new U.S. government.

1789 **David Ramsay**'s *History of the Revolution* is published.

In April, **George Washington** is sworn in as the first U.S. president.

In July, the French Revolution begins in Paris. King **Louis XVI** will be beheaded in 1792 during this revolution.

In September, the U.S. Army is established by Congress.

1791 The Bill of Rights, written by **James Madison,** is passed by the U.S. Congress.

Pierre Charles L'Enfant is appointed to design the new federal capital, Washington, D.C.

1792 **Judith Sargent Murray** writes an essay stating that women are born equal to men and have the capability to enter all professions if properly educated.

1797 **John Adams** becomes the second U.S. president.

1801 **Thomas Jefferson** becomes the third U.S. president.

1912 The discovery of five skeletons near her property seems to prove true the legend that **Nancy Morgan Hart** killed five Tory soldiers during the American Revolution.

Words to Know

A

Abolitionism: The belief that measures should be taken to end slavery.

Absolutism: Also known as absolute power; a system in which one person—usually a king or queen—rules without any kind of restrictions on his or her actions.

Agent: A person who conducts business on another's behalf.

Allegiance: Loyalty to king, country, or a cause.

Articles of Confederation: An agreement among the thirteen original states, approved in 1781, that provided a loose form of government before the present Constitution went into effect in 1789.

Artillery: The science of using guns; a group of gunners in an army; or the weapons themselves, especially cannons that throw bombs across a battlefield.

Assemblies: One of the names used by the colonies for their lawmaking bodies.

B

Boston Massacre: An encounter between British troops and townspeople in Boston in 1770, before the Revolutionary War. The British fired into a crowd and five Americans were killed.

Boston Tea Party: An incident on December 16, 1773, in which Boston patriots dumped 342 chests of English tea into Boston Harbor to protest British taxes.

Boycott: A refusal to buy, sell, or use certain products from a particular company or country, usually for a political reason.

Brigadier general: A military position just below major general.

Bunker Hill, Battle of: The first great battle of the Revolutionary War, fought near Boston in June 1775. The British drove the Americans out of their fort at nearby Breed's Hill to Bunker Hill; the Americans gave up only when they ran out of ammunition, proving they were willing to take on trained British soldiers.

Burgesses: An old term for members of the British Parliament; the lawmaking body of colonial Virginia called itself the House of Burgesses.

C

Coercive Acts: The British name for the Intolerable Acts.

Colonel: A military rank below brigadier general.

Colonial: Relating to the period before the United States declared independence.

Colonial agents: Men appointed by lawmaking bodies in the colonies to live in London, England, circulate among important people, and report back on what was happening in the British Parliament. Benjamin Franklin served as an agent for several colonies.

Colonies: Territories that are settled by emigrants from a distant land and remain subject to or closely connected with the parent country.

Committees of Correspondence: Colonial groups that shared information, coordinated the activities of colonial agitators, and organized public opinion against the British government.

Committees of Safety: One of many colonial committees that had the authority to call up militias (groups of volunteer soldiers) when they were needed.

Common Sense: A pamphlet written by Thomas Paine in 1776 in which he urged the colonies to declare independence immediately.

Confederacy: A union of states.

Confederation: A group of states united for a common purpose.

Conservatives: People who wish to preserve society's existing institutions.

Continental army: An army of American colonists formed during the American Revolution.

Continental Congress: An assembly of delegates from the American colonies (later states). The delegates governed before and during the Revolutionary War and under the Articles of Confederation. The Continental Congress first met in 1774.

The Crisis: Also known as *The American Crisis,* a series of pamphlets written by Thomas Paine in which he discussed issues of the American Revolution.

D

Declaration of Independence: The document establishing the United States as a nation, adopted by the Continental Congress on July 4, 1776.

Delegates: Representatives.

Democracy: A system of government in which power belongs to the people, who rule either directly or through freely elected representatives. See also **Republic.**

"Don't fire until you see the whites of their eyes": A famous command said to have been given by either William Prescott or Israel Putnam, American officers at the Battle of Bunker Hill. In order for colonial weapons to be effective, the shooter had to be close to his victim.

Duties: Taxes on imported or exported goods.

E

Essays: Short pieces of writing that deal with a single subject.

F

Federalist: One who supports a strong central government instead of a loose organization of states.

Founding Fathers: A general name for male American patriots during the Revolutionary War, especially the signers of the Declaration of Independence and the drafters of the Constitution.

Freedom of the press: The right to circulate opinions in print without government interference.

French and Indian War: A series of military battles between Great Britain and France (and France's Indian allies) that took place on the American frontier and in Canada between 1754 and 1763.

French Revolution: An event lasting from 1789 to 1799 that ended the thousand-year rule of kings in France and established France as a republic. The American Revolution and the American experiment with democracy was an inspiration to many French people, but while the American experiment thrived, the French Revolution ended in chaos.

G

Great Britain: The island off the western coast of Europe made up of England, Scotland, and Wales. Also called "Britain" or "England."

Grievances: Complaints.

H

Hessians: Citizens of Hesse-Cassel, once a part of Germany. German soldiers (mercenaries) were hired by King George III to fight for the British in the American Revolution. Many came from Hesse-Cassel; as a result, all German soldiers were called Hessians.

I

Intolerable Acts: Four laws passed by the British government in 1774 to punish Boston for the Boston Tea Party.

Iroquois Confederacy: A union of the Mohawk, Oneida, Onondaga, Cayuga, Seneca, and Tuscarora tribes. Members were sometimes called "Iroquois" instead of their tribal names.

L

Lexington and Concord, Battle of: The first battle of the Revolutionary War, a minor skirmish fought in Massachusetts on April 19, 1775.

Loyalists: Colonists who remained loyal to England during the American Revolution; also known as Tories.

M

Martial law: Temporary rule by military authorities imposed upon regular citizens in time of war or when civil authority has stopped working. The British-appointed governor of Virginia became so angry at Patrick Henry's "give me liberty or give me death" speech that he declared martial law in Virginia.

Mercenaries: Soldiers for hire; see **Hessians.**

Militia: A military force consisting of citizens rather than professional soldiers.

Minutemen: Armed American citizens (nonmilitary) who promised to be ready to fight alongside regular soldiers at a moment's notice.

Monarchy: Rule by a king or queen.

N

Neutral: Not committed to either side of an issue.

New England: The region in the northeastern United States that includes present-day Connecticut, Maine, Massachusetts, New Hampshire, Rhode Island, and Vermont.

The name was probably given by English explorer Captain John Smith, one of the original settlers of Jamestown, Virginia (1607), because the region resembled the coast of England.

"No taxation without representation": A popular phrase of the Revolutionary War era. The colonists were not allowed to choose representatives to Parliament, which passed laws taxing the colonists. This offense against colonial rights is one of the main grievances against Great Britain listed in the Declaration of Independence.

P

Pamphlets: Reading material with paper covers.

Parliament: The British lawmaking body.

Patriot: A person who loves, supports, and defends his country.

Petition: A formal document.

Privateer: A privately owned ship authorized by the government during wartime to attack and capture enemy vessels. Privateer may also refer to the person who commands the ship.

Propaganda: Information and argument designed to influence public opinion about political matters.

Q

Quaker: A member of the religion known as the Society of Friends. Quakers oppose all violence and warfare.

Quota: A share assigned to a group. During the American Revolution, when too few men volunteered to be soldiers in the Continental army, Congress assigned a quota to each colony, representing the number of men the colony was expected to round up and send to serve in the army.

R

Radical: A person who favors revolutionary changes in a nation's political structure.

Rebel: A person who resists or defies ruling authority.

Redcoats: British soldiers who wore red uniforms.

Repealed: Done away with; especially referring to laws.

Republic: A form of government in which people hold the power and exercise it through elected representatives. Today, the words "republic" and "democracy" are used interchangeably, but in the early days of the United States, they differed in meaning. "Republic" was used to mean a system of government in which the will of the people was interpreted by representatives who might be wiser or better educated than the average person. Back then, the elected representatives had to own property.

Resolution: A formal statement of a decision or expression of opinion put before or adopted by a lawmaking assembly.

Revenue: Money collected to pay for the expenses of government.

Revolution: A sudden political overthrow; a forcible substitution of rulers.

Revolutionary War: The war for American independence from Great Britain. The fighting began with the Battle of Lexington and Concord in 1775 and lasted through the Battle of Yorktown in 1781.

S

Saratoga, Battle of: A major battle of the Revolutionary War, fought in northern New York state. It is often called the turning point of the war because the American victory there convinced France to send aid.

Satirical writing: Writing that ridicules individuals or groups by pointing out their stupidities or abuses.

Sedition: Acts or language leading to rebellion.

Self-evident: Something requiring no proof or explanation.

Separation of church and state: The principle that government must maintain an attitude of neutrality toward religion. The relationship between church and state has been the subject of argument since the first European settlers arrived in America to escape religious persecution at home.

"Shot heard 'round the world": A phrase from a July 4, 1837, poem by Ralph Waldo Emerson about the Battle of Lexington and Concord. He wrote of the determination of the colonists in standing up for their rights. This led to the establishment of a new kind of democratic nation and encouraged other peoples of the world to move toward democracy.

Skirmish: A minor encounter in war between small bodies of troops.

Stamp Act: A law passed by the British government in 1765 that required the payment of a tax to Great Britain on papers and documents produced in the colonies.

T

Thirteen colonies: The colonies that made up the original United States on the signing of the Declaration of Independence in 1776: Connecticut, Delaware, Georgia, Maryland, Massachusetts, New Hampshire, New Jersey, New York, North Carolina, Pennsylvania, Rhode Island, South Carolina, and Virginia.

Tories: Colonists who remained loyal to England during the American Revolution; also called Loyalists.

Townshend Acts: Laws passed by the British government in 1767. They included a Quartering Act, which ordered the colonies to house British troops, and a Revenue Act, which called for taxes on lead, glass, paint, tea, and other items.

Treason: Betrayal of king and country.

Tyranny: Absolute power, especially power exercised cruelly or unjustly.

U

Unalienable rights: Rights that cannot be given away or taken away.

V

Valley Forge: A valley in eastern Pennsylvania that served as quarters for the Continental army in the winter of 1777–78. General George Washington had been forced to leave the comfort of Philadelphia, and his soldiers suffered from cold and lack of supplies.

W

West Indies: A group of islands between North and South America, curving from southern Florida to Venezuela. Much trade was carried on between colonial America and British-owned islands in the West Indies. The French, Spanish, and other nations owned islands in the West Indies, too. Some Revolutionary War battles were fought there between the French and Spanish navies and the British navy.

Y

Yankee: Once a nickname for people from the New England colonies, the word is now applied to anyone from the United States.

Yorktown, Battle of: The last battle of the Revolutionary War, fought in 1781 near the Virginia coast. General Charles Cornwallis surrendered his army to General George Washington.

Thaddeus Kosciuszko

Born February 12, 1746
Breescin, Lithuania (then part of Poland)
Died October 15, 1817
Soleure, Switzerland

Polish-born American military leader

"A statesman ... must strive to give unity of action to his nation and to establish [its] respectable and strong character."

Portrait: Thaddeus Kosciuszko. *Reproduced courtesy of the Library of Congress.*

Thaddeus Kosciuszko is one of Poland's most honored patriots as well as one of America's most honored heroes. Kosciuszko came to America during the Revolutionary War to help create a new independent nation. He built vital forts, then went on to become widely admired for his kindness and military skill. Back in Poland, he led his comrades in an effort to rid his country of Russian domination. Even today, his name stands as an international symbol of the fight for liberty and human rights.

Thaddeus Kosciuszko (pronounced THAD-ee-us ko-SHOE-sko) was born in the Lithuanian region of Poland on February 12, 1746. His parents were Ludwig Kosciuszko, an army colonel (pronounced KER-nuhl) and member of the minor nobility, and Thecla Ratomska Kosciuszko. As the youngest of four sons, Kosciuszko could share in but not inherit control of the family estates, so he chose to make his career in the army.

Kosciuszko's father died in 1758, during the years Kosciuszko was being tutored by his uncle and attending Roman Catholic schools near his home. In 1765 the bright

Foreign Soldiers in the Continental Army

Throughout the Revolutionary War, General George Washington faced constant manpower and supply shortages. The situation improved after Silas Deane (1737–1789; America's first ambassador abroad) went to France in 1776 to request military assistance. The French sent supply ships, and soon there was an influx of foreign officers from throughout Europe into the American army.

Deane was not qualified to sort out the good soldiers from the bad, and he was inclined to say yes to anyone who had a noble title. The foreign officers proved to be a mixed blessing. Many were adventurers searching for fortune or reputation. Most found it difficult to adjust to American conditions, and few were willing to accept any but the highest ranks. Their arrogance caused trouble among Americans. Nevertheless, they brought with them a professional military knowledge and competence that the Continental army sorely needed. Once the misfits had been identified and placed where they could do the least harm, the foreign officers' skills were exploited by the Americans to considerable advantage.

It took time for these foreign volunteers to make their presence felt. Louis du Portail, a Frenchman, and Thaddeus Kosciuszko, a Pole, did much to advance the art of engineering in the Continental army. **Casimir Pulaski** organized its first real cavalry unit. Johann de Kalb and Friedrich Wilhelm von Steuben, both Germans, and the **Marquis de Lafayette** (see entries), a French nobleman, made valuable contributions as trainers and leaders of the Continental forces.

youth entered the Royal Military School in Warsaw, Poland, in time becoming an instructor of students. In 1768 he was made a captain, and he graduated the following year.

Kosciuszko earned a scholarship and borrowed money from his family to attend military school in Paris, France, where he studied engineering and artillery (the science of using guns). For one year he attended an art school in Paris, which helped him develop his skills as an artist and draftsman. Many of his sketches have been preserved.

Brokenhearted, leaves Poland for America

In 1774 Kosciuszko returned to Poland. Two years earlier, Prussia (a state in Germany), Russia, and Austria, three countries that surrounded Poland, had achieved a bloodless takeover of the country. They divided various sections of Poland, leaving a greatly diminished nation. Russia took over Lithuania, where the Kosciuszko family lived. Kosciuszko came home to find that the Polish army was now almost nonexistent and that his brother had squandered most of the family fortune.

While in Poland, Kosciuszko fell in love with Ludwika Sosnowska (pronounced lewd-VEE-ka sos-NOV-ska), the daughter of a wealthy nobleman. But her father, fearing that Kosciuszko had no prospects for making much money, put an end to the relationship. The brokenhearted Kosciuszko never married.

Kosciuszko lacked the funds to buy a commission (position as an officer) in the army. Seeing no future for himself in Poland, he sailed to America to obtain an officer's commission from the Continental Congress, the governing body during the American Revolution (1775–83). American Charles Henry Lee, who had served in the Polish army for five years and later held a military position in America, helped Kosciuszko obtain a commission with the Continental army, the army of the American rebels. Kosciuszko got involved in America's fight for independence out of a desire to help people resist unjust rule—a cause that he strongly supported all his life.

Serves in the American Revolution

Kosciuszko arrived at Philadelphia, Pennsylvania, in 1775, and soon went to work for the Pennsylvania Committee of Defense as an engineer. Engineers were responsible for designing and building fortifications, bridges, and other structures. He used his engineering talents to help plan and supervise the construction of forts along the Delaware River. The forts were vital to thwarting any attempt by the British navy to attack the city of Philadelphia, then America's capital city. In October 1776, Congress made Kosciuszko a colonel of engineers in the Continental army.

Later that year, Kosciuszko took part in the Battle of Ticonderoga, New York. There he advised American general Horatio Gates to fortify a site known as Bemis Heights. This was done, and the British were unable to take Bemis Heights.

Their failure played a major role in the great 1777 victory of the Americans over the British forces of General **John Burgoyne** (see entry) at Saratoga, New York.

In the spring of 1778, Kosciuszko went to West Point, New York, to oversee the construction of forts there. In 1780 he went to serve in the south under General Nathanael Greene in the Carolina campaign. He stayed there as a fighting officer and an engineer until the capture of Charleston, South Carolina, by the British in 1782.

Receives American honors, returns to Poland

In October 1783, after the Treaty of Paris was signed and the war was officially over, the Continental Congress showed its thanks to Kosciuszko. He was promoted to brigadier general, made an American citizen, and granted 500 acres of land in Ohio. General George Washington presented him with a sword and two pistols to show his appreciation for Kosciuszko's help. Washington welcomed him into the Society of the Cincinnati, an exclusive club for former Revolutionary War officers. The society was named for the heroic Roman citizen-soldier Cincinnatus. Washington also presented Kosciuszko with the antique cameo ring the Society had given to Washington.

Kosciuszko stayed for a time in New York City. With no duties to perform, he left for a brief vacation in Paris, and in 1784 returned home to Poland. There he spent several restless years in retirement in the Polish countryside. Though much of Poland was still divided among Prussia, Austria, and Russia, there had developed a strong desire for liberty among Poland's common people.

In 1789 King Stanislas of Poland asked Kosciuszko to return to active duty in the Polish army as a major general and help train young soldiers. When Russia declared war on Poland in the spring of 1792, Kosciuszko led a small and poorly supplied unit in an attempt to defend his country. But his troops met with quick defeat; he was forced to flee Poland and went to France. There he sought financial help for the rebel Poles. But France was in the middle of a revolution and could not help.

In 1794 Kosciuszko returned to Poland, where he led a victorious uprising of Polish citizens. He was chosen to be the country's leader. He instituted reforms that granted much greater freedom to individuals than had previously been permitted. But before long, a large and well-armed Russian force defeated his soldiers and put down the rebellion.

Kosciuszko was captured and sent to a prison near St. Petersburg, Russia. He was released by Russian Czar (emperor) Paul I in November 1796. After he promised never again to take up arms against Russia, he was exiled. Kosciuszko traveled to several European countries, then returned to a hero's welcome in America in 1797. Congress gave him a considerable amount of back pay it owed him. Kosciuszko used the money to buy black slaves in America and give them their freedom.

Works for freedom of Poland

In 1799 Kosciuszko returned to France. There he wrote an account of his war experiences in America, a major study of the horse artillery, and a variety of articles, including one concerning democracy.

From 1799 to 1815 Napoleon Bonaparte engaged in a series of battles, called the Napoleonic Wars, to establish a French empire throughout Europe. In 1806 Napoleon asked for Kosciuszko's help in the invasion of Russia, but Kosciuszko, having given his word to the Russian czar, refused. Poland did join in the fighting.

The Napoleonic Wars ended in 1815 with the downfall of Napoleon, by then the emperor. During that time, Kosciuszko met in Paris with Czar Alexander of Russia (who succeeded Paul I in 1801). He tried to gain the czar's support for the restoration of an independent Polish nation and an amnesty (forgiveness without penalties) for Polish patriot prisoners of Russia. But despite his agreement and promises to Kosciuszko, the czar failed to deliver.

The Congress of Vienna, made up of representatives of various European powers, met in Austria in 1815. There they signed a peace treaty that settled the wars. The treaty readjusted territories throughout the continent and restored the European monarchies Napoleon had overthrown. It also established the "Kingdom of Poland," a tiny country that belonged to Russia and was subject to its laws, and distributed the rest of Poland among Russia, Austria, and Prussia.

During that time, Kosciuszko spoke out in favor of Polish democracy. In 1816 he freed the serfs on his Polish estate. Serfs were workers, often farm laborers, who were bound to the land by the lord who owned it. They could neither be thrown off the land nor leave it voluntarily.

Final years in Switzerland

Kosciuszko decided that he could no longer bear to live in his greatly diminished homeland. On a visit to Switzerland, he became friends with Francis Xavier Zeltner, brother of the Swiss ambassador, who invited him to come and stay with his family in Soleure (pronounced so-LUR), Switzerland. Soleure was a pretty city at the base of the Jura Mountains.

Kosciuszko took up residence with the Zeltners, and before long he was like a member of the family. He spent his time riding horses and reading history and geography books. On October 15, 1817, Kosciuszko died after a brief illness. His remains were returned to Poland and buried at the cathedral at Cracow.

The people of Poland mourned Kosciuszko as a national hero. He had directed in his will that his lands in Ohio be sold and the profits used to free American slaves. The money also went to found the Colored School at Newark, New Jersey, one of the first schools for black students established in the United States.

Thomas Jefferson (see entry), who was a friend of Kosciuszko, once wrote of his admiration for "the purity of [Kosciuszko's] virtue, the [kindness] of his heart, and his sincere devotion to the cause of liberty." The French Duke de la Rochefoucauld-Liancourt (pronounced ROWSH-foo-ko LEE-en-cor) wrote about the Polish hero in his personal diary: "There is no heart friendlier to liberty, or an admirer of virtue and talent, in whom the name of Kosciuszko does not excite sentiments of interest and respect.... Elevation and sentiment, grandeur, sweetness, force, goodness, all that commands respect and homage, appear to me to be concentrated in this celebrated and interesting [man]."

For More Information

Abodaher, David J. *Warrior on Two Continents: Thaddeus Kosciuszko.* New York: Julian Messner, 1968.

"Kosciuszko, Tadeusz." *Webster's American Military Biographies.* Springfield, MA: G. & C. Merriam Co. Publishers, 1978, pp. 221-22.

"Kosciuszko, Thaddeus." *Who Was Who During the American Revolution.* Compiled by the editors of *Who's Who in America.* Indianapolis: Bobbs-Merrill Co., Inc., 1976, p. 502.

Pula, James S. *Thaddeus Kosciuszko: The Purest Son of Liberty.* New York: Hippocrene Books, 1999.

"Tadeusz Andrzej Bonawentura Kosciuszko." *Encyclopedia of World Biography.* Suzanne M. Bourgoin and Paula K. Byers, eds. Detroit: Gale Research, 1998, vol. 9, p. 88.

Ward, Harry M. "Kosciuszko, Tadeusz Andrzej Bonawentura." *American National Biography.* John A. Garraty and Mark C. Carnes, eds. New York: Oxford University Press, 1999, vol. 12, pp. 884-85.

Marquis de Lafayette

Born September 6, 1757
Chavaniac, France
Died May 20, 1834
Paris, France

French military leader, politician

"At the first news of this quarrel my heart was enrolled in it."

Portrait: Marquis de Lafayette. *Reproduced by permission of the National Portrait Gallery.*

Among the heroes of the Revolutionary War (1775–83), only the name of **George Washington** (see entry) ranks higher than that of the Marquis de Lafayette, the renowned Frenchman who put his life and fortune at the disposal of the American rebels in their fight with England. Although his political skills were sometimes not equal to his lofty purposes, he had an important influence on the creation of new governments in both America and his French homeland. Lafayette supported social equality, representation of the common people in government, religious tolerance, and freedom of the press, which was unusual for a person of his time and class in society.

For centuries, members of the wealthy Motier (pronounced mo-TYAY) family of French nobles lived at the family mansion in the province of Auvergne (pronounced oh-VAIRN), France. There Marie Joseph Paul Yves Roch Gilbert du Motier (pronounced Muh-REE jo-SEFF pole eve rowsh jheel-bair duh mo-TYAY) was born on September 6, 1757. The Motiers were known by their noble title of La Fayette; the American spelling of the family's title is Lafayette, and the American pronunciation is lah-fee-YET. Marie Joseph Motier is usually called simply Lafayette.

When Lafayette was two years old, his father was killed in a military battle. His mother died of an illness some years later. From his mother and her family, the young man inherited the title of marquis (pronounced mar-KEE) and a sizable fortune.

The wealthy orphan boy was shy and awkward. He was educated at the highly respected College du Plessis in Paris, and in 1771, he joined the French army. At that time in history, when the average life span was much shorter than it is today, important life events such as beginning a career and marriage typically took place at much younger ages than they do now.

In 1773, at age sixteen, Lafayette married fourteen-year-old Adrienne de Noailles (pronounced ay-dree-EN duh no-ELL), who was the daughter of a wealthy noble family and a relative of French royalty. Lafayette retired from the army after only five years, with the rank of captain. He then became part of the court life at Versailles (pronounced ver-SIGH), France, the extravagant castle where the royal family lived.

The tremendously wealthy teenager was not content to simply settle into the life of luxury at the court. When the Revolutionary War (1775–83) broke out in America, Lafayette decided to put his talents and military experience in the service of America against England, France's historic enemy.

Young noble goes to America

As a member of nobility, Lafayette had to request the king's permission to go to America and fight. Lafayette's father-in-law opposed the idea, and King **Louis XVI** (see entry) refused the request. Lafayette sailed off anyway, using his own money to buy and equip a ship. When the seventeen-year-old Frenchman presented himself to America's Continental Congress, the revolutionary government, Congress was cool to him. But when he offered to serve in the army at his own expense, Congress relented and made him a major general, with the understanding he would not command any soldiers. He was sent to serve as the chief aide to General **George Washington** (see entry), head of the Continental army.

By this time, the red-haired Frenchman had reached his full height of six feet tall. He was graceful and had angular features, smiled easily, and was said to excel at conversation because he devoted his entire attention to the person with whom he was speaking.

Lafayette soon grew to love and respect Washington, who became a father figure to him. He was always ready and willing to do whatever his commander requested to help the American cause. In return, the general took an immediate liking to the young man, but at first he did not know what to do with him. At that point, Lafayette spoke little English and had never engaged in active warfare, but he was most anxious to command American troops in battle. Lafayette spent the difficult winter of 1777–78 with Washington and his troops at Valley Forge, Pennsylvania. He used the time to improve his English and his knowledge of military tactics.

Takes command of division, returns to France

Lafayette turned out to be a good fighter and a wise adviser to Washington. He performed well at battles in New Jersey and Pennsylvania, but in September 1777 he was shot in the thigh. The wound established his bravery in the eyes of American soldiers, and on his recovery, Lafayette was placed in charge of a division of American troops. In helping him to get that appointment Washington had written to Congress, "it appears to me, from a consideration of his ... important connexions, [and] the attachement which he has [shown] for our cause ... that it will be advisable to gratify his wishes [to gain a command].... Besides, he is sensible, [has fine manners], has made great [strides in mastering] our language,... and possesses a large share of bravery and military ardor."

In 1778 George Washington sent Lafayette back to France to try to drum up support for the American cause. When he arrived in his homeland in 1779, Lafayette immediately went to the Palace of Versailles, where his wife and family were living. Lafayette was placed under arrest because he had disobeyed the king and gone to America. But because he was able to give the king a first-hand report about what was happening in America (instead of just rumors), all was forgiven.

Lafayette insisted that more financial aid should be granted to the Americans. The king honored this request. Lafayette had also suggested that France invade England, Ire-

Lafayette was wounded at the Battle of Brandywine in September 1777. Lafayette bravely endured his injury, stayed with his troops, and assisted their retreat. Upon his recovery, he was placed in charge of a division of the American troops. *Reproduced by permission of Archive Photos, Inc.*

land, or Canada to divert England from the war in America; that soldiers be hired from the Swedish navy to serve in America; and that a large loan be gotten from Holland to help finance the war. The King refused these schemes. Lafayette returned to America in April 1780.

Plays important role in final days of war

In 1781 General Washington placed Lafayette in charge of the defense of Virginia. When the major fighting of the war moved from the North to Virginia, Lafayette played a crucial role in trapping the English commander, General Charles Cornwallis, at Yorktown, Virginia. On October 19, 1781, Cornwallis surrendered, an event that brought America's war of independence to a military conclusion.

Yorktown was the high point of Lafayette's career as a soldier. He returned to France in 1782, where he was honored as a hero and made a general in the French army.

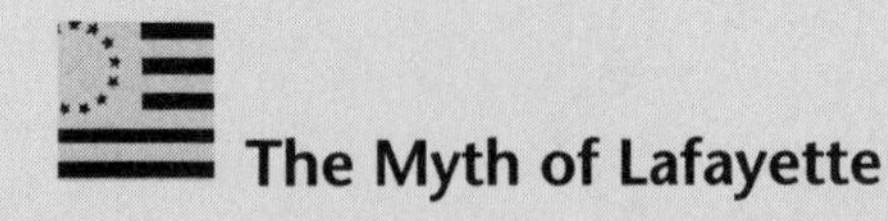

The Myth of Lafayette

The Marquis de Lafayette has long been celebrated in America as a French noble who came to fight out of love for the ideals of liberty. But according to research done by Louis R. Gottschalk, one of Lafayette's biographers, this is an exaggeration. Gottschalk claimed that Lafayette came to America because he was frustrated and dissatisfied with affairs in France at the time. Gottschalk also pointed out that Lafayette desired glory and the opportunity to get revenge on France's long-time enemy, England.

Gottschalk claims that the image of Lafayette as the idealistic hero was the product of Americans who wanted to use him for purposes of propaganda (as a tool to influence people to have positive ideas about the American Revolution) and to obtain military aid from France. But other historians go further. In its *Guide to the Study of the U.S.A.: Representative Books Reflecting the Development of American Life and Thought,* the Library of Congress stated: "Once Lafayette became the symbol, he lived the role to such an extent that the symbol became the reality, and in later years, Lafayette deserved the [honor] of being the outstanding liberal of his day." A liberal is a person who supports forms of government in which rule is by the common people and their representatives, rather than by kings and queens or absolute rulers.

In 1784, George Washington invited Lafayette back to the United States for a visit. Over the next several years, the friendship Lafayette had established between America and France proved valuable to the new nation. For example, Lafayette was able to assist **Thomas Jefferson** (see entry), then U.S. Minister to France, with several political and economic matters.

Arrives home in time for French Revolution

Lafayette had a love of liberty and equality that was not common among noble Europeans of his time. He was wildly enthusiastic about America, where his ideals of freedom were becoming a reality. His time in America had only served to strengthen Lafayette's commitment to democratic principles.

Lafayette returned to France at a time when the system of rule by kings and queens was being challenged in Europe.

He became a political leader in the movement against absolutism (pronounced ab-so-LUTE-ism) in France. Absolutism is a system in which one person—usually a king or queen—rules without any kind of restrictions on his or her actions. In such a system, common people are easily abused by wicked or thoughtless leaders. This was the case in France, where the citizens suffered from unfair taxation and a terrible shortage of food. Lawlessness had reached such a point that French citizens were often the victims of armed bands of criminals roaming the countryside.

In 1787 and 1788 Lafayette joined a group of French nobles who were in favor of a new way of governing in France. In 1789 he was present at a meeting of nobles, clergymen, and representatives of the common people. The meeting was called to decide what should be done about the terrible financial difficulties France was facing at that time. At the end of the meeting, the common people declared themselves the true rulers of France, and the French Revolution (1789–99) began.

When the king seemed resistant to the idea of the common people ruling France, French workers stormed the Bastille (pronounced bah-STEEL), a prison in Paris where for centuries inmates had been held and tortured. That same day, June 14, 1789, Lafayette, then the most popular man in France, was appointed head of the National Guard, an organization of citizen-soldiers formed to carry forward the French Revolution.

Lafayette's opinions were widely listened to and respected during the first months of the French Revolution. On his recommendation, the French Declaration of the Rights of Man and the Citizen, a document patterned on the American Declaration of Independence, was adopted. But as French mobs grew more unruly and Lafayette seemed to go against them, popular opinion towards him changed.

Supports parliamentary monarchy, loses National Guard post

Lafayette's popularity began to wane after he rescued Queen Marie-Antoinette (pronounced an-twah-NET) from a mob attack on the Palace of Versailles on October 5, 1789. Lafayette may have been a foe of absolutism, but he also opposed violence toward the royal family. His popularity declined further when he voiced his support for a new type of government like the one used in England, a parliamentary monarchy.

In a parliamentary monarchy, a king or queen performs ceremonial functions but is not the head of the government. The government is ruled by parliament, a group of representatives who have the power to make and carry out laws on behalf of all the people. The type of parliamentary monarchy favored by Lafayette would be based on a formal written constitution, like the one adopted in the United States in 1789.

In discussions about what form a new government would take, Lafayette had to deal with people who held very extreme views. They wanted to see a new form of government put in place, but they also wanted to see violence done to the king and queen. Lafayette's was a voice of reason in arguing for a parliamentary monarchy and against doing violence to the king and queen, but his views did not endear him to the radicals.

In the spring of 1791, King Louis XVI and his wife tried to escape from France. In a show of support for the revolutionaries, Lafayette issued orders to stop them. The pair were arrested and imprisoned. A period of even greater chaos followed the end of the monarchy, a period that tested Lafayette's political skills to the utmost. He was very disturbed by the growing violence of the revolution.

On October 8, 1791, Lafayette ordered his National Guard troops to put down a mob in Paris. His troops refused to follow his orders, and Lafayette was forced to retire from command of the National Guard.

Falls further out of favor with radical French leaders

In 1792 a war pitted France against Austria and Prussia (a former German state). For a short time, Lafayette was popular again, until he led 52,000 troops in an unsuccessful invasion of Belgium. He returned with his troops to Paris to protest to the government about a July 20 mob attack on the French royal family. His protest was not well received by either the government or his troops.

By that time, France was being ruled by a radical group called the Jacobins (pronounced JACK-uh-bins). They accused

Lafayette of planning to turn his troops against them, and on August 10, 1792, they proclaimed Lafayette a traitor. To escape arrest and possible execution, Lafayette fled to Belgium with a number of fellow officers.

In Belgium, Lafayette was treated as a prisoner-of-war and held captive by the Austrians and Prussians for five years. For two of the five years, his beloved wife Adrienne stayed with him in prison. The hardships she suffered there forced her to leave and led to her death in 1807 at the age of forty-eight. She left behind four children. Henriette (pronounced hen-ree-ET) was born in 1775; Anastasie (pronounced on-uh-STAH-zee) was born in 1777; George Washington was born in 1779; and Virginie (pronounced ver-jhuh-NEE) was born in 1782.

Lafayette was released from prison in 1797 at the request of Napoleon Bonaparte, a French general and political leader. Napoleon had risen through the ranks of the French army and crowned himself Emperor of France in 1804. Though he released him, Napoleon would not allow Lafayette to return to France; he may have looked upon the former hero as a threat to his hold on France.

Returns to France and lives quietly there

Lafayette returned to France without permission in 1799. With the rise of Napoleon, Lafayette no longer held any political power and his personal fortune had been lost. The French military provided him with a military pension (a yearly payment for his service) as a retired general and he went to live quietly at his country estate at Lagrange, forty-three miles from Paris. Bonaparte softened his position toward Lafayette and offered him opportunities to become a senator, receive the French national award called the Legion of Honor, or become minister to the United States. But Lafayette turned them all down because he did not approve of Napoleon. To show his disapproval, in 1802 he was one of only a small number who voted against granting Napoleon's wish to be made First Consul, head of the government of France for life.

In 1805 Lafayette rejected an offer by President Thomas Jefferson that he become Governor of Louisiana in the United States. He preferred to stay in his beloved France and did not want it to appear that Napoleon could drive him out.

Lafayette did not resume public life in France until 1814, when he was elected to the Legislative Chamber, France's lawmaking body. He was the first to demand Napoleon's final and permanent departure as head of the government. Napoleon was overthrown in 1815 after a disastrous defeat by the British army at Waterloo, Belgium. Napoleon was then permanently exiled (forced to live away from France).

Serves in French government, revisits America

In 1815 the Bourbon family returned to the French throne with the crowning of King Louis XVIII. He was the brother of Louis XVI, who with his wife Marie-Antoinette had been beheaded during the French Revolution. Their son, Louis XVII, had died in a prison cell. Upon the death of Louis XVIII, his older brother ascended to the throne, ruling as Charles X until his death in 1830. During the two kings' reigns, from 1818 to 1824, Lafayette served in the branch of the French government called the Chamber of Deputies. He was a member of the party that opposed royalty.

In 1824 Lafayette stepped down from public life when the government of the United States invited him to visit America. During his fifteen-month tour, he met with wide acclaim and appreciation. The U.S. Congress presented Lafayette with a gift of $200,000 and a large piece of land, which, in time, brought him a sizable profit. Lafayette returned to France in 1825 hailed as a hero on both sides of the Atlantic.

Lafayette returned to public life in 1830, at the outbreak of a second revolution in France, after the people decided they no longer wanted their country ruled by a monarchy. At that time, Lafayette became the symbol of moderate republicanism (a system in which the power is held by voters, whose policies are carried out by representatives elected by them). Lafayette was asked to head the National Guard that had driven Charles X from France. He refused a demand by the French public that he become president of the new republic. Instead, he decided to support a man named Louis Phillipe, who was called the "citizen king." Louis Phillipe was supposed to rule according to a constitution, but over time he became an authoritarian leader who started demanding unquestioning obedience to his wishes. His reign was marked by corruption, and he was finally forced to leave office.

Death of the hero

Lafayette died in Paris on May 20, 1834, at the age of seventy-six. By that time, he no longer had many followers. The royalists, supporters of rule by kings and queens, considered him a traitor to the privileged class, and the radical revolutionaries considered him half-hearted in his support of changes in the social structure.

Lafayette's greatest legacy was in serving as a symbol of friendship between France and America. In 1825, when Lafayette was preparing to leave America for the last time, then-President John Quincy Adams made a farewell speech to him. He said: "We shall look upon you always as belonging to us, during the whole of our life, and as belonging to our children after us. You are ours by that more than patriotic self-devotion with which you flew to the aid of our fathers at the crisis of our fate; ours by that unshaken gratitude for your services which is a precious portion of our inheritance; ours by that tie of love, stronger than death, which has linked your name for the endless ages of time with the name [George] Washington."

For More Information

Boatner, Mark M., III. "Lafayette, Marquis de" and "Lafayette Myth." *Encyclopedia of the American Revolution.* Mechanicsburg, PA: Stackpole Books, 1994. pp. 591-94.

Bourgoin, Suzanne M. and Paula K. Byers. "Lafayette, Marquis de." *Encyclopedia of World Biography.* Detroit: Gale, 1998, vol. 9, pp. 151-52.

Gerson, Noel B. *Statue in Search of a Pedestal, The Biography of Marquis de Lafayette.* New York: Dodd, Mead & Co., 1976.

Guide to the Study of the U.S.A.: Representative Books Reflecting the Development of American Life and Thought. Washington, D.C.: U.S. Library of Congress, 1960.

Whitlock, Brand. *La Fayette.* New York: D. Appleton & Co., 1929.

Web Sites

"The Marquis de Lafayette." The LIBERTY! website. PBS Online and Twin Cities Public Television. [Online] Available http://www.pbs.org/ktca/liberty/chronicle/lafayette.html (accessed on 9/6/99).

"Marquis de Lafayette, French Soldier & Statesman." [Online] Available http:///www2.lucidcafe.com/lucidcafe/library/95sep/lafayette.html (accessed on 9/6/99).

"Who Served Here? The Marquis de Lafayette." Historic Valley Forge. [Online] Available http://www.ushistory.org/valleyforge/served/lafayette.html (accessed on 9/7/99).

Pierre Charles L'Enfant

Born August 2, 1754
Paris, France
Died June 14, 1825
Near Bladensburg, Maryland

Architect, engineer, city planner, army officer

Pierre Charles L'Enfant was a French-born architect and engineer. Although he had little formal training, he designed the brilliant plan for the city of Washington, D.C., as well as other public and private buildings. His designs became models for city planners. His grand ideas and haughty attitude caused problems with many of his clients, however, and his life ended in poverty and bitterness.

A plan for the design of Washington, D.C., "must leave to [those who come after] a grand [memorial] to the patriotic interests which promoted it."

Pierre Charles L'Enfant (pronounced pee-AIR sharl LON-FON) was born in Paris, France, on August 2, 1754. His father, Pierre, was a painter of battle scenes and landscapes. His mother, Marie Charlotte Leullier (pronounced luh-LYAY), was the daughter of a French military officer. Pierre had a brother, Pierre Joseph, who died in 1758, and a sister about whom nothing is known.

Young L'Enfant grew up among artistic people and was educated at Paris's Royal Academy of Painting and Sculpture, where his father taught. He learned to draw battle scenes and forts. L'Enfant also studied with André LaNotre (pronounced luh-NOTE), who designed the famous gardens at the beautiful Palace of Versailles (pronounced ver-SIGH), the extravagant

Portrait: Pierre Charles L'Enfant. *Reproduced permission of the National Archives and Records Administration.*

home of the French royal family. L'Enfant also served in the French army, where he held the rank of lieutenant.

L'Enfant went to America in 1777, at the age of twenty-three, and volunteered to serve in **George Washington**'s (see entry) army in the fight for independence from Great Britain (the American Revolution was fought from 1775 to 1783). Although France had not yet entered the war on the American side, many idealistic men from France and other countries were inspired by the aims of the American revolutionaries and volunteered to serve in the American army.

L'Enfant was assigned to work with General Frederick von Steuben (pronounced von-SHTEW-ben), a German general who had volunteered to train American army troops. L'Enfant first met George Washington during the difficult winter of 1777–78 at Valley Forge, Pennsylvania. L'Enfant kept General Washington and his fellow officers entertained by drawing pictures and sketches of them. Before long, L'Enfant attained the rank of captain in the U.S. Army Corps of Engineers. He helped to supervise the building of forts and also engaged in combat.

In the *Taggart Collection of Miscellaneous L'Enfant Papers,* Hugh T. Taggart describes L'Enfant as "fully six feet in height, finely proportioned, nose prominent, of military bearing, [with a] courtly air, and polite manners, his figure usually enveloped in a long overcoat ... a man who would attract attention in any assembly."

L'Enfant was present at the siege of Savannah, Georgia, in 1779, and suffered a serious wound that required months of recovery. He was later captured and held prisoner by the British until January 1782, when he was released in exchange for a British prisoner-of-war. He then served under George Washington, who promoted him in 1783 to Major of Engineers in the Continental army.

L'Enfant designed his first building while he was still in the Continental army. It was done at the request of the French foreign minister to America, a man named La Luzerne. He wanted to arrange a grand banquet in Philadelphia, Pennsylvania, in honor of the 1781 birth of the first son of King **Louis XVI** of France (see entry), Louis-Joseph, who was himself in line to become king. La Luzerne had L'Enfant design and supervise the building of a magnificent hall in which to hold the banquet. The French government paid for the hall.

Visits France, returns and opens architectural firm

After the Continental army was disbanded in 1783, L'Enfant was invited to join the Society of the Cincinnati. The society was named for Cincinnatus, a Roman general of ancient times. The society aimed to keep alive the spirit of the revolution and the friendships of the men who had fought in the war. L'Enfant's handsome design for the society's medal greatly enhanced his reputation among America's early leaders and spread his fame as an artist. When L'Enfant returned to Paris to visit his dying father in 1783, he started a French branch of the Society of the Cincinnati.

While in Paris, L'Enfant learned that France had decided to grant him a pension, a small annual payment in recognition of his services and the wounds he received during the American Revolution. He never bothered to take the steps necessary to collect the pension. All his life, L'Enfant would be plagued by financial problems, in part because of his neglect of such details.

L'Enfant returned to America in April 1784 and began working as an architect, establishing a private practice in New York City. He had met many rich and well-known people in America, and he soon had a long list of clients. He was hired to design, build, and restore buildings and monuments, and he also worked as an interior designer.

New York projects

Among L'Enfant's famous New York projects were St. Paul's Chapel, Erasmus Academy in Brooklyn, Gracie Mansion (now the residence of New York's mayor), and private homes for such prominent New Yorkers as wealthy businessman John Jacob Astor, furniture designer Duncan Phyfe, and U.S. president-to-be **Alexander Hamilton** (see entry).

In 1789 L'Enfant was hired by the City of New York to remodel city hall for possible use as the nation's capitol building. New York failed in its bid to become the permanent capitol, but the building did witness George Washington's swearing-in as the nation's first president. City officials offered L'Enfant ten acres of land near the city in payment for his work, but he refused. He claimed the complicated and chal-

In 1791, L'Enfant was chosen by George Washington and Thomas Jefferson to design America's capital, Washington, D.C. Washington (on horseback) and L'Enfant surveyed the new site and discussed L'Enfant's vision of the new city. *Reproduced by permission of the Granger Collection, New York.*

lenging project was worth far more than that. Ten years later he was offered $750; again he refused. In the end, he and the American government never reached an agreement and he was never fairly compensated for the excellent work he had done.

Draws up plans for new capitol in Washington, D.C., but loses job

At the urging of Virginian **Thomas Jefferson** (see entry), it was decided by the U.S. Congress that a new capital city would be constructed on the Potomac River, not far from Jefferson's home. It would be built on a ten-mile-square piece of land, called the District of Columbia, that would be federal territory, rather than belonging to any particular state.

In 1789 L'Enfant wrote to George Washington with his suggestions for the design of the new capital. He said the plan "should be drawn on such a scale as to leave room for that [expansion] and [decoration] which the increase of the wealth of the nation will permit it to pursue at any period, however remote." With those words L'Enfant showed himself to be a visionary, a man who looked beyond the present to the nation's future needs. In 1791 Washington and Thomas Jefferson chose L'Enfant to draw up plans for the new capital city on the Potomac River.

L'Enfant worked on the plan for more than a year. His final design was based partly on the Gardens of Versailles in France and partly on the restoration of the city of Rome, Italy, in 1585. L'Enfant's plan for the nation's capital used the grid pattern of streets that he pioneered. The design included the use of long avenues that joined at key points marked by important buildings, monuments, or parks. In this way the city became a symbolic representation of power radiating from a central source.

Personality stands in way of career success

L'Enfant was a stubborn man with a quick temper and a large ego. He always had problems staying within a budget, and he was often fired from jobs for his free spending. His work on Washington, D.C., was no exception. In 1792 President Washington dismissed L'Enfant from the project. After only six months on the job, L'Enfant was well over his budget. He quarreled bitterly with his superiors over expenses and insisted on complete control of the project.

Despite this very public dismissal, L'Enfant was asked to do other jobs. In 1792 he created a design for the new city of Paterson, New Jersey. It would be the nation's first city designed to be a manufacturing center. Within a year L'Enfant lost the job of supervising the construction of the city because of his haughty attitude and the fact that it would have been impossible to carry out his plans and stay within a budget.

The pattern of Lafayette's being hired and then soon fired continued. In 1794 he was hired as an engineer at Fort Mifflin on the Delaware River. But once again he was fired when his plans for the fort turned out to be far grander than the budget would allow. Later in 1794, he designed a magnificent mansion in Philadelphia for Robert Morris, a wealthy man who had contributed a good deal of his own money to finance the American Revolution. Morris ran into financial dif-

L'Enfant Honored after Death

The remains of Pierre Charles L'Enfant lay in a poorly marked grave at Digges Farm, near Bladensburg, Maryland, for nearly a century after his death in 1815. Meanwhile, attention turned to the incomplete condition of the nation's capital. In 1902 both the Parks Commission of the City of Washington, D.C., and the U.S. Senate presented reports on what steps should be taken to improve and develop the city. Both groups said that the plans made by L'Enfant a century earlier had been carefully reviewed and had met with the approval of all concerned.

In 1908 the U.S. Congress finally got around to recognizing L'Enfant's achievements and directed that his remains be removed to a special site in Arlington National Cemetery in Virginia. The cemetery is a public monument for people who have made sacrifices in their lives for the public good. Congress ordered that a monument be erected at the gravesite.

On April 22, 1909, L'Enfant's remains were unearthed, placed in a metal-lined casket, covered with the American flag, and moved to Mount Olivet Cemetery in Washington, where they rested for six days. On April 28, 1909, a military escort conveyed the casket to the U.S. Capitol building, to honor the distinguished man. The casket lay in state (displayed formally to the public before burial) in the U.S. Capitol Rotunda (a place in the Capitol Building used for ceremonial purposes) from 9 A.M. until noon. The casket was then taken to Arlington National Cemetery, where it was buried on the slope in front of the Custis-Lee Mansion, which had been built as a memorial to George Washington by his adopted grandson, George Washington Parke Custis.

A ceremony to honor L'Enfant was held at the cemetery and featured dedication addresses by President William Howard Taft and Ambassador J. J. Jusserand of France. The group of 350 that attended the ceremony included the Chief Justice of the U.S. Supreme Court, other justices, senators and members of Congress, high-ranking military and city and national officials, and patriotic organizations, including representatives of the Society of the Cincinnati.

The monument constructed for L'Enfant's burial site is made of white marble (now very rough due to weather erosion). The top of the monument features an engraving of L'Enfant's design

ficulties and the project was never completed. Later, though poor and dependent on others, L'Enfant refused to sue Morris for money due him, as the two men had become fast friends.

In 1812 L'Enfant was asked to accept the position of professor of engineering at the U.S. Military Academy at West Point, New York, but he declined the position. He said that he did not think he would be a good teacher, he preferred to work actively rather than teach, and he had some problems with the English language.

Retirement and poverty

During the War of 1812 (1812–15), which pitted the United States against England over who would control the seas in North America, L'Enfant was employed to design and supervise the construction of Fort Washington, which was to stand several miles from the U.S. capital. Its purpose was to defend the city of Washington, D.C. At some time during the project, he had bitter disagreements with his superiors there and the construction of the project was taken over by another officer. L'Enfant then retired.

L'Enfant continued to neglect his own personal financial affairs. His father left him a small farm in Normandy, France, but L'Enfant never took the steps necessary to claim his inheritance. From 1815 to 1824 L'Enfant, now nearly broke, lived with the family of his friend, William Dudley Digges, near Bladensburg, Maryland.

Appeals to Congress for fair payment for work on capital

To the end of his days, L'Enfant believed he had been treated unjustly by his clients, both private individuals and the federal government. He haunted the halls of Congress applying for payment for his work on the Capital. He claimed he was owed $95,500 for his work, but George Washington and other federal officials figured the amount due him was between $2,500 and $3,000.

In trying to collect the money he felt was owed him, L'Enfant sent a series of memos to the U.S. Congress. In them, he recalled his accomplishments on the nation's behalf despite his personal misfortunes. Biographer Elizabeth S. Kite explained in *L'Enfant and Washington:* "He also wrote of 'the absolute destruction of his family's fortune in Europe,' owing to the French Revolution, his being reduced 'from a state of ease and content to one the most distressed and helpless,' living as he did, upon 'borrowed bread'; but he would not doubt of 'the [nobility of mind] and justice of Congress.'" To the end of his life L'Enfant never gave up hope that in time the United States would fairly compensate him for his brilliant work, but his hope went unfulfilled.

When the seventy-five-year-old L'Enfant died in 1815, his body was buried at the Digges' home at the foot of a tree. According to Elizabeth S. Kite, the goods he left behind consisted of "three watches, three compasses, some books, maps, and surveying instruments, the whole being valued at forty-six dollars."

L'Enfant's plans are realized

Seventy-four years after L'Enfant died poor and forgotten, his plan for Washington, D.C., was unearthed from the federal archives, and its brilliance was finally recognized. In 1901 plans went forward to develop the nation's capital according to L'Enfant's vision.

For all of his difficulties in getting along with people, L'Enfant was a man of honor. George Washington had once expressed his fear that L'Enfant might publicly denounce the Washington, D.C., project because he was fired from it. But reflecting later on L'Enfant's character, Washington wrote that he had never shown any "disloyalty to the creation of his genius [the capital city]. He bore his honors and disappointment in humility and poverty."

For More Information

Boatner, Mark M., III. "L'Enfant, Pierre Charles." *Encyclopedia of the American Revolution.* Mechanicsburg, PA: Stackpole Books, 1994, pp. 615-16.

Caemmerer, H. Paul. *Life of Pierre Charles L'Enfant.* New York: De Capo Press, 1950.

Kite, Elizabeth S. *L'Enfant and Washington.* New York: Arno Press, 1970, pp. 1-29.

Taggart, Hugh T. *Taggart Collection of Miscellaneous L'Enfant Papers.* Records of the Columbia Historical Society, XI, p. 216.

Web Sites

"L'Enfant, Pierre Charles." *The Cambridge Dictionary of American Biography.* J. S. Bowmen, ed. Cambridge, England: Cambridge University Press, 1995. [Online] Available http://search.biography.com (accessed on 9/6/99).

Meehan, Thomas. "Pierre-Charles L'Enfant." From the *Catholic Encyclopedia.* Encyclopedia Press, Inc., 1913. Electronic version copyright 1997 by New Advent, Inc. [Online] Available http://www.knight.org/advent/cethen/09150a.htm (accessed on 9/2/99).

"Pierre Charles L'Enfant: Major, United States Army, and Designer of Washington, D.C." Arlington National Cemetery Website [Online] Available http://www.arlingtoncemetery.com/l-enfant.htm (accessed on 9/6/99).

Louis XVI

Born August 23, 1754
Versailles Palace, France
Died January 21, 1792
Paris, France

King of France during the American and French revolutions

"I die innocent of all the crimes I am accused of. I forgive the authors of my death and I pray to God that the blood you are about to spill may never fall upon the head of France."

Portrait: Louis XVI.
Reproduced by permission of AP/Wide World Photos.

France's King Louis XVI started life in the majesty of the French royal court and ended it with a horrible death among the jeering crowds of Paris. History has often portrayed Louis XVI as simple-minded and cowardly. But some historians contend that Louis XVI was a dynamic, dedicated leader who tried to act in the interests of the French people during very turbulent times, and was an unfortunate victim of circumstances.

Louis-Auguste (pronounced lew-EE oh-GOOST), who later became King Louis XVI, was born in 1754 to the French royal family known as Bourbon. Their ancestors had ruled France since 897. Louis-Auguste's father was the son of King Louis XV. His mother, Marie-Joseph, was the second wife of Louis XV and a daughter of the King of Poland. Louis-Auguste had three brothers and two sisters who lived beyond infancy.

Louis-Auguste's older brother, the self-confident young Duc de Bourgogne (pronounced DOOK duh-ber-GOYNE), was his parents' favorite. When the ten-year-old heir to the throne got ill and died of a respiratory disease in the spring of 1761, the family was devastated.

Louis-Auguste, next in line to become king, was a fair-skinned, rather awkward boy with blue eyes and heavy eyebrows. He was encouraged by his tutors to be reserved and restrained, because those were considered good traits for a future king. All his life, Louis-Auguste enjoyed riding and hunting, and worked for hours making keys and locks and drawing maps. He does not seem to have been overly proud, despite his royal upbringing. In his biography, *Louis and Antoinette,* Vincent Cronin called Louis-Auguste "that rare creature, a prince with a poor opinion of himself."

Louis-Auguste's parents died of respiratory disease in the mid-1760s. On April 27, 1774, after his grandfather's death from smallpox, nineteen-year-old Louis-Auguste became the King of France. He was henceforth known as Louis XVI.

Marriage and children

In 1770, then sixteen-year-old Louis Auguste married the Archduchess Marie-Antoinette (pronounced an-twah-NET), youngest daughter of the Holy Roman Emperor Francis I and Maria Theresa of Bohemia and Hungary. (The Holy Roman Empire dissolved in 1806.) The slim, blue-eyed, blonde Marie-Antoinette, a bride at sixteen, was mostly interested in fashion, the theater, and court gossip. The French people distrusted her devotion to her native land, Austria, and blamed France's financial problems on her free-spending ways.

The couple had three children. They were Marie-Therese, born in 1778; Louis-Joseph, a much-loved oldest son who was born in 1781 and died in 1789; and Louis-Charles, who was born in 1785.

Common people get angry over finances

A French king was called an absolute monarch, but his powers were really rather limited. He directed and paid for adventures in foreign lands and declared war if necessary to preserve the country. He made decisions together with a State Council. His ability to impose taxes was limited by the group of thirteen courts known as the parlements (pronounced PARL-mahns). The parlements were made up of nobles, who opposed any of Louis's efforts to take away their tax-free status. As a result, the tax burden fell on the people who were least able to pay.

When Louis XVI became king, France's treasury was empty and the country was hugely in debt. Heavy taxes on the common people had caused widespread misery. Gradually the peasants (the common people) became angry with the ruling class, the cause of their unhappiness.

Taxation problems, reforms

Between 1774 and 1789, Louis XVI had several finance directors who tried to manage the treasury of France. Each in his turn proposed various financial reforms, but finally concluded that France's privileged classes must be taxed in order to prevent the country from going bankrupt. The privileged classes included members of the royal court, the nobles, members of parlements, and Roman Catholic clergymen. Louis XVI repeatedly bowed to pressure from those people and rejected any talk of taxing them. After the king rejected his proposals, each finance minister was forced to resign.

During this period of revolving finance directors, Louis XVI approved limited reform measures. For example, he approved the taxing of rich people for road repairs, rather than forcing the common people to repair them for free in their spare time. The reforms led to a brief period of popularity for Louis. But the common people continued to simmer with resentment. They lived lives of grinding poverty, and they resented being forced to send their sons to serve in the military.

Meeting of the Estates General proposed

Chaos erupted in France in 1788. Bad weather had ruined the harvest and people were starving. The peasants were forced to pay higher and higher taxes and make large payments to the Roman Catholic Church. Punishment for crimes was very harsh. For example, if a man were caught killing a gamebird to feed his starving family, he was executed.

In 1788 some people who were interested in solving France's financial crisis pressured Louis XVI to call a meeting of the Estates General to discuss the country's problems. France had three social classes, known as estates. The First Estate was the clergyman of the Roman Catholic Church, the Second Estate consisted of noblemen, and the Third Estate was made up of the common people. A meeting of all three classes had not taken place for 175 years.

The king at first refused to call such a meeting, but public pressure forced him to do so. He ordered the meeting for May 1789. The man who was then finance director, Brienne (pronounced bree-EN), publicly asked all Frenchmen to send him suggestions on how best to conduct the Estates General meeting. This kind of free speech had never been allowed in France before. Instead of offering useful suggestions, though, people took the opportunity to insult Brienne and the royal family. The king was angry about this and dismissed Brienne in August 1788. But it was too late to stop France's peasants from expressing their displeasure with their lives.

National Assembly formed

In May 1789 the Estates General met at the Palace of Versailles (pronounced ver-SIGH), which was located in the town of Versailles, twelve miles west of Paris. It was a huge, magnificent structure where the French royal family lived in great luxury, surrounded by ten thousand relatives, nobleman, and an enormous staff of servants. There the Third Estate (commoners) formed itself into a National Assembly.

In June 1789 the National Assembly vowed to stay together until it produced a new constitution and saw it firmly established in France. But Louis XVI resisted the assembly's demands for political independence, equal rights, and freedom for all French citizens. On June 23 he threatened to dismiss the Assembly at once if it did not take back its claims to national power.

The assembly then rose up and declared that the king no longer *could* dismiss them, because they now held the power in France. They vowed to leave "only at the point of a bayonet." The king responded by ordering troops to force the assembly to disband. But Louis's troops refused to attack their countrymen. A few days later the king, fearing bloodshed, backed down and ordered all three estates to work together to draw up a new constitution.

Storming of the Bastille

On July 11, 1789, Louis XVI dismissed finance minister Jacques Neckar, who had urged him to make many reforms that would help the peasants. By that time, the king had sur-

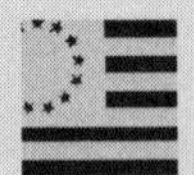

Louis XVI and the American Revolution

When Louis XVI became King of France in 1774, the American Revolution (1775–83) was in its very early stages. As a king himself, Louis did not feel sympathetic toward the American rebels, who were rising up against their lawful king. So why did he agree to help the Americans? As long as the American cause seemed doomed to failure, he did not want to. For a time he refused to see **Benjamin Franklin** (see entry), who had been sent to France to request its help. But in late 1777, Louis changed his mind.

Louis had a number of reasons for agreeing to help the Americans in their conflict with France's longtime enemy. One reason was economic. He knew that England wanted France's most valuable overseas possessions, some islands in the West Indies (an area in the Caribbean Sea between the United States and South America). A war with England over these possessions might be avoided if France helped American revolutionaries to achieve a quick victory. Another reason Louis agreed to help was pressure from French soldiers, who were eager to go to war against Great Britain to avenge earlier war losses and to gain glory for themselves.

For the first three years of the war, King Louis pretended to be neutral (non-involved) while secretly helping the Americans. He okayed a large loan from his government and persuaded Spain to advance money as well. The money was used to supply the Americans with 200 cannon, 25,000 muskets, 200,000 pounds of gunpowder, 20 brass mortars (a type of cannon), and clothing and tents for 25,000 men.

rounded Paris and the Palace of Versailles with 25,000 Swiss and German mercenaries (pronounced MER-sa-naireez; soldiers for hire) to protect him in case of an uprising.

The uprising began early on July 14, 1789, when Parisian peasants armed themselves with pitchforks and shovels to defend against a rumored assault on them by French and foreign soldiers. Soon realizing that these weapons were inadequate, the revolutionaries set out to find guns of their own. They seized 30,000 muskets from an old military hospital, but they still needed gunpowder. Word got out that a large quantity of gunpowder was being stored at the Bastille (pronounced bah-STEEL) in Paris.

When the Americans scored a stunning victory over the British at Saratoga, New York, in October 1777, Louis was finally moved to act openly. He now feared that if England lost to the Americans, the two countries might band together and attack France. In February 1778, France signed the French Alliance with Benjamin Franklin. Without this alliance, it is doubtful that America could have won the Revolutionary War.

France became engaged in a costly worldwide naval war with England, capturing from her islands in the West Indies and Africa. In April 1779, the king sent 5,500 French troops to help the American rebels. In October 1781, British General Charles Cornwallis, head of British troops in America, surrendered his 7,000 officers and men to the Americans, bringing an end to the fighting.

Louis XVI had gone to war mainly for the benefit of France, but many Americans hailed him as a selfless champion of freedom. Benjamin Franklin himself praised the king. In a letter to French Foreign Minister Vergennes in 1783, the American patriot wrote, "May I beg the favour of you, sir, to express respectfully for me to his Majesty, the deep sense I have of all the inestimable benefits his goodness has conferr'd on my country." It is ironic that the ideas of liberty championed by the American revolutionaries were taken up by French revolutionaries, which led to the loss of King Louis's head.

The Bastille was Paris's ancient prison, a gray stone structure with nine-foot-thick walls and high gun towers that stood as a symbol of France's oppressive government. For centuries, people had been sent to serve time in the prison, whether or not they were convicted of any crimes. On July 14, an angry crowd forced its way into the Bastille, demanding gunpowder. Arguments between the people and Bastille officials continued throughout the day, and tensions mounted.

Finally, in the afternoon, soldiers inside the Bastille fired their cannons and hundreds of peasants were killed or wounded. The crowd went wild. Hungry for revenge, they rampaged through the Bastille, destroying whatever they could find and killing some of the soldiers. The building was torn apart, stone by stone. Today, French people throughout the world commemorate the July 14 anniversary of the storming of the Bastille as Bastille Day, a celebration of French independence.

Changes in the government

After this explosion of violence, many nobles and members of the royal family escaped from France. But the king was trapped at the Palace of Versailles and could not escape. On August 27, the National Assembly issued the Declaration of the Rights of Man and the Citizen. The document declared that "men are born and remain free and equal in rights." It announced the aims of the French Revolution and called on other countries to throw off their chains and demand liberty for themselves.

The assembly declared that King Louis must share his power with them and with the Parlements. No longer could he dictate laws and have them put in place unchallenged. Now laws could be made only through agreement with the other branches of government. Likewise, laws could not be enacted by the assembly without the king's approval.

Louis XVI claimed that he shared the assembly's belief in a republican form of government, but few people were convinced of his sincerity. (A republic is a government with a chief of state who is not a monarch. Supreme power rests in a body of citizens who are entitled to vote.)

King forced back to Paris

On October 15, 1789, a group of rowdy citizens from Paris broke into the Palace of Versailles to bring their complaints directly to the king. They were particularly angry about the widespread lack of food. They demanded that Louis XVI return to Paris, where he could keep himself informed about their plight and show his dedication to changing the situation. Louis XVI and his family made the journey to the dark old palace of the Tuileries (pronounced TWEE-ler-eez) in Paris. The Assembly moved there with him.

A period of peace

After the king's move to Paris, his subjects' hostility abated. The fall harvest turned out to be better than expected, and people felt empowered by what they had accomplished in demolishing the Bastille and bringing their king back to Paris. For a while they calmed down and peace descended on France.

The National Assembly prepared a constitution that called for power to be divided between the king and the Assembly. It contained a system of checks and balances, like that of the U.S. Constitution, to make sure one department of government did not exercise too much power over the others. The assembly introduced other measures such as freedom of speech and open trade. It also demanded that members of the clergy take oaths of loyalty to the Revolution.

During the years 1789 to 1791, the Assembly made adjustments to the new constitution. As for Louis XVI and Marie-Antoinette, they were humiliated at their forced move to Paris. They felt like prisoners. They hated the gloomy Tuileries Palace, where commoners often pressed up against the windows to observe the royal family's activities. Marie-Antoinette urged Louis to go to her native Austria and bring back an army to destroy the revolutionaries and take back his monarchy.

King fails to escape France, signs constitution

In 1791, the king and queen tried to flee the country but were caught and forced to return to Paris. With his capture, the king's hopes of reestablishing his authority were dashed.

The members of the National Assembly publicly forgave the king for his attempt at escape. They had worked hard at coming up with a constitution, and that document said that they had to share power with the king. Some assembly members feared that without a king at their head, commoners might get out of hand and destroy the entire social system of France.

On September 14, 1791, the king signed the new constitution, and swore his allegiance to it. It appeared that the revolution was over and France could look forward to a bright future. But worse times were in store.

In 1791 Louis XVI took an oath of loyalty to uphold the new French constitution. This new constitution stated that governmental power would be shared between the king and the National Assembly. *Reproduced by permission of Archive Photos, Inc.*

Legislative Assembly forms, war is declared

On October 1, 1791, the National Assembly was replaced by the Legislative Assembly, made up mostly of people hostile to the king. The Legislative Assembly faced many problems, including food shortages. When faced with problems at home, governments throughout history have often gone to war to divert the attention of their people from the problems. Members of the Legislative Assembly turned to this tactic. They warned French citizens of the very real possibility of France being invaded by Austria and Prussia.

King Louis favored a war too. He hoped it would result in his being restored to his throne. In April 1792, Louis XVI exercised one of his few remaining powers and declared war against Austria and Prussia.

King found guilty and executed

The war went badly for France, and the king was blamed. In August 1792, Louis XVI and his family were permanently confined in the Temple, a dark, damp, twelfth-century fortress that had long served as a prison.

In September 1792, the French government declared France a republic and abolished the monarchy. King Louis XVI and his wife were now considered commoners and were charged with various crimes. Imprisonment was hard on Louis, who became depressed, stopped exercising, and grew quite fat.

In December 1792, Louis XVI was placed on trial by the government. He was ordered to defend himself on charges of repeated acts of treason against the Republic of France. On January 20, 1793, the king was found guilty and was sentenced to death.

On the following day, to the jeers of noisy crowds, King Louis XVI was guillotined (pronounced GILL-uh-teened; put to death by having his head cut off) in a public square in

Paris. His head was displayed in a basket and his remains were carted off, thrown into a pit, and dissolved with a powerful chemical called quicklime. Years later a chapel was erected in the king's memory at the site of his final resting-place.

Fate of the king's family

Marie-Antoinette met her death on the guillotine on October 16, 1793. The couple's eight-year-old son, Louis-Charles, was kept in solitary confinement in a dark cell, where he developed a disease and died in June 1795. His sister, Marie-Therese, spent two years in prison but was then released in December 1795, in exchange for an Austrian prisoner. She later married a royal cousin.

Biographer Vincent Cronin recognized the noble aspects of the doomed king's character. Cronin wrote, Louis XVI "brought to [his reign as king] the principle of justice that had characterized the French monarchy at its best, and also something of his own: a respect for other people's opinions, symbolized in [a journey he once took through the French countryside] when the crowds shouted, 'Long live the King!' and Louis called back 'Long live my people!'"

For More Information

Boatner, Mark M. "Louis XVI." *Encyclopedia of the American Revolution.* Mechanicsburg, PA: Stackpole Books, 1994, p. 660.

Bourgoin, Suzanne M. and Paula K. Byers, eds. "Louis XVI." *Encyclopedia of World Biography,* 2nd ed. Detroit: Gale, 1998, vol. 9, pp. 534-35.

Cronin, Vincent. *Louis and Antoinette.* New York: William Morrow & Co., Inc., 1975.

Fay, Bernard. *Louis XVI.* Translated by Patrick O'Brien. Chicago: Henry Regnery Co., 1966.

Hardman, John. *Louis XVI.* New Haven, CT: Yale University Press, 1993.

Purcell, L. Edward. *Who Was Who in the American Revolution.* New York: Facts on File, 1993, pp. 300-01.

Flora Macdonald

Born 1722
South Uist, Hebrides
Died March 4, 1790
Kingsburgh, Scotland

Musician

"Her name will be mentioned in history, and if courage and fidelity be virtues, mentioned with honor."

A quote engraved on a monument at Macdonald's gravesite

Portrait: Flora Macdonald. *Reproduced by permission of the Granger Collection, New York.*

Flora Macdonald became famous in Scotland and England by helping Charles Edward Stuart escape from his enemies in Scotland in 1746. Stuart believed himself to be legally entitled to become King of England. As a result of that adventure, Macdonald has been celebrated in many songs and legends. Macdonald later moved to America, where she took part in unsuccessful British efforts to defeat the American colonists in the Revolutionary War (1775–83).

Flora Macdonald was born in 1722 on Milton Farm in South Uist (pronounced YEW-ist) in the Hebrides (pronounced HEB-ruh-deez), a group of Scottish islands west of Scotland. Her last name is sometimes spelled MacDonald or McDonald. She and two older brothers were the children of Ranald Macdonald, a farmer who died when Flora was only two years old. Their mother, Marion Macdonald, remarried and had a second family with her new husband. Flora lived with her older brother Angus until age thirteen, when she was adopted by a relative, Lady Clanranald, the wife of a local clan chief. In Scotland, a clan was a social group made up of several families who claimed to descend from a common ancestor, bore the same family name, and followed the same leader, known as a chieftain.

While living with the Clanranalds, Flora became an accomplished singer and player of the spinet, a piano-like instrument. According to some accounts she traveled to Edinburgh, Scotland, to finish her education, returning to the Isle of Skye in 1745. It was here she was to become involved in the rescue of Charles Edward Stuart, an incident that would make her one of the most famous heroines of Scottish history.

Stuart family's claim to the British throne

In 1745, Charles Edward Stuart and his supporters made the last of several mismanaged attempts to take back the throne of England that had once belonged to the Stuart family. Charles Edward Stuart, known as "Bonnie Prince Charlie" (bonnie is a Scottish term for handsome), was the grandson of the last King of England from the Stuart family. (Kings and queens of England also hold the title King or Queen of Scotland and Ireland.) Stuart considered himself to be the rightful heir to the English throne, and his followers agreed.

In those days, it was dangerous to be a king or queen; plots against the lives of royalty were common. When James II, the last Stuart king, fled England for France in 1688, driven out by his enemies, many of his subjects still regarded him as their lawful king. They were called Jacobites (pronounced JAY-cub-ites; *Jacobus* is the Latin word for James). In 1714, a man from the German Hanover family was invited to become the King of England. He accepted, taking the name George I, and was succeeded by his son, George II, in 1727.

George II's followers were known as Hanoverians (pronounced HAN-oh-VAIR-ee-uhns). They rejected the notion that the Stuart family had any right to the English throne. They called the son of James II "The Old Pretender," and they referred to Charles Edward Stuart, born in 1720, as "The Young Pretender," because the two laid claim to the throne of England.

In 1745, the tall, lean, and freckle-faced Charles Edward Stuart landed on the coast of Scotland, determined to take back the English throne on behalf of his family, whose original homeland had been Scotland. The handsome young man charmed the Scottish chieftains by wearing a kilt, the native formal dress of men in Scotland, and by trying to speak Gaelic (pronounced GAY-lick), the Scottish language. In a short time, nearly 2,000 Highlanders (men from the Scottish Highlands, the mountainous region in northern and western Scotland) pledged to fight for the Stuart kingship.

Hanoverians win conflict, Stuart flees

In attempting to seize back the English throne, the Highlanders fought many battles with the Hanoverian army. The final battle took place at the Scottish town of Culloden in 1746. There, the 5,000 soldiers of Charles Edward Stuart's army were defeated by the Hanoverian army, which numbered 9,000 and was led by the Duke of Cumberland, King George II's youngest son. Because of the brutality of the Hanoverians, the Duke gained the name of the "Butcher."

At the end of the lost battle, Charles Edward Stuart advised his followers to scatter. The Hanoverians then began an intensive manhunt and put a price on the head of Stuart that equaled 2 percent of the cash available in the entire country of Scotland. Despite this enormous reward, it is said that not one single Scot betrayed Stuart in the five months in which he stayed in hiding in Scotland. With the help of hundreds of his supporters, Stuart then managed to escape to continental Europe. Young Flora Macdonald played a major role in Stuart's escape.

Macdonald helps Stuart escape to France

Flora Macdonald's biographer, Elizabeth Gray Vining, described her in *Flora, A Young Woman* as "slight and short, 'well-shaped,' with wide dark eyes and the dazzlingly fair skin and bright color of the [Hebridean] island girls." In 1746, when Macdonald was visiting the Clanranalds in the Hebridean Island of Benbecula (pronounced BEN-be-koo-luh), Charles Stuart arrived there. Stuart's companion proposed to the family that they help the young man escape to the Isle of Skye. Flora Macdonald agreed to cooperate. She later said that she did so because she would offer a hand to any person who was in distress.

At the time of Stuart's attempted escape, British authorities on the lookout for him would not allow anyone to leave the island of Benbecula without the permission of the local citizen soldiers. Pretending that she was going to visit her mother,

Flora Macdonald obtained a passport for herself, her manservant, an Irish maid named "Betty Burke," and a crew of six men. Betty Burke was actually Charles Edward Stuart, disguised in a gown, a cloak, and a white cap.

The party set sail and landed at Kilbride. Macdonald left Stuart and her servant hiding there in a cave and went to the home of Sir Alexander Macdonald of Sleat. Many families in the area were known by the last name Macdonald, because they were part of the same clan. Flora Macdonald revealed her secret to his wife, Lady Margaret Macdonald, who agreed to aid in the escape.

Exiled Jacobite Charles Edward Stuart escaped Scotland with Flora Macdonald's help, thus avoiding capture by British forces. Stuart never regained the English throne, but stories of Macdonald's bravery spread throughout Scotland. *Reproduced by permission of Archive Photos, Inc.*

The next day, September 20, 1746, Charles Stuart left Scotland aboard the French ship that took him to safety. Before leaving he had returned the fancy garters from his Betty Burke outfit to Macdonald, and she later had a piece of jewelry made from one of the buckles. Some legends say that Stuart and Flora Macdonald shared a romance and that Charles presented Flora with his portrait in a golden locket. Whatever took place, the two were never to meet again.

Stuart's parting words to the young woman were, "For all that has happened, I hope, Madam, we shall meet at St. James's [the court of the English king] yet and I will reward you there for what you have done." Stuart spent his life traveling throughout Europe; he never succeeded in regaining the English throne.

Jail, freedom, and honors

When the boatmen who had smuggled Stuart out of Scotland returned to Benbecula, they were arrested and forced to reveal their secret mission. Soon Flora Macdonald was called before British authorities and questioned about her involvement in the plot. Although she provided the facts, she did her best to protect her friends. For her involvement in the escape, Macdonald spent several weeks on prison ships and finally was imprisoned. Legend says that she spent some time in the Tower of London, a famous prison, but no formal records support that rumor.

Elizabeth Gray Vining pointed out that like other prisoners of some importance, Macdonald was lodged in a messenger's house. According to Vining: "Messengers were government officials who escorted prisoners and witnesses from one place to another and sometimes carried mail. They were permitted to turn their own houses into private [jails] for profit." Macdonald stayed at the home of William Dick, who ran one of the best of them. Other prisoners who stayed there during her confinement included Charles Edward Stuart's barber and wig maker and other of his supporters.

During her time in London, an article about Flora Macdonald appeared under the title *Some Particulars of the Life, Family, and Character of Miss Florence Macdonald, now in Custody of one of his Majesty's Messengers in London, in 1747.* She was described as "a graceful person, [with] a good complexion, and regular features. She has a peculiar sweetness mixed with majesty in her [face], ... even under confinement she betrays nothing of sullenness or discontent and all her actions bespeak a mind full of conscious innocence."

Macdonald was released from captivity one year later, in 1747, as part of a general pardon of prisoners by the British government. She then stayed for a time at the home of the widow Lady Primrose. There she was visited by many important people of the day, because the story of her helping Charles Edward Stuart had become well known, and Stuart still had many friends. Lady Primrose's home was the center of the now ruined but still hopeful Jacobite movement. Macdonald was honored at a banquet attended by many families from the Isle of Skye.

Marriage and relocation to America

In 1750, Flora Macdonald married Allan Macdonald (no relation to Flora's family). Allan, a tall, handsome, vigorous, and intelligent man, was the son of Macdonald of Kingsburgh in Skye, Scotland. During their long marriage, the couple produced five sons and two daughters.

In time, British landlords took over the lands of those who had supported the cause of Charles Edward Stuart. This, along with bad crops, loss of cattle, high food prices, bad weather, and disease epidemics, caused many Highlanders to leave their homeland rather than live there under British rulers hostile to their way of life. In 1774, Flora Macdonald, with her husband and two of their sons, moved to North Carolina, one of the American colonies. The Highlanders were drawn to North Carolina because their former countrymen who settled there had sent back glowing reports. Some of them had received generous grants of land from the British government.

Macdonalds rally the Highlanders

The American Revolutionary War broke out in 1775. At that time, British-appointed governor of North Carolina Josiah Martin made an effort to assert British control over the area. Martin wrote to British Lord Dunmore, Governor of Virginia, that he could gather loyal Highlanders from the interior counties of North Carolina and slaves, who would support the British in exchange for the promise of freedom.

Flora Macdonald's husband Allan helped raise a group of Highlanders to fight for the British against the American colonists. Allan Macdonald became a brigadier (pronounced BRIG-a-deer) general (a position just below major general). Meanwhile, Flora Macdonald rallied the Scots there to stand behind Donald McDonald, the elderly British officer who was to play a major role in the battle at Moore's Creek Bridge, North Carolina, in 1776.

Historian Tom Steel pointed out in *Scotland's Story: A New Perspective* that the Macdonalds were an example of an interesting occurrence: "Scots once loyal to the Stuart monarchy, who after the failure of the [1745 attempt by Charles Stuart to recapture the throne] transferred loyalty to an equally strong British monarchy they had once [tried] to overthrow."

Why did Highlanders, who had suffered so severely at the hands of the Hanoverian army, take their side in the conflict in America? Elizabeth Gray Vining explained that some were former military men still receiving soldiers' pay from the British army; they believed that they owed their loyalty—and their paychecks—to the British army. Others "remembered the fearful penalties that attended an unsuccessful rebellion against the Hanoverians.... The merchants among them were afraid of losing trade.... Many of the Scots, like Allan [Macdonald] himself, had come to North Carolina too recently to have developed firm ties to the land. All of them looked on monarchy as the form of government ordained by heaven and considered [the type of government proposed for America] horrid and unnatural."

The Battle of Moore's Creek Bridge

In North Carolina, with Flora Macdonald's help, eighty-year-old Donald McDonald had successfully recruited both Scottish and non-Scottish supporters of the British. On February 15, 1776, more than 2,500 troops showed up at Cross Creek to rally around Governor Martin. But learning that Martin was not there and they would have to march to far-away Brunswick, where Martin awaited them aboard a ship, many of the men immediately deserted, until there were finally only 1,300 Highlanders and about 300 Loyalists.

On February 26, 1776, the Highlanders arrived at Moore's Creek Bridge, where American revolutionaries had set up camp at the bridge over the creek to stop the Scots.

Early on the morning of February 27, the Highlanders charged and were met by American fire. Lillian B. Miller described the scene in *The Dye Is Now Cast.* To the music of bagpipes and drums, and the sound of battle cries, the Loyalists began their attack. "As the Scots attempted to cross the beams of the bridge, many fell into the water and drowned. Those who managed the perilous crossing encountered the murderous fire of [revolutionary leader Richard] Caswell's well concealed men. In a few moments, between thirty and seventy Tories [Loyalists] were either killed or wounded ... The rebels suffered only two wounded, one of whom later died."

The rest of the Tories fled. The battle had lasted only three minutes. Soon after, Allan Macdonald and his son, Alexander, were taken prisoner and jailed in Halifax, Virginia.

Their battle lost, family returns to Scotland

In 1777, the family's plantation was taken away because Flora Macdonald would not take an oath of allegiance to America, as commanded by the North Carolina Congress. Soon after, Flora returned to Scotland. A popular tale says that during her trip, pirates attacked the ship she was on, but she stayed on deck to offer encouragement to the sailors and suffered a broken arm. In fact, she slipped and dislocated her arm while she was leading other women to safety below decks.

Upon returning to Scotland, Flora Macdonald traveled to Milton, where a brother built her a cottage; after two years her husband joined her there. The couple then settled once again in Kingsburgh, where they mourned the death of relatives and rejoiced in the birth of new grandchildren. She died there on March 4, 1790.

Flora Macdonald's funeral was unique to the Isle of Skye, where loyalty to Charles Edward Stuart ran deep. Thousands of mourners honored her in a funeral procession that extended more than a mile. Her body was wrapped in a sheet that had been slept on by Bonnie Prince Charlie, and she was buried at a churchyard in Kilmuir. Over time, admirers carried Macdonald's original gravestone away bit by bit. In 1871, a memorial consisting of a tall stone cross with a circle was erected at her gravesite. When it was blown down in a violent storm, a sturdier one was erected; it still stands there today.

For More Information

Fry, Plantagenet, and Fiona Somerset Fry. *The History of Scotland.* London: Routledge & Kegan Paul, 1982, p. 198.

Miller, Lillian B. *The Dye Is Now Cast.* Washington, DC: Smithsonian Institution Press, 1975, p. 207-09.

Prebble, John. *Culloden.* New York: Atheneum, 1962.

Purcell, L. Edward. "McDonald, Flora." *Who Was Who in the American Revolution.* New York: Facts On File, 1993, pp. 306-07.

Steel, Tom. *Scotland's Story: A New Perspective.* London: William Collins Sons and Co., Ltd., 1985, pp.169-72.

Vining, Elizabeth Gray. *Flora, A Biography.* Philadelphia: J. B. Lippincott Co., 1966.

Web Sites

"Bonnie Prince Charlie, The 1745 Jacobite Rising." [Online] Available http://ourworld.compuserve.com/homepages/CSOUCHON/jacobris.htm (accessed on 6/24/99).

James Madison

Born March 16, 1751
Port Conway, Virginia
Died June 28, 1836
Orange County, Virginia

President of the United States, secretary of state, congressman

"The right of electing the members of the government constitutes ... the essence of a free and responsible government."

Portrait: James Madison. *Reproduced by permission of AP/Wide World Photos.*

James Madison was a wealthy man with a careful but creative mind who gave his whole life to public service. He worked to gain American independence and helped establish the nation's new government. Madison is known as the person most responsible for making the Bill of Rights part of the U.S. Constitution.

James Madison, the first of ten children, was born in 1751 to a wealthy young couple, James and Eleanor Conway Madison. Members of the Madison family were longtime residents of Virginia and owned a great deal of land. Although he was frail and sickly, James Madison was an excellent student. He was brought up in Orange County, Virginia, and entered what is now Princeton University in New Jersey in 1769, graduating in a mere two years. While at college, he was a member of a student club that favored colonial resistance to British taxation policies. Ever since the passage of the Stamp Act in 1765, colonists had been complaining about British attempts to raise money by taxing them.

After graduation, Madison considered becoming a Protestant minister. Instead, he returned home to Virginia, depressed and uncertain what to do with his life.

Begins political career

Madison regained his zest for living in 1774, at age twenty-three, when he began serving on Orange County's committee of safety, which was responsible for local defense. Citizens of Virginia and Massachusetts were among the first to imagine the possibility of a war of independence between the colonies and Great Britain. Madison was part of a group of early Virginia patriots that included **Patrick Henry** (see entry). They enthusiastically supported the separation of the American colonies from England.

Madison's political career moved to a new level with his appointment to the 1776 Virginia Convention. Virginia was always a leader in discussing individual rights and liberties and passing laws to guarantee them, and Madison played a large role in getting such laws passed. In May 1776 he and the other delegates at the Virginia Convention voted to propose a resolution to the Second Continental Congress in Philadelphia, Pennsylvania. The Congress was a meeting of representatives from all thirteen colonies; the topic of discussion was the tense situation between the colonies and Great Britain. The Virginia resolution stated: "Resolved, that these United Colonies are, and of right ought to be, free and independent States, that they are absolved from all allegiance to the British Crown, and that all political connection between them and the State of Great Britain is, and ought to be, totally dissolved."

Madison helped write the Virginia constitution, which was adopted on June 28, 1776. It was a vital step in breaking all ties with England and embarking on independence. On July 2, 1776, Congress accepted the Virginia resolution, and two days later, Congress adopted the Declaration of Independence, the document that broke all ties between all the colonies and England and established the United States as a nation.

Helps write Declaration of Rights; serves in Virginia government

In 1776 the Virginia Convention adopted the Virginia Declaration of Rights; it would later serve as the model for the first ten amendments to the U.S. Constitution (discussed below). The Declaration of Rights laid out some basic principles of republican government, the type that Madison favored.

Republican government is a system in which power is held by the people, who exercise their power through elected representatives. Madison helped **George Mason** (see entry), the primary author of the Declaration, to strengthen the section on religious freedom (see box on p. 308).

Virginia's new constitution had established the Virginia House of Delegates as its lawmaking body. Madison began serving in the House in October 1776. He lost his elected seat there in April 1777, reportedly because he refused to furnish liquor to the voters. Buying votes with liquor was a common practice at that time. But the House recognized his leadership abilities and appointed him to serve on the Virginia Council of State, the official group of advisers of the Virginia governor.

At Williamsburg, then Virginia's capital, Madison worked closely with **Thomas Jefferson** (see entry) and Patrick Henry. At that time most of the talk was about war, and the men threw their energies into the war effort. Thomas Jefferson became governor of Virginia in June 1779. By that time, he and Madison had developed what proved to be a lifelong friendship.

Assumes national leadership role

In March 1780, the twenty-nine-year-old Madison won a three-year term to represent Virginia in the Continental Congress. Although he was the youngest member of the Congress, Madison quickly became one of its leaders. He realized that the new American nation would have to collect taxes and make treaties with foreign governments in order to grow and become a respected world power. Madison worked out a way for Congress to raise money by collecting taxes on imported goods. He wrote the arguments that **John Jay** (see entry) took to Spain in 1780; Jay was seeking the right of free navigation of the Mississippi River, then controlled by Spain. Jay had little luck with the Spanish, in part because America's form of government was too disorganized and the states could not agree on treaties. Seeing this, Madison became an early supporter of a strong central government.

In the spring of 1784, Madison redirected his attention to state politics when he was elected to the Virginia General Assembly. He served from 1784 to 1786. When talk turned to a new form of government for America, Madison paved the way for the Constitutional Convention, held in Philadelphia, Pennsylvania, in 1787. Representatives of all the states met there to write a new constitution.

Plays role in adoption of U.S. Constitution

At the Constitutional Convention, Madison presented the Virginia Plan, his state's version of a new constitution. The plan called for larger states like Virginia to have more representatives in government than smaller states had. Naturally, the larger states supported the Virginia Plan, while the smaller states supported another, called the New Jersey Plan, which gave the smaller states equal representation with the larger ones. After a bitter fight, the delegates compromised on a system in which the states would be equally represented in a senate, and a state's representation in a house of representatives would be proportional to the state's population. This system remains in place today.

Madison believed that the challenge of building a new nation required the strong central government proposed in the Constitution. He worked tirelessly to get it accepted by the other delegates. Madison also took notes at the convention, and although an official record was kept of the proceedings, Madison's notes serve as an interesting and valuable addition.

Madison's opponents were people who supported a loose alliance of states instead of a strong central government. They raised objections to the proposed constitution. To explain why the proposed form of government was necessary, Madison joined with **Alexander Hamilton** (see entry) and John Jay to write a document called *The Federalist Papers*. It remains today the best explanation of the U.S. Constitution.

A Constitution forming a strong central government was finally adopted by the convention delegates and was sent around to the individual states for their approval. Passage by Virginia and New York was crucial, because they were the largest states. Madison fought hard to get the Constitution passed in his home state. He then traveled to New York to urge delegates there to ratify the constitution. The U.S. Constitution was eventually ratified by all the states and was adopted in 1789.

Dolly Madison, the First "First Lady"

Dolly Payne Madison's first husband died in 1793, and she married James Madison in 1794. Despite the fact that she was twenty years younger than Madison, the couple enjoyed a happy marriage. Although the Madisons had no children of their own, James Madison became the stepfather of Dolly's young son by her first marriage, Payne Todd.

Dolly Madison first became the darling of Washington society when she began hosting parties and dinners for President Thomas Jefferson, a widower. At that time, her husband was serving as Jefferson's secretary of state. The friendly and lively Dolly Madison was immensely popular and earned the honorary title "first lady" of the land. She continued to function in that role until 1817, when her husband James Madison ended his second term as president.

Following James Madison's death in 1836, Dolly Madison faced financial difficulties, brought on in part by the foolish spending of her son. She was forced to sell the family's Montpelier estate to raise money; the sale remained a heartache to her for the rest of her life. Friends sometimes had to supply her with the necessities of life.

Dolly Madison lived in poverty until Congress purchased her husband's historical papers. She moved into a home across the street from the White House and died there at the age of eighty-one on July 12, 1849. She was buried next to James Madison on the grounds of Montpelier.

Writes Bill of Rights, joins Republican Party

In 1789 Madison was elected to the U.S. House of Representatives, where he served throughout the eight years of President **George Washington**'s (see entry) term. He made many contributions to the formation of a stable government. He helped form the U.S. Departments of State, Treasury, and War. His major accomplishment in Congress was writing the Bill of Rights, the name given to the first ten amendments to the U.S. Constitution. During this period, Madison witnessed the birth of the two-party system in the United States.

When he first ran for national office, Madison was a member of the Federalist Party. Federalists believed that the rich and well educated should have more influence in government than ordinary citizens. As time went on, Madison found himself objecting to the financial plans proposed by the Federalist Secretary of State, Alexander Hamilton. He was particularly disgusted by Hamilton's followers in Congress, who were using Hamilton's financial setup for their own personal profit. His disgust grew, and over time, Madison became strongly allied with Thomas Jefferson and the newly forming Republican Party, which called itself the party of the common man.

Marries; enjoys brief retirement

In 1794 Madison's life took a happy turn when he married a pretty young widow named Dolly (or Dolley) Payne Todd (see box). Historian Henry Adams described James Madison at this time as, "a small man, quiet, somewhat precise in manner, pleasant, fond of conversation, with a certain mixture of ease and dignity" in the way he presented himself.

In 1797 Madison retired from the U.S. House of Representatives, and went to live at Montpelier (pronounced mon-PEEL-yer), his grand Virginia estate. But still he remained a strong figure in his party. He came out of his brief retirement in 1798 to draft the Virginia Resolutions that argued that individual states had the right to reject acts of Congress as unconstitutional.

Serves as U.S. secretary of state

Madison returned to the national scene in 1801 when new President Thomas Jefferson appointed his old friend to serve as U.S. secretary of state. He was responsible for helping to plan and carry out American foreign policy. Madison held the office throughout Jefferson's eight-year presidency and also served as Jefferson's chief adviser.

The great achievement of their partnership was the 1803 Louisiana Purchase, in which the United States paid France less than fifteen million dollars for a territory that stretched from the Mississippi River to the Rocky Mountains. It doubled the size of the United States.

At the time Madison became secretary of state, England and France were at war. Neither France nor England could move trade goods out of their countries, so the United States was doing it for each of them. American ships were often

Madison's Role in the Separation of Church and State

Ever since the first settlers came to the New World to escape religious persecution, the relationship between church and state has been the subject of countless arguments. In the Old World, it was common for nations to have official religions; frequently, people who did not belong to the official religion were persecuted.

At the time when Virginia was working on its Declaration of Rights, the Protestant Anglican Church was the official church of Virginia. James Madison favored freedom of religion and strongly opposed any state religion. He played an important role in making the Virginia Declaration of Rights more supportive of the personal freedom of individuals.

The committee that drafted a proposed Declaration of Rights adopted an article by George Mason on the subject of religion. It stated that "all men shou'd enjoy the fullest toleration in the Exercise of Religion, according to the dictates of conscience." But Madison tried to get the word "toleration" stricken from the document to prepare the way for total liberty of conscience and separation of church and state in Virginia. Madison wanted the declaration to read "all men are equally entitled to the full and free exercise of [religion] according to the dictates of conscience; and therefore that no man or class of man ought, on account of religion to be invested with [special payments] or privileges."

stopped by the French or British navy, who took over their cargoes. In addition, the British often kidnapped American sailors and forced them to serve in the British navy. Jefferson and Madison protested this behavior by the French and the British and finally cut off trade with both countries.

Becomes fourth U.S. President

In 1808 Madison ran for president as a Republican and was elected to succeed Jefferson as President of the United States. His election victory was celebrated by a grand ball, which then became an American tradition.

As Madison took office in 1809, England and France were still at war with one another and their conflict threatened

But the adoption of Madison's words would have had serious consequences for the Anglican Church and many of the Virginia representatives opposed that notion. So Madison offered an alternate wording that read, "all men are equally entitled to enjoy the free exercise of religion, according to the dictates of conscience, unpunished and unrestrained by the [courts], unless the preservation of equal liberty and the existence of the State are manifestly endangered."

This change satisfied most of the convention members, and the key part of Madison's revision was adopted. The final article read that "religion, or the duty which we owe our Creator, and the manner of discharging it, can be directed only by reason and conviction, not by force and violence; and therefore, all men are equally entitled to the free exercise of religion, according to the dictates of conscience, and that is the mutual duty of all to practise Christian forbearance, love, and charity towards each other."

The change Madison made to this document was very important because it made freedom of conscience a right that did not depend on some authority figure granting his approval. Freedom of conscience now existed on its own, belonged to all men, and was a right that could not be taken away. According to historian Ralph Ketcham, "Madison ... made possible complete liberty of belief or unbelief, and the utter separation of church and state."

the peace in America. In 1810 the United States agreed to resume trade with both England and France. But both countries violated their agreements with the United States and continued to seize American ships and sailors.

England became even more hostile, threatening to unite with the Indians in the Great Lakes region in a war with the United States. Madison himself had little enthusiasm for the war, but the "war hawks" in his own party largely forced his hand. They were primarily westerners who feared Indian attacks in the Northwest, backed by money and supplies from Great Britain. In 1812 Madison recommended to Congress that the United States declare war on Great Britain and on June 18 the War of 1812 (1812–15) began.

The friendly and lively Dolly Madison was immensely popular and earned the honorary title "first lady" of the land. She continued to function in that role until 1817, when her husband James Madison ended his second term as president. *Reproduced by permission of Archive Photos, Inc.*

"Mr. Madison's War"

Madison was reelected president in 1812. As the war progressed, British soldiers occupied large sections of the Great Lakes region and support for the war was high among westerners. But New Englanders largely opposed the war. America's conflict with England, the world's major naval power, interfered with the profitable shipping-related activities that were a vital part of the New England economy. The Federalist Party had its base in New England and referred to the war as "Mr. Madison's War."

According to Mark M. Boatner III, writing in the *Encyclopedia of the American Revolution,* "The disgraceful performance of an unprepared and disunited country in the War of 1812 ... cost [Madison] popularity." In the summer of 1814, the British invaded Washington, D.C., set the White House on fire, and took over the city. A popular story credits Dolly Madison with saving a life-size portrait of George Washington from the fire. The Madisons fled to safety in the surrounding area. When they returned to Washington five days later, they found the White House in need of rebuilding. The War of 1812 came to an end with the Treaty of Ghent (Belgium) on December 24, 1814.

Growth of Republican Party, decline of the Federalist Party

Although most historians see the War of 1812 as a draw between America and Great Britain, the Americans of the time saw the war as a great victory. As a result, a feeling of national pride swept the country. The Republican Party of James Madison was given credit for the victory and thrived after the War of 1812.

During the war, New England Federalist leaders had

met secretly in Hartford, Connecticut. Many people suspected that they were plotting to have New England secede (break off from) the United States. After the war, the Federalists were called disloyal. Suspicion of the Federalist Party was so great that it soon declined and disappeared.

By the end of Madison's second term of office, he had come to believe that the nation needed a national bank. He had opposed the creation of a national bank in 1791, but now, with his support, a national bank was created.

Has productive retirement

Madison retired in 1817 at the end of his second term and retired to Montpelier. He remained an active citizen. From 1826 to 1834 Madison served as headmaster of the University of Virginia and arranged that after his death his personal library would go to the institution.

Madison's later years were marked by illness, but he always retained his quick mind. He enjoyed entertaining but soon found himself in debt. Economic circumstances forced Madison to scale down his way of life and sell off some of his land to raise money to live on. In his final months, Madison was confined at home because of illness. He died at Montpelier in the summer of 1836.

American historian and secretary of state Daniel Webster said of James Madison, "He had as much to do as any man in framing the Constitution, and as much to do as any man in administering it."

For More Information

Boatner, Mark M., III. "Madison, James." *Encyclopedia of the American Revolution.* Mechanicsburg, PA: Stackpole Books, 1994, pp. 668-70.

Bourgoin, Suzanne M. and Paula K. Byers. "Madison, James." *Encyclopedia of World Biography.* Detroit: Gale, 1998, vol. 10, pp. 121-23.

Ketcham, Ralph. *James Madison: A Biography.* Charlottesville: University Press of Virginia, 1980.

Web Sites

"James Madison: Fourth President 1809–1817." [Online] Available http://www.whitehouse.gov/WH/glimpse/presidents/html/jm4.html (accessed on 9/21/99).

George Mason

Born 1725
Fairfax County, Virginia
Died October 7, 1792
Fairfax County, Virginia

Political leader, judge, plantation owner, writer

Mason urged his descendants to prefer "the happiness and independence [of] a private [life] to the troubles and [annoyances] of public business [unless] the necessity of the times should engage [you] in public affairs."

Portrait: George Mason. *Reproduced by permission of Archive Photos, Inc.*

George Mason was one of the most important Americans of Revolutionary times. The intelligent and thoughtful man made a great impact on the development of the American government. He is especially remembered for the passionate arguments he made in favor of freedom for individuals at the Federal Constitutional Convention in Philadelphia, Pennsylvania, in 1787. There the Constitution of the United States was written and passed.

George Mason was born in 1725 on the Virginia plantation of his parents, George and Ann Thomson Mason. His father drowned when Mason was ten. With the approval of Mason's mother, his uncle, a lawyer named John Mercer, took charge of bringing up the boy. Mason had access to his uncle's large library of law books and was taught by private tutors. He gained a good grasp of the classics, the writings and languages of the ancient Greeks and Romans.

In his late teens, the wealthy young man began running the family plantation, one of the largest in Virginia. He had a cranky personality, and he tended to be overly concerned about his health. Still he became a popular and important person in his community. In 1750 he married Anne Eilbeck, with whom he had five sons and four daughters. Between 1755 and 1758 he designed and supervised the building of his own grand home, Gunston Hall.

Fights in French and Indian War

In 1752 Mason and fellow Virginian, **George Washington** (see entry), became part owners of a business called the Ohio Company, which bought and sold land for profit in the Great Lakes region. Through this venture, both Virginia aristocrats became familiar with what was then the American frontier, and they soon got caught up in a frontier war.

In the mid-eighteenth century, France and England were engaged in a worldwide war that in 1754 spilled over onto the North American frontier. The French saw the Ohio Company's colonizing efforts in America's west as a challenge to their claims to the region. Rivalry between France and England and her colonies over the western lands led to the French and Indian War (1754–63).

In that war, American militia (pronounced ma-LISH-a) men fought with the British against the French and their Indian allies. (Militia men were volunteer soldiers; America did not have a regular army.) Mason acted as a supply agent for troops commanded by George Washington. He also served as a captain in the war and earned the rank of colonel (pronounced KER-nuhl) in the Virginia militia.

Mason maintained a lifetime interest in the development of the Great Lakes region. He was a leading member of a committee that approved the expedition of explorer George Rogers Clark into the region now known as the Midwest. Clark carried out the first survey of the area and he later supervised settlement there.

Joins with colonial groups to protest taxation

During this time, Mason began to take an interest in public life. Between 1754 and 1779 he served on the board of directors of the city of Alexandria, Virginia, and was a justice of the Fairfax County Court. In 1758 he was elected to the Virginia House of Burgesses, the representative assembly of colonial Virginia, where he served with George Washington. But he grew tired of the routine and retired in 1760 after two terms.

At the end of French and Indian War, England was heavily in debt and began to pass tax laws to raise money in the colonies to pay off those war debts. As a private citizen, Mason voiced his opposition to the Sugar Act of 1764 and the Stamp Act of 1765. Mason wrote a letter to England's King **George III** (see entry) expressing the outrage of the American colonists and their opposition to what they viewed as unfair taxation.

In the years before the outbreak of the Revolutionary War (1775–83), the colonies set up "committees of correspondence." These were groups of people who aroused public opinion and organized acts of defiance against Great Britain. George Mason became involved in the Virginia committee after the passage of the Townshend Acts in 1767. These Acts imposed taxes on glass, lead, paints, paper items, and tea. To protest these taxes, Mason helped form an association that agreed to stop buying British goods until British merchants joined the colonists in demanding a repeal of the taxes.

Suffers personal tragedy, begins political writing

Between 1767 and 1773, Mason concentrated on running his plantation and raising his family. His wife, Anne, fell ill in 1772 and died a year later at age thirty-nine. That same year Mason wrote his first important public paper, "Extracts from Virginia Charters, with Some Remarks upon Them."

The paper examined the legal rights of the Ohio Company and showed Mason's skill in analyzing legal and political matters. It was one of many such writings that appeared in the days before the American Revolution, writings that explained how American colonists had the same rights as English citizens. It was also one of several papers written by Mason that would influence the writers of later documents such as the Declaration of Independence and the 1783 Treaty of Paris that ended the Revolutionary War.

Serves at Virginia Convention

By 1774 American colonists were becoming openly rebellious against Great Britain. Mason took on an important role in national politics when he helped patriot **Patrick Henry** (see entry) draft the "Fairfax Resolves." These papers stated the legal position of the American colonies in relation to Great Britain, pointing out how British taxation policies were violating colonial rights.

In July 1775 Mason was elected to the Virginia Convention as Virginia prepared to take part in the upcoming struggle to gain freedom from Great Britain. He replaced George Washington, who had been named commander-in-chief of the newly formed Continental army.

Opinion in the Virginia Convention was sharply divided over the question of going to war with the mother country, and quarrels were frequent. Mason later wrote to Washington, "I was never in so disagreeable a situation, and almost despaired of a cause which I found so ill conducted. Mere [annoyance] and disgust threw me into such an ill state of health that before the convention rose, I was sometimes near fainting in the House." Mason helped set the House session back on course when it began to fall apart due to political disputes and confusion about how to proceed.

Throughout his lifetime, Mason never enjoyed serving on committees and often arrived late for meetings. He expressed contempt for those he called "babblers," people who talk on and on and are commonly found in politics. But no other Virginia lawmaker was as respected and carefully listened to. His reputation grew, and the other delegates wanted Mason to succeed Washington as their representative to the Continental Congress. The Continental Congress was a group of representatives from the American colonies who met to express grievances against British colonial policy; they had created the Continental army to fight against the British. Mason avoided serving in the congress by pleading that he had to take care of his motherless children.

Writes Virginia's Bill of Rights and Constitution

Even before July 1776, when America declared its independence from England and the thirteen colonies officially became states, Virginia had already begun the hard work of forming a new government. In April 1776 Mason was elected to the Virginia Constitutional Convention to help write the constitution for his home state. He spent the spring studying and discussing forms of government with other prominent leaders.

Mason was elected to the Virginia Constitutional Convention to help write the state constitution. His Bill of Rights became the model used by other colonies and by Thomas Jefferson when he wrote the first section of the Declaration of Independence.
Reproduced courtesy of the Library of Congress.

Virginia's convention voted "to prepare a Declaration of Rights and such a plan of government as will be most likely to maintain peace and order in this colony and secure substantial and equal liberty to the people."

Over a mere six weeks, Mason took part in discussions and wrote the first draft for the Virginia Declaration of Rights, which was adopted as the Virginia Bill of Rights by the convention on June 12, 1776. Mason's declaration laid out some basic principles of republican government (a system in which voters hold the power and elect representatives to carry out the voters' wishes). It also affirmed the right to trials by jury and it supported religious tolerance. It became a model used by other colonies and guided **Thomas Jefferson** (see entry) when he wrote the first section of the U.S. Declaration of Independence.

Writes Virginia Constitution, helps form federal government

James Madison (see entry), later a U.S. President, called George Mason the "master builder" of Virginia's 1776 constitution. During the six-week period in which he wrote the Virginia Declaration of Rights, Mason also wrote the first constitution of the independent Commonwealth of Virginia. It passed with no opposition on June 29, 1776.

About this event, Edmund Pendleton, the head of the delegates at that convention, wrote to Thomas Jefferson, "the political cooks are busy in preparing the dish, and as Colonel Mason seems to [be in charge of] the great work, I have [confidence] it will be framed so as to answer its end."

During the war years from 1776 to 1780, the former British colonies, now American states, were busy forming a new national government. Much lawmaking activity took place in Philadelphia, then the nation's capital. George Mason played a major role in helping to establish a national government independent of Great Britain. He was also active in organizing military affairs for the new nation, especially in the western frontier.

Retires from public life, then returns to it

The Revolution officially ended in 1783 with the signing of the Treaty of Paris. By that time, Mason believed the new American government was on firm footing and decided to retire from public life. With his second wife, Sarah Brent, whom he had married three years earlier, he went to live quietly at Gunston Hall. When people tried to get him involved in government affairs, he explained that their efforts were an invasion of his personal liberty.

But Mason cared too much about his country to stay completely out of politics. Gunston Hall was located on the main road from Richmond, Virginia, to Philadelphia. State and national leaders often passed by Mason's house and stopped to get his advice on political matters.

In 1785 Mason emerged from semi-retirement to participate in talks about the Articles of Confederation, which were used to govern the United States during the war. The Articles were not considered adequate to govern the new nation. Finally it was decided that a constitution was needed, and a Federal Constitutional Convention was held in Philadelphia in 1787 to draw one up.

Suggests changes to proposed U.S. Constitution

In 1787 Mason was one of Virginia's representatives at the Federal Constitutional Convention. He became one of the major speakers, forcefully presenting his point of view. The delegates to the convention had many different views about how a government should be organized. Mason believed that all men—both rich and poor—are born with certain natural rights to life and freedom; protecting these rights for all, he said, must be the cornerstone of government policies.

Some delegates, led by George Washington and others, wanted a strong central government. This view was supported by several different factions, many of them made up largely of wealthy men. Businessmen, traders, and ship owners, who suffered financially when the states argued about taxes, favored a strong central government. Men who had lent money to the government thought a strong central government would be more likely to pay them back. Some rich men were afraid that if poor men ran the states, they might issue large sums of worthless money or protect people with bad debts. Westerners who lived on the wild frontier wanted a powerful central government to protect them from possible Indian, Spanish, and British invasions.

Mason expressed his opposition to the strong central government proposed by the new constitution in a paper, "Objections to the Proposed Federal Constitution." It is considered one of his best pieces of writing. In it, Mason stated that the U.S. House of Representatives proposed by the new constitution did not really represent all the people. He believed that the proposed U.S. Senate would be too powerful. He also said that the proposed justice system would allow the rich to oppress the poor. He expressed his fear that the country might be ruled by kings and queens or could fall into the hands of corrupt, rich citizens.

Mason also objected to a provision in the U.S. Constitution that allowed the slave trade to continue until 1808. Mason, like many Southern landowners, relied on slaves to work his farm. Still, he recognized that slavery was an evil institution and urged that the slave trade be ended as soon as possible. His view lost out to those who wanted more time before the slave trade was discontinued.

Proposes Bill of Rights, refuses to sign Constitution

In order to protect individual rights, Mason proposed that a bill of rights be added to the Constitution, and he was highly disappointed when his proposal was defeated. His proposal that a second convention be held was also voted down.

In the end, Mason refused to sign the U.S. Constitution adopted by the Convention. According to the notes of James Madison, Mason stated he "would sooner chop off his right hand than put it to [sign] the constitution as it now stands."

Opposes Virginia's adoption of the U.S. Constitution

When the Federal Constitutional Convention completed its work, conventions were held in each state to decide whether or not to adopt the U.S. Constitution. At the Virginia convention, held in June 1788, James Madison supported it. George Washington and Thomas Jefferson also added their support in writing, although they were not able to attend the convention. Mason and Patrick Henry opposed it.

Lively debate on the topic took place. Virginia finally approved the Constitution by a vote of 89-79. Upset and angry after his lost political battle, George Mason went home to Gunston Hall. He turned down several government job offers, because he preferred to offer his advice in a more casual way to leaders who came to visit him.

But Mason left his mark on the U.S. Constitution. A Bill of Rights was included in the version of the Constitution that was finally adopted on December 15, 1791. The Virginia Declaration of Rights, written by Mason, served as the basis of the Bill of Rights of the U.S. Constitution. The Bill of Rights is made up of the first ten amendments (additions) to the Constitution and protects basic rights of individuals from being stepped on by the federal government.

Final years

In the 1790s, Mason retired from state and national politics for good. But being a man of strong opinions, he spent his last years feuding with other members of the Fairfax County Court over the location of a new courthouse and other local affairs. Mason died on October 7, 1792, and was buried at Gunston Hall. In February 1795, the Eleventh Amendment to the U.S. Constitution was put in place. It addressed Mason's demand that the court system have some limits placed on its powers.

Several presidents of the United States honored George Mason as an outstanding thinker. Thomas Jefferson once referred to him as "the wisest man of his generation," and James Madison praised him as "a powerful reasoner, a profound statesman, and a devoted republican."

For More Information

Allison, Robert J. "George Mason." *American Eras: The Revolutionary Era, 1754-1783.* Detroit, MI: Gale, 1998, pp. 192-93.

Boatner, Mark M., III. "Mason, George." *Encyclopedia of the American Revolution.* Mechanicsburg, PA: Stackpole Books, 1994, pp. 682-83.

Garraty, John A. and Mark C. Carnes. "Mason, George." *American National Biography.* Oxford: Oxford University Press, 1999, vol. 14, pp. 645-647.

Web Sites

"A Biography of George Mason, 1725-1792." Text copied from National Archives and Records Administration: The Founding Fathers' Page for The American Revolution—an .HTML project, 1997. Department of Humanities Computing. [Online] Available http://odur.let.rug.nl ~usa/B/gmason/mason.htm (accessed on 9/12/99).

"George Mason Writings and Biography." *National Archives and Record Administration.* Copyright at Common Law by LEXREX, 1998. [Online] Available http://www.lexrex.com/bios/gmason.htm (accessed on 9/12/99).

Williams, Gary. "George Mason." *The Freeman,* May, 1992. Copyright 1988 by Foundation for Economic Education, Inc. The American Revolution—an .HTML project. [Online] Available http://odur.let.rug.nl /~usa/B/gmason/gmasxx.htm (accessed on 9/12/99).

Mary McCauley ("Molly Pitcher")

Born October 13, 1754
Trenton, New Jersey
Died January 22, 1832
Carlisle, Pennsylvania

Domestic servant, camp follower

Mary McCauley ran a household and tended to children, the typical duties of a woman of the late eighteenth and early nineteenth centuries. But when her country needed her, she showed independence of thought and action. Nicknamed "Molly Pitcher," Mary McCauley demonstrated courage under fire and helped save American lives at a critical Revolutionary War battle.

"You girls should have been with me at the battle of Monmouth and learned how to load a cannon."

The woman believed to be the Molly Pitcher of Revolutionary War fame was born Mary Ludwig on October 13, 1754. Her parents were dairy farmers who lived on a small farm outside of Trenton, New Jersey. In some documents the name "Ludwig" is spelled "Ludwick." Many people in Colonial times were illiterate and so could not correct others who misspelled their names. Mary herself could not read or write, and signed documents as an adult with a simple "X."

Mary Ludwig's father was John George Ludwig. (Some historians believe the family's actual last name was Hass or Has, a name that was dropped when John arrived in America.) John Ludwig immigrated to America in about 1730 from an area in southwest Germany that was home to many people

Painting: "Molly Pitcher at the Battle of Monmouth" by C. Y. Turner. *Reproduced by permission of the Corbis Corporation (Bellevue).*

who practiced a Protestant religion. This fact is interesting first because many German American groups have claimed Mary Ludwig (Molly Pitcher) as a German heroine. Second, like the Pilgrims in the New England colonies, many Protestants also immigrated to America because of religious persecution in Europe.

Moves to Pennsylvania

Mary Ludwig's life was fairly uneventful until 1769, when at the age of fifteen she moved to Carlisle, Pennsylvania, to become a servant to the family of Dr. William Irvine. Ludwig's father apparently arranged for his daughter to have this job, even though it meant she would move far away (about 125 miles) from her parent's home. As a domestic servant, Mary cleaned house, washed clothes, and cared for the Irvine children.

Life as a soldier's wife

In July 1769, Mary Ludwig married William Hays, who had been born in Ireland, immigrated to America, and worked as a barber in Carlisle. William enlisted as a gunner in the Pennsylvania State Regiment of Artillery in May 1777. This date is significant because the Revolutionary War had been underway for about a year, and the American need for soldiers had grown.

Artillery is a term that includes weapons such as cannons that throw projectiles (bombs) across the field of battle. As an artillery man, William "served" the cannons. He prepared cartridges (cloth packets full of gun powder), hauled and stacked cannon balls, loaded the guns, aimed and fired them, and swabbed them out to wash away any lingering traces of gunpowder before reloading. It was heavy, hot, smoky, dangerous work, especially in the heat of battle.

As a soldier's wife who accompanied her husband from battlefield to battlefield, Mary Hays had many duties. She had to take care of her own and her husband's belongings and be ready to pack them at a moment's notice when the army was on the move. Hays also had to keep her family and clothing clean while on the move and find food wherever the army stopped. When her husband or an unmarried soldier became ill, Hays nursed them in addition to her other duties.

The Battle of Monmouth

Historical records report that William Hays and his regiment served with distinction at the Battle of Monmouth, New Jersey, in June 1778. It was the last major battle fought in the North during the Revolutionary War. When Hays's regiment was ordered from Pennsylvania to New Jersey, Mary Hays followed the army to stay with her husband. The move also allowed her to be near her family.

The stage for the battle was set when the British army evacuated Philadelphia on June 18, 1778, and marched eastward across New Jersey to the Atlantic coast. Their goal was to load their army and baggage onto British ships and sail north to New York City, a city still in the hands of the British.

American General **George Washington** (1732–1799; see entry) received news of the movements of the British army, however, and attacked on June 28. Washington claimed a victory, since the Americans forced the British from the field of battle. The British disagreed, pointing out that they escaped during the night after the battle and saved most of their men and belongings. The Americans lost an estimated 500 men, while the British lost about 1,000 men killed or wounded.

The Other "Molly Pitcher"

The name "Molly Pitcher" is sometimes applied to other Revolutionary War heroines. One such heroine was Margaret Cochran Corbin (see entry) or "Captain Molly," a woman who fought in the Battle of Fort Washington, New York, in 1776. "Molly" was a common nickname given to girls named Mary or Margaret. The "Pitcher" name was given because of the water they carried to soldiers on the battlefield.

Over the years, many historians have tried to verify which parts of the "Molly Pitcher" story are true. They have consulted official documents from Colonial and Revolutionary War times, including property deeds (certificates of ownership of homes and animals), letters, pension applications, newspaper articles, and congressional and military records. A good historical case can be made that Mary Ludwig Hays McCauley, sometimes called "Sergeant Molly," is the "Molly Pitcher" of legend.

Molly Hays's courage at the Battle of Monmouth

Mary Hays was a young woman of twenty-four at the time her husband William served as a gunner at Monmouth. The battle actually took place in the small town of Freehold in northeastern New Jersey and is more accurately called the Battle of Monmouth County Courthouse.

When Mary McCauley's husband was overcome with heat during the Battle of Monmouth, she loaded the cannons in his stead. *Reproduced courtesy of the Library of Congress.*

The day of the battle was extremely hot and humid. Mary Hays helped her husband's regiment by carrying pitcher after pitcher of cool water from the Monmouth Courthouse well and serving the water to the thirsty soldiers. They began to call her "Molly Pitcher." She also offered first aid to the soldiers who fell in battle. And when her husband was overcome with the heat, she replaced him, helping his gun crew keep up their firing pattern. General Washington himself is said to have stopped after the battle to thank and congratulate "Molly Pitcher" on her brave service to his soldiers.

Receives army pension

After the war, Mary and her barber husband settled down in Carlisle. William died in 1788, leaving behind Mary and a young son, John, aged five. A year later, in 1789, Mary Hays married John McCauley. Many records indicate that this second marriage was not a happy one for Mary McCauley. She continued to work as a domestic servant. A tax record from around this time stated that the McCauleys owned a house, a half-lot, two cows, and a half-dozen teaspoons. John McCauley died about 1813, and Mary McCauley did not marry again.

Mary McCauley continued to work as a domestic servant for the rest of her life. Various people described her as a short, heavy-set woman who had an abrupt manner. She often wore the style of clothing that was popular in her youth, a white dress covered by a striped skirt that was split in the middle and gathered to each side, along with a white cap with a broad frilled edging. She was a talkative woman who loved children and was a tender, careful nurse to the sick. Mary McCauley did have a rough side, however. As the wife of a soldier, she had learned to swear and usually spoke her mind with some bluntness.

Among the households where Mary McCauley was employed was the Miles home in Carlisle. Mary tended Mrs. Miles, who was ill for a year before she died in 1822. In addition to nursing Mrs. Miles, Mary cared for the family's two young sons. One son, Wesley Miles, published his recollections of "Molly Pitcher" in the May 18, 1876, edition of *The Carlisle Herald,* the town newspaper.

Years after the war ended, state governments began to grant money to soldiers and their widows, many of whom had fallen on hard times. In 1822, the Commonwealth of Pennsylvania passed a bill that immediately granted Mary McCauley forty dollars and the promise of forty dollars per month for the remainder of her life. At first, this pension was applied for because Mary McCauley was the widow of a soldier. However, the final wording of the bill makes it clear that McCauley received the pension in recognition of her own services. The act read: "For the relief of Molly McKolly for her services during the revolutionary war."

U.S. census records show that McCauley spent the last years of her life living in the Carlisle home of her son, John L. Hays, and his wife, Elizabeth. The Hayses had seven children, providing Mary with many opportunities to be with the children she loved.

Buried with full military honors

Mary McCauley is buried in the Old Graveyard in Carlisle. Her gravesite is marked by a stone that reads: "Mollie McCauley. Renowned in History as Molly Pitcher, the heroine of Monmouth. Died Jan. 1832. Aged 79 Years. Erected by the Citizens of Cumberland County. July 4th, 1876."

On June 28, 1905, the Patriotic Order of Sons of America unveiled an additional monument, a cannon planted over her grave. In Monmouth, New Jersey, a battle monument shows "Molly Pitcher" with a cannon and a pail of water.

Legend grows

Eyewitness accounts of the Battle of Monmouth were given by some of the soldiers who fought there, by their wives who heard the stories from their soldier husbands, and by the friends and family of Mary McCauley. It is difficult to prove which stories are true because of the large gap in time between the battle and when the stories began to be published.

Nevertheless, the stories do paint an exciting picture. One tale describes how Mary Hays carried an injured soldier on her back, away from the battlefield while under heavy fire from British cannons. Another tale tells how Mary Hays was servicing her husband's cannon. As she reached over for a cartridge, a British cannonball passed between her legs, leaving her uninjured but carrying away part of her skirt. Some believe that General Washington made Mary the only woman officer in the Continental army.

In 1876, at the one-hundred-year anniversary of the founding of the United States, many people became very interested in the Revolutionary War. They loved to retell stories of bravery from the war, and were fond of tracing their ancestors' activities during the war. At this time, the story of Molly Pitcher was retold and added to.

Molly Pitcher's story is retold

The story of Molly Pitcher is celebrated in numerous children's books, and she has an entry in most U.S. encyclopedias. She is also the subject of at least three plays. Edward Martin Walsh produced *Molly Pitcher, the Monmouth Girl,* a four-act play, in 1900, in Detroit, Michigan. In 1928, Molly Pitcher's story was retold in *La Capitaine,* which was published in *Short Plays from American History and Literature,* by Olive M. Price. "La Capitaine" is French for "the captain." In 1971, Marjory Hall published *Molly Meets the General: Two Patriots of the American Revolution.*

Mary McCauley's bravery at the Battle of Monmouth is also the subject of paintings and at least one poem, entitled "Molly Pitcher: The Battle of Monmouth—28 June 1778." The poem tells how General Washington's army survived the brutal winter at Valley Forge, Pennsylvania, and then marched to the Jersey Shore to fight the British in the heat of summer. The poem describes Molly Pitcher, her nursing of the wounded, her pitchers of cooling water, and her firing of her husband's cannon after he fell ill from the heat.

For More Information

Malone, Dumas. *Dictionary of American Biography*. Vol. 6. New York: Charles Scribner's Sons, 1933, pp. 574-675.

Purcell, L. Edward. *Who Was Who in the American Revolution*. New York: Facts on File, 1993, p. 219.

Rome, Ellen. "Molly Pitcher. An Ohio Schoolgirl's Essay." *Daughters of the American Revolution Magazine*. Vol. 109, 1975, pp. 903-05.

Smith, Samuel Stelle. *A Molly Pitcher Chronology*. Monmouth Beach, NJ: Philip Freneau Press, 1972.

Stevenson, Augusta. *Molly Pitcher: Young Patriot*. New York: Aladdin Paperbacks, 1986.

Web Sites

Lopez, Lilli. *Molly Pitcher: The Battle of Monmouth, 28 June 1778*. [Online] Available http://www.midmaine.com/~lopez/page 96.html (accessed on March 9, 1999).

U.S. Field Artillery Association. *The Story of Molly Pitcher.* [Online] Available http://sill-www.army.mil/pao/pamolly.html (accessed on February 19, 1999).

Jane McCrea

Born c. 1752
Lamington, New Jersey
Died July 27, 1777
Fort Edward, New York

American captive

As the Revolutionary War (1775–83) raged, dramatic tales were told of how Jane McCrea died. Her capture and murder led people in New York and New England to rally against the British forces stationed there. McCrea's story continued to arouse patriotic feelings among Americans for more than a century after her death.

Jane McCrea (pronounced Ma-CRAY) was the daughter of James McCrea, a Presbyterian minister from New Jersey, and Mary Graham McCrea. Jane McCrea was born the sixth of seven children, and the younger of two daughters. After her mother's death, her father remarried and had five more children.

When her father died (date unknown), Jane McCrea went to stay with her brother, John McCrea, a lawyer living in northern New York State. He served in the Continental army during the Revolutionary War. Few other facts are known about Jane McCrea's early life. Like many families at the time of the American Revolution, her family was divided by the war. Two of her brothers and one half-brother served in the Continental army, while two other half-brothers were Loyalists and fought on the side of the British.

Portrait: Jane McCrea.
Reproduced by permission of Archive Photos, Inc.

Leaves for Fort Edward to meet fiancé

In 1776 McCrea became engaged to David Jones, whose family lived near Fort Edward in New York State. Jones was a Tory (an American colonist who was loyal to England) and he served in the British army under General **John Burgoyne** (see entry). Some stories say the two young lovers had known each other as children, while other accounts say the couple met as young adults. Even though her brother John, with whom she lived, supported the patriots, Jane McCrea chose to support the cause of her intended husband. In her book *White Captives: Gender and Ethnicity on the American Frontier,* June Namias mentions how the stories of Jane's choice differ: "According to most renditions, Jane deliberately did not go with her brother's family to fight for the rebel cause, but chose instead her lover, David, and thus the Tory side. The fiction, histories and biographies of Jane give mixed messages regarding her decision to desert her patriot brother (or father) for her Loyalist lover." Namias also indicates that "many of the [facts of the story] remain in dispute to this day."

In the summer of 1777 Burgoyne launched an invasion against the colonists in New York. His men marched southward from New York's Lake Champlain toward the Hudson River. Fearing for their safety, most people living along the route immediately left their homes and moved elsewhere.

John McCrea urged his sister to go with his family to the relatively safe area of Albany, New York. But she chose not to go, instead setting out for Fort Edward, hoping to meet her fiancé there. David Jones had written her a letter, saying, "In a few days [my unit] will march to Fort Edward,... where I shall have the happiness to meet you." According to popular legend, the couple was intending to marry at Fort Edward after their reunion.

A mysterious death

There are many versions of what happened next, but it seems clear that on the morning of July 27, 1777, McCrea arrived at the home of her friend, Sarah McNeil, an elderly woman and a cousin of the British general Simon Fraser.

Together the two women went on to Fort Edward. Their timing was disastrous. They arrived at the fort in the afternoon, at the same time as did a group of Indians scouting on behalf of General Burgoyne, about two days ahead of the main body of the British troops. The Indians seized McCrea and McNeil, not realizing that their prisoners were friendly to the Tory cause. They intended to take the women back with them to General Burgoyne, who was at British army headquarters in New York's Fort Ann, and claim a reward for having caught them.

But when the Indians arrived at Fort Ann, only Mrs. McNeil was with them. The next day, Jane McCrea's scalped and bullet-ridden body was found near Fort Edward. The circumstances surrounding her death remain a mystery.

Differing explanations

In one story describing McCrea's fate, she was stripped of her clothing, shot, and scalped by her Indian captors. That version spread rapidly and was believed by many patriots as well as supporters of the British in America and overseas. Another commonly repeated story of McCrea's death is based on the account of a man named Samuel Standish, who claimed to be an eyewitness being held in the area by Indians. Standish testified that several Indians got drunk and fell into an argument about who would serve as McCrea's guard. In the scuffle that followed, McCrea was shot. According to a third version of the story, as told later by Mrs. McNeil's granddaughter, a member of a party that was pursuing the Indian group accidentally shot McCrea.

Murder shocks both Americans and British

Accounts disagree regarding Jane McCrea's physical appearance. At the time of her death, she was somewhere between seventeen and twenty-four years of age. McCrea has often been portrayed as an attractive young woman, tall, with hair that reached the floor when tied in a braid. In his 1853 biography of McCrea, combining historical fact and romantic fiction, David Wilson refers to her as "a young lady of fine accomplishments, great personal attraction, and remarkable sweetness of disposition."

Whatever the actual circumstances of her death, Jane McCrea apparently was scalped and her long hair displayed in

triumph by the Indians before the British army. Not long after the murder, David Jones, McCrea's fiancé, was said to have applied for a military discharge. When it did not come through, he deserted Burgoyne's army and fled to the Canadian wilderness, where he lived as a bachelor for the rest of his life.

Loyalist Jane McCrea was captured by Indian scouts, killed, and scalped. *Reproduced by permission of Archive Photos, Inc.*

General Burgoyne was said to have been shocked by the violent murder, which reportedly was committed by a Wyandot Indian named Panther, who took the young woman's scalp as evidence for his claim that he had captured her. Although Burgoyne wanted to discipline the man, he did not, because he feared his Indian troops would abandon the British and leave them without guides in a strange wilderness. However, he apparently asked that the Indians stop taking scalps. His request backfired on him when many of the warriors left the battlefields and returned home. Others deserted the British army to make their own war on the New York settlers.

The British, too, were deeply affected by the young woman's murder. The London *Annual Register* for 1777 wrote that McCrea's death "struck every breast with horror." **Edmund Burke** (see entry), a famous British politician of the eighteenth century, denounced the British policy of making use of Indian allies.

Murder results in growth of the American army

Burgoyne's American enemies used the opportunity presented by the murder of Jane McCrea to whip up anti-British feelings among the American colonists. General **George Washington** referred to the McCrea death to remind New Yorkers and New Englanders that the British could not be trusted. **Horatio Gates** (see entries), a general in the Continental army, used the incident to influence popular opinion against the Indians.

The story of Jane McCrea prompted large-scale enlistments in the Continental army. Hearing the account of her death, many Americans who until then had remained neutral (non-involved) in the conflict between the Tories and the American patriots swung to the side of the patriots. They feared that if they did not, enemy victories on the battlefield might expose their own families to similar dangers. In a short time, the American army saw a surge in the number of new recruits to the cause of American independence. Within three months after McCrea's death, Burgoyne and his forces would surrender to the patriots.

McCrea's name becomes an American battle cry

At the time of McCrea's murder, General Horatio Gates had taken command of the American troops in the northern part of the colonies. He quickly did what he could to transform McCrea into a martyr (pronounced MAHR-ter) for her support of the American cause.

In a strange turn, the name of Jane McCrea, the Tory fiancé of a British soldier, became the war cry of many American military men. Burgoyne's British soldiers were often met on the battlefield by patriot soldiers yelling her name as they charged.

General Burgoyne helps McCrea's half-brother

In 1777, with great sadness, Continental army soldier John McCrea buried his sister at Moses Kill, New York, near Fort Edward. Some time later, one of Jane McCrea's half-brothers, who was serving as a captain in the British Army under General Burgoyne, asked the general's help in obtaining charge over a company of soldiers. Shortly thereafter Burgoyne received a letter from the young captain thanking him for the help he had provided.

In the margin of Captain McCrea's letter, Burgoyne noted that he had been accused of encouraging the Indians to act in a savage manner. In his own defense Burgoyne wrote: "It was a great pleasure to me to be thought of so differently by that lady's [Jane's] brother, as five years afterwards, when he had other and more able supporters, to be singled out as the person whom he wished to act as his patron. From a man of Captain McCrea's character, this selection was not only a pleasing evidence of my innocence," it also showed McCrea understood Burgoyne's hatred of Jane's murder.

McCrea becomes a celebrity in death

A short time after Jane McCrea's death, she became a legendary figure—a martyr of the American Revolution. The tale of her murder was retold in songs, poems, plays, and newspaper stories and at patriotic events. Writer Philip Freneau, who had himself been treated cruelly when held captive by the British, used McCrea's story as the basis of an angry poem he wrote in 1778 called "American Independence, an Everlasting Deliverance from British Tyranny." In her 1805 *History of the American Revolution,* **Mercy Otis Warren** (see entry) accused General Burgoyne of being responsible for McCrea's murder. Joel Barlow wrote in his 1807 poem, "The Columbiad": "Eternal ages [should] trace [the incident of McCrea's death] with a tear," and Delia Bacon made it into a play called *The Bride of Fort Edward* in 1839.

In 1852 a businessman in Fort Edward cut down the tree under which McCrea's body was supposed to have been found. He advertised "elegant canes and boxes manufactured from this world-renowned tree," believing that "an event [filled with] so much interest ... will meet with a hearty

The Practice of Scalping

Scalping is the cutting and removal of the scalp. The severed scalp was thought to give the victor the enemy's power and often served as a trophy, something kept in remembrance of a victory. Scalping was practiced in Europe and Asia and among some Native American tribes.

During the eighteenth century the French and British in America encouraged the spread of scalping by offering Indians bounties, payments of goods in exchange for scalps. The number of scalps taken would help the Europeans determine how many enemies had been killed. In time Indians began to make fake scalps out of horsehair, preparing them in the same way as human scalps. Once the French and English figured this trick out, they examined the scalps brought to them more carefully before making payment and reduced the amount of money they would pay for them.

In his diary written in the eighteenth century, a French soldier known only as J.C.B. wrote about the process of scalping: "When a war party has captured one or more prisoners that cannot be taken away, it is the usual custom to kill them by breaking their heads with the blows of a tomahawk.... When he has struck two or

response from every American." It is not known if he was successful in these marketing attempts.

One hundred years after the murder, Chrisfield Johnson, in his *History of Washington Co., New York,* pointed out that the power of Jane McCrea's story did not lie merely in her murder: "Thousands of men, women, and children have been massacred during the wars between the Indians and the colonists ... [and] during the Revolution and subsequent conflicts, but not another case among them all has attracted so much attention as that of lovely Jane McCrea." Wilson believed that the popularity of McCrea's story could be due to "the youth, beauty, and social position of the victim ... [and] the romance that mingled with the tragedy."

Incident inspires artworks

The death of Jane McCrea was depicted in drawings and paintings by many popular artists of the eighteenth and three blows, the [Native American] quickly seizes his knife, and makes an incision around the hair from the upper part of the forehead to the back of the neck. Then he puts his foot on the shoulder of the victim, who he has turned over face down, and pulls the hair off with both hands, from back to front.... This hasty operation is no sooner finished than the savage fastens the scalp to his belt and goes on his way. This method is only used when the prisoner cannot follow his captor; or when the [Native American] is pursued.... He quickly takes the scalp, gives the deathcry, and flees at top speed.... When a savage has taken a scalp, and is not afraid he is being pursued, he stops and scrapes the skin to remove the blood and fibres on it. He makes a hoop of green wood, stretches the skin over it like a tambourine, and puts it in the sun to dry a little. The skin is painted red, and the hair on the outside combed. When prepared, the scalp is fastened to the end of a long stick, and carried on his shoulder in triumph to the village or place where he wants it put. But as he nears each place on his way, he gives as many cries as he has scalps to announce his arrival, and show his bravery. Sometimes as many as 15 scalps are fastened on the same stick. When there are too many for one stick, they decorate several sticks with the

nineteenth centuries. John Vanderlyn's 1804 painting, the *Death of Jane McCrea,* was praised by art critics of the time as one of the first major American works of art.

In 1822 the remains of Jane McCrea were moved to the old cemetery at Fort Edward amid a patriotic ceremony. Her remains were moved to Union Cemetery near Hudson Falls, New York, in 1852. Throughout the 1890s, supporters raised funds to surround the grave with a decorative iron fence. During a celebration of Fort Edward in 1927, a play by Philip Henry Caroll was presented there entitled *Jane McCrea: A Tragedy in Five Acts*. Jane McCrea's legend lived on, even 150 years after her death.

The changing, lesser status of women

According to June Namias, who examines relationships of power between men and women in her writings, one picture of the McCrea murder "after another shows Jane's body pulled, dragged, or thrown from horseback and pushed to the ground by two or more Indians. It appears that they often take turns stabbing her ... with knives and tomahawks.... Each works as a reminder of enemy brutality, female weakness, and the need to restrict women's choice."

Namias noted that the legend of Jane McCrea helped to define the role of white women in American life following the American Revolution. She wrote that "creators of culture ... centered her in a compelling plot, transformed [McCrea] into a romantic legend, and finally left her as both a local legend and a victim of 'savages' in need of protection and direction." Namias believes that the widespread images and stories about Jane McCrea contributed to the idea that women need protecting and encouraged them to remain dependent on men for generations after the American Revolution.

For More Information

Anburey, Lt. Thomas. *Travels through the Interior Parts of America,* Vol. 1. Boston: Houghton Mifflin, 1923.

Boatner, Mark M., III. "McCrea Atrocity." *Encyclopedia of the American Revolution.* New York: David McKay, 1994, pp. 688–90.

Booth, Sally Smith. *The Women of '76.* New York: Hastings House Publishers, 1973.

Bush, Martin H. "Jane McCrea." *Notable American Women, 1607–1950,* Vol. 2. Edited by Edward T. James et al. Cambridge, MA: Harvard University Press, 1971.

Johnson, Chrisfield. *History of Washington Co., New York.* Interlaken, NY: Hearts of the Lake, 1979.

Leary, Lewis. Introduction to *Miss McCrea, A Novel of the American Revolution.* Written by Michel Rene Hilliard-d'Auberteuil, 1784; reprinted, Gainesville, FL: Scholars' Facsimiles & Reprints, 1958.

Lunt, James. *John Burgoyne of Saratoga.* New York: Harcourt Brace Jovanovich, 1975.

Namias, June. *White Captives: Gender and Ethnicity on the American Frontier.* Chapel Hill: University of North Carolina Press, 1995.

Wilson, David. *The Life of Jane McCrea, with an account of Burgoyne's Expedition in 1777.* New York: Baker, Goodwin, 1853.

Zeinert, Karen. *Those Remarkable Women of the American Revolution.* Brookfield, CT: The Millbrook Press, 1996, p. 53.

Web Sites

Bray, George E., III. "Scalping During the French and Indian War." [Online] Available http://earlyamericacom/review/1998/scalping.html (accessed on 8/1/99.)

Judith Sargent Murray

Born May 1, 1751
Gloucester, Massachusetts
Died July 6, 1820
Natchez, Mississippi

Writer and editor

"I expect to see our young women forming a new era in female history."

Portrait: Judith Sargent Murray. *Reproduced by permission of the Sargent-Murray-Gilman-Hough House Association.*

Judith Sargent Murray was an eighteenth-century writer known for her essays on education for women, on equality, and on economic independence for all people. Murray was the first American woman to self-publish a book, one of the first American writers of plays, and the first woman to have a play produced on stage in America. Her personal letters, discovered only in modern times, offer valuable insights into life in revolutionary America.

Judith Sargent Murray was born in 1751 in Gloucester (pronounced GLOSS-ter), Massachusetts, to Captain Winthrop Sargent, a wealthy ship owner and merchant, and his wife, Judith Saunders, who was from a well-known seafaring family. Murray was the oldest of eight children. Her father supported her desire to learn, and she received an excellent education. Murray was tutored along with her brother, Winthrop, as he was preparing to attend Harvard College (now Harvard University, in Cambridge, Massachusetts). The two young people studied literature, science, history, economics, and religion.

On October 3, 1769, when Murray was eighteen, she married Captain John Stevens of Gloucester. At the time of their marriage Stevens was a wealthy merchant, but in time the couple ran into financial problems. John Stevens fled to the West Indies in the Caribbean, where he died in 1786, leaving Murray with the bills he owed.

Begins writing, remarries

To support herself, Murray began her writing career by composing poems and essays (short pieces of writing that deal with a single subject), some of which appeared in the 1784 *Gentleman's and Lady's Town and Country Magazine,* published in Boston, Massachusetts. She wrote under the pen name "Constantia."

In the early 1780s, Judith Sargent Murray's family converted to the Universalist sect, which taught that all individuals would enter heaven. The minister who converted them was John Murray. He began the Gloucester phase of his religious career in 1774 as pastor of the first Universalist meeting house in America. In time, the friendship between the widow Sargent and Murray grew into love. The couple married on October 6, 1788.

Essays put in print

John Murray believed that women should be educated. He wisely supported Judith Sargent Murray in her writing career, and when the family faced financial troubles, the money she earned from her writings helped support them. She shared her husband's interest in religious issues of the day, and accompanied him on preaching tours around the East. She wrote an account of a tour to Philadelphia in letters that were printed nearly a century later in the April 1881 and 1882 issues of *Universalist Quarterly.*

In 1789, Judith Sargent Murray had the first of several poems published in *Massachusetts Magazine.* She later began writing a column of monthly essays called *The Gleaner,* which appeared in the magazine between February 1792 and August 1794. In the essays, Murray examined such topics as current events, religion, marriage, child-rearing methods, the status of women, and equal education for women. At the time she wrote, Murray's views were considered extreme, since she called for a change in society's accepted treatment of women.

Hannah Adams: America's First Professional Woman Writer

Historian Hannah Adams was born in 1755 in Medfield, Massachusetts. Her father, a businessman, lost most of his money during the time of the American Revolution, and the family was forced to take in boarders to make ends meet. At her father's urging, the young woman was taught Greek, Latin, literature, geography, and logic by the students who rented rooms at her house.

Hannah Adams succeeded in her writing career despite many obstacles. After her mother died when she was only ten years old, her father remarried and had more children. After his death, while Hannah was a young woman, her half-brother moved his family into the home where Hannah had lived with her father, forcing her to leave the house and find a way to support herself.

Adams then began to make lace, braid straw, and write history books to make a living. In her 1787 pamphlet *Women Invited to War,* she discussed how women could help in war emergencies and argued that women should not carry on warfare like men, but should direct their energies toward dealing with their own spiritual and private challenges.

Adams went on to compose a historical dictionary of religious groups, *A View of Religions,* that was published in both Boston, Massachusetts, and London, England. Her other major works were the 1799 *A Summary History of New England* and *A History of the Jews,* written in 1812. After their publication, the master of a girl's school in Newark, New Jersey, dedicated the school's Quarterly Catalogue to her. He wrote: "In [Adams's] researches

Champions education for women

Murray wrote that women were capable of more than "contemplating [thinking about] ... sewing the seams of a garment." She hoped that America's hard-won political independence would encourage a spirit of self-reliance and inspire women to prepare to earn a living independent of men. It was her opinion that parents should teach daughters "to [get] for themselves the necessaries of life; independence should be placed within their grasp."

In Murray's 1792 essay *On the Equality of the Sexes,* she denied the popular notion that women were born inferior to men. She declared that women have the capabilities to enter after useful and important knowledge, she has long been a model of patience and [persistence that] the young ladies of America [should imitate]."

Adams's history of New England, published in 1804, was designed to be a text for schoolchildren. Shortly after its appearance, two ministers, Jedidiah Morse and Elijah Parish, published books on New England history that were based largely on her work. Adams believed they had treated her unfairly. In a highly unusual move for a woman of the time, Murray hired a lawyer to plead her case in court. One of the books partly copied from hers was used in a number of schools. Judges agreed that her work had been used without her permission, but she was paid no money to make up for damages done her.

In a letter, one of the men who copied her work wrote that woman should not be engaged in writing at all. This was his way of excusing his unfair publishing practices. In the end, Adams received no money whatsoever for the work stolen from her, nor did she receive an apology from the men who plagiarized (to steal another's ideas and pass them off as one's own) her work.

Other writers of the time appreciated Adams's work, and she was admitted into the Boston Athenaeum (pronounced ath-uh-NEE-um), a society for esteemed writers. Her portrait still hangs at the group's headquarters. In her later years, Adams wrote a few other books, including her *Memoir*, published in 1831. Later that year she died in Brookline, Massachusetts.

all fields and professions. After comparing male and female mental abilities in the areas of imagination, memory, reason, and judgment, she concluded that if girls had the same educational opportunities as did boys, then they too could further develop their reasoning abilities. She defended curiosity, a trait for which women were known, as "the origin of every mental" achievement, and asked without it, "in what [utter] ignorance would mankind have been wrapped"?

Murray's essay on equality faced strong criticism from some religious leaders. They objected because she failed to mention the section in the Bible that says that women should not teach men. She also failed to discuss the story of the first couple Adam and Eve, whom God cast out of paradise because they sinned against God by seeking the apple of knowledge. In response, Murray added an introduction to the work's second edition that addressed these complaints.

How women might progress

Murray described her ideal woman as "a sensible and informed woman—companionable and serious ... —blest with competency—and rearing to maturity a promising family of children." She stated that if the equality of women's minds with those of men was more widely recognized, women might assume more responsibility in society and play a larger role in national life.

Murray believed that if young women were to feel a sense of worthiness, they needed knowledge of the contributions made by women of earlier times. She thought women were strong, and she gave examples of the lives of women throughout history to illustrate that "Courage is by no means *exclusively* a masculine virtue."

Promotes marital equality, the necessity of mental stimulation

Murray also wrote about the institution of marriage. She said she regretted that young women were forced to rush into marriage in order to gain financial security. She rejected the opinion put forward by Enos Hitchcock that the aim of a young girl's life should be to get married. Instead, she believed, that for girls "marriage should not be presented as their [highest aim], or as a certain, or even necessary event; they should learn to respect a single life, and even regard it as the most [desirable, unless] a warm, mutual [two-way] and [wise] attachment" came into their lives.

In Murray's short novel *The Story of Margaretta,* she stated her belief that marriages should be based on "mutual esteem, mutual friendship, [and] mutual confidence"—a genuine sharing on the part of both men and women. Men were instructed to treat their wives as "reasonable creatures." Murray believed that if proper methods of educating females were adopted, "the term *helpless widow,* might be rendered as unfrequent and inapplicable as that of *helpless widower."*

In *Margaretta* Murray pointed out that domestic chores are not enough to occupy a woman's mind. She declared that women ought to occupy themselves with matters of greater importance than housework, or their idle minds might get them into mischief of various sorts.

Plays presented, book published

In addition to writing essays, Murray also wrote plays. Her first drama, *The Medium, or A Happy Tea-Party* (which was called *The Medium, or Virtue Triumphant* in print), was presented at Massachusetts's Boston Federal Street Theatre on March 2, 1795. British plays were usually presented there; Murray's was probably the first play produced there that was written by an American. Her second play, *The Traveller Returned,* was presented in March 1796. Neither play was very successful.

In February 1798 Murray collected the two plays, along with her essays and some other short pieces of prose and poems, and published them herself. They appeared in three volumes under the title *The Gleaner,* and she advertised and sold them by subscription in local newspapers. A subscription is the agreement to pay for a publication for a certain period of time. Her friend, writer **Mercy Otis Warren** (see entry), offered Murray her advice and support, and helped her to sell eight hundred subscriptions to *The Gleaner.* The subscribers included Martha and **George Washington, John** and **Abigail Adams,** and **John Hancock** (see entries).

Later writing and editing

Except for several poems that appeared in Boston magazines, Murray's later writing consisted of essays. As her husband's health began to fail, she helped him prepare and edit for publication his *Letters, and Sketches of Sermons.* They appeared in three volumes in 1812 and 1813. After his death in 1815, she released the final three chapters of his autobiography under the title *Records of the Life of the Rev. John Murray, Written by Himself, with a Continuation by Mrs. Judith Sargent Murray.*

During her final years, Murray went to Natchez, Mississippi, to live with her daughter, Julia Maria Bingaman, the only one of Murray's two children who lived into adulthood. Judith Sargent Murray died there on July 6, 1820.

Judith Sargent Murray has not been forgotten. Her writings remain in print, and the Sargent House Museum in Gloucester, Massachusetts, offers tours of the home of Murray and her husband, who live on as two of Gloucester's most honored citizens.

For More Information

Kerber, Linda K. *Women of the Republic: Intellect and Ideology in Revolutionary America.* Chapel Hill: University of North Carolina Press, 1980, pp. 189, 204–05, 210–11, 227, 259.

Malone, Dumas, ed. "Murray, Judith Sargent Stevens." *Dictionary of American Biography.* New York: Charles Scribners Sons, 1934, pp. 364–65.

McHenry, Robert, ed. "Murray, Judith Sargent Stevens." *Liberty's Women.* Springfield, MA: G & C Merriam, 1980, p. 297.

"Murray, Judith Sargent Stevens." *Who Was Who in American History, Historical Volume, 1607–1896.* Chicago: Marquis Who's Who, rev. ed. 1967, p. 444.

Norton, Mary Beth. *Liberty's Daughters: The Revolutionary Experience of American Women, 1750–1800.* Boston: Little, Brown, 1980, pp. 234–35, 238–39, 252, 254, 271, 280.

Williams, Selma. *Demeter's Daughters: The Women Who Founded America, 1587–1787.* New York: Atheneum, 1976, pp. 310–12.

Web Sites

"Judith Sargent Murray, 1751–1820." *Sunshine for Women,* 1999. [Online] Available http://www.pinn.net/~sunshine/march99/murray3.html (accessed 5/99.)

Sedgwick, Jeanette, and Kristen Vogel. "Remember the Ladies: Revolutionary Women Writers." [Online] Available http://gda.org/gda/archon/RTLADIES.HTML (accessed on 5/4/99).

Jonathan Odell

Born September 25, 1737
Newark, New Jersey
Died November 25, 1818
Fredericton, New Brunswick, Canada

Clergyman, physician, essayist, satirist, spy

"Thou hast supported an atrocious cause Against thy King, thy country, and the laws."

Jonathan Odell, a multitalented American who stayed loyal to England during the American Revolution, is best remembered for the poetry he wrote in support of England. A strong believer in the authority of the church and state in society, Odell feared that the leaders of the American Revolution (1775–83) were bringing evil on America. He was a stern and serious man with strong opinions, and he wrote about the Revolution with grimness and bitterness.

Jonathan Odell was born in New Jersey in 1737 to John Odell, a carpenter, and Temperance Dickinson, the daughter of the first president of the school that became Princeton University in New Jersey. He was a descendant of William Odell, one of the founders of the Massachusetts Bay Colony.

Jonathan Odell graduated from Princeton in 1754 with a bachelor's degree. For a short time, he ran the college's elementary school, taking two-thirds of that school's profits as a salary. In 1756 he continued his studies at Princeton, and in 1759 he received his master's degree in medicine. He then joined the British Army and served in the West Indies (islands in the Caribbean Sea, between the United States and South America) as an army surgeon.

Next Odell decided to become an Episcopal minister, even though his family had strong ties to the Congregationalist Church. In 1763 he traveled to England to study for the ministry. At the same time, he taught at a school there and published his first poems. In England, he met **Benjamin Franklin** (see entry), who was working there as an agent for New Jersey and Pennsylvania. He also began a lifelong friendship with Franklin's son, William, who was living in England with his father but was soon to be appointed governor of New Jersey. Benjamin Franklin used his influence to help Odell gain an appointment by the Anglican Church (a Protestant religious group in England) to become a Christian missionary to America. (A missionary is a person sent by a church to preach and teach in a foreign country)

After Odell officially became a minister in 1767, he sailed back to America and went to see his new friend, William Franklin. Franklin helped him obtain a position as pastor of St. Ann's Church in Burlington, New Jersey. Odell later served as a minister to other churches across the Delaware River in Pennsylvania.

Gains distinctions, marries and has family

While Odell was at St. Ann's, talk of revolution against England was spreading. Those who opposed a revolution and remained loyal to England were called Loyalists. Odell promised New Jersey colonial authorities who supported American independence that he would keep his Loyalist leanings to himself rather than stir up members of his congregation. At the time just prior to the Revolutionary War, feelings ran high among the Loyalists and their opponents, the American supporters of rebellion against British rule.

Odell was soon recognized for his multiple talents. In 1768 he was chosen to be a member of the American Philosophical Society, an exclusive group that only accepted individuals who were accomplished in several fields. The society asked him to translate into English some French studies of silkworms. He supplemented his minister's pay by returning part-time to the practice of medicine. Twice in the 1770s he had the honor of being elected to membership in the New Jersey Medical Society.

In 1772 Odell married Anne de Cou of Burlington, New Jersey. She bore him two children. The couple's daughter, Mary, became the wife of a British army officer. Their son, William Franklin Odell, named after Odell's longtime friend, had a successful career as a Canadian politician.

Goes into hiding, flees to New York

When the Revolutionary War began in 1775, Odell tried to remain neutral (not take sides). But several letters he had written to friends in England fell into the hands of the New Jersey Provincial Congress. In the letters, he had voiced his opposition to the revolution. His Loyalist views were soon common knowledge.

In 1776 Odell gave up trying to stay neutral. He openly became friends with captured British officers who were being confined on an island in the Delaware River. To entertain them, he wrote a poem in celebration of the June 4 birthday of King **George III** (see entry) of England. Before long, the Burlington Committee of Safety, a pro-revolutionary group, learned of Odell's activities. Because of his pro-Loyalist poetry and his friendship with Loyalist soldiers, they considered him a dangerous influence and feared he might stir up Loyalist support. They ordered him to be confined near the town of Burlington, where they could keep an eye on him.

American revolutionaries came to believe that Odell's activities had progressed from poetry writing to harboring enemy soldiers. In December 1776, supporters of the Revolution searched his house for enemy troops. When he heard that the rebels had been ordered to hunt him down and take him dead or alive, Odell fled and went into hiding at the home of a friendly Quaker woman (Quakers opposed all types of warfare). He hid in a small windowless apartment that could only be entered, as he later recalled in his diary, by "entering a linen closet in the adjoining room, drawing out the shelves, prying up the movable back, and creeping in through the opening."

As soon as it seemed safe, Odell escaped to New York City, leaving behind his wife and three small children. New York had been taken by the British in September 1776. The following year, he moved to Philadelphia, Pennsylvania, after its capture by the British in September 1777. In Philadelphia, he and a friend, Joseph Stansbury, began to publish satirical political poems. (Satires are writings that make fun of others' stupidities, vices, or abuses.) Odell's satirical verse ranks among the best written during the American Revolution (see box). His satires were collected and published in *The Loyal Verses of Joseph Stansbury and Doctor Jonathan Odell* in 1860.

Life in Philadelphia and New York

In Philadelphia, Odell served as a minister to a group of Loyalist soldiers. They helped him to survive by paying him a small salary and sharing their food with him. Later, he supplemented this income by running the British government's printing press and publication program.

When the British left Philadelphia in May 1778, Odell returned to New York City. He continued to write political poems for various newspapers. They often focused on the frustrations felt by Loyalist and British soldiers toward the lack of military skills of their commander, Sir Henry Clinton.

During the first years of the war, Odell remained confident that the great British army was sure to stamp out the American rebellion. The year 1778 had started out badly for the British; they had suffered embarrassing defeats at Trenton and Princeton, New Jersey, in December 1777. Odell wrote a poem welcoming 1779; in it he spoke of the turnaround in the course of the war that he expected to take place soon.

The poem began:

> Last year rebellion proudly stood
> Elate, in her meridian [highest] glory;
> But this [year] shall quench her pride in blood—
> [King] George will avenge each martyred Tory [Loyalist].

Produces Loyalist writings, helps spy

Seventeen-seventy-nine was busy for Odell. That year, Odell and writer Samuel Seabury produced several long poems and a series of essays that tried to encourage the Loyalists and discredit the Continental Congress, America's revolutionary government. The essays were signed under the pen name "Britannicus." Some of Odell's writings appeared in **James Rivington**'s (see entry) *New-York Gazetteer,* a Loyalist newspaper.

In their writings, Odell and Seabury made fun of the finances of the American revolutionaries, which were in terrible disarray, and Odell suggested that his readers think back to the origins of the American Revolution. They would see that the British had made mistakes in dealing with the colonies. He proposed that America let bygones be bygones and remain a part of the British Empire while being governed in a way that would benefit loyal colonists.

In 1779 Odell befriended the American general **Benedict Arnold** (see entry), who became America's most famous traitor. Arnold was unhappy with the way he was being treated and decided to go over to the British side. Odell carried Arnold's note offering to change sides to British General Henry Clinton. But the note got damp, the invisible ink ran, and Clinton could not make out most of the note. After that incident, British officer John André rewrote Arnold's treasonous letters into code form, and Odell decoded them for Clinton. When the negotiations between Arnold and Clinton faltered, Odell intervened, encouraging both sides to keep up their efforts.

Goes to London

In 1781 Odell became assistant secretary to the Board of Directors of the Associated Loyalists, a political group headed by his close friend William Franklin. (Unlike his father, William Franklin was a supporter of the British.) That year fighting ended, but British soldiers remained in America under the command of Sir Guy Carleton until the peace treaty was signed in 1783. In 1782 Odell joined Carleton's staff, first as a chaplain, then as assistant secretary to Carleton.

In December 1783, Odell left New York and traveled to London, taking his family with him. He would never live in America again. In England, Odell sought repayment for the financial losses he suffered by being a Loyalist. As a reward for his services, he was appointed to the well-paying position of provincial secretary of the newly formed province of New Brunswick, Canada (Canada was then a British possession).

While some Loyalists were able to reconcile with their former enemies after the war, Odell never could. He became one of many former Loyalists who made new lives in England or other parts of the British Empire. According to historian Moses

Jonathan Odell's Poetry

Jonathan Odell wrote Loyalist poetry full of fury against the American rebels. In *Who Was Who in the American Revolution,* L. Edward Purcell wrote that Odell's "satire on the patriots caused much squirming among rebels in the early days of the Revolution."

According to *American Writers Before 1800: A Biographical and Critical Dictionary,* Odell's lasting reputation is based mainly on poems he wrote during the time he lived in New York City. In *Inscription for a Curious Chamber Stove,* Odell satirized Benjamin Franklin's Revolutionary activities, using imagery that refers to Franklin's invention of the stove. Odell wrote that Franklin caught:

> "A Spark, that from Lucifer [the devil] came and kindled the blaze of Sedition [rebellion]."

During the early years of the Revolutionary War, Odell admitted that changes needed to be made by England in the matter of rights within the colonies, but he thought that such change could take place slowly and steadily, without the need for a rebellion.

One of Odell's most famous poems, *The Congratulation,* was written in 1779 to celebrate British military successes. Aimed at ridiculing the Continental Congress, it begins with a tone of mock congratulation:

> Joy to great Congress, joy hundred fold;
> The grand cajolers [kidders] are themselves cajol'd!
> The farce of empire will be finished soon,
> And each mock-monarch dwindle to a loon.
> Mock-money and mock-states shall melt away,
> And the mock-troops disband for want of pay....
> Myriads of swords are ready for the field;
> Myriads of lurking daggers are conceal'd;
> In injur'd bosoms dark revenge is nurst;
> Yet but a moment, and the storm shall burst....
> Now Boston trembles; Philadelphia quakes;
> And Carolina to the center shakes....

Coit Tyler, Odell was motivated by a "deathless love" for Great Britain and a "deathless hate" for an American republic.

Life and death in Canada

In 1784 Odell moved his family to Canada and took on his new position in New Brunswick. He was upset when high-level government officials in Canada soon demanded more

Hate[d] now [by] men, and soon to be
the jest —
Such is your fate, ye monsters of the
West!

Odell's satire in three parts entitled *The American Times,* published in 1780, is his longest and most famous poem. It appeared under his pen name Camillo Querno, a name he had chosen for its reference to an early court jester (a person who is hired by a king to behave foolishly for entertainment purposes). By 1780, according to Percy H. Boynton in his book *American Poetry,* "Odell had lost all hope for any but the most bitter solution [to the war], and ... had become filled with hatred as the result of his own indefensible hardships," which included financial problems, separation from his family, and fear for his life.

The American Times charges leaders of the American Revolutionary movement with various crimes. Odell's targets included revolutionary writers, generals, governors of the states, leaders, such as **Thomas Paine**, and members of Congress, such as **John Jay** (see entries). In the poem, Odell refers to the American revolutionaries as a "faction, pois'nous as the scorpion's sting" that "infects the people and insults the King."

In this excerpt from Part One, Odell questions the motives of **George Washington** (see entry) for his involvement in the Revolution. He wrote:

Hear thy indictment, Washington, at large
Attend and listen to the solemn charge
Thou hast supported an atrocious cause
Against thy King, thy Country, and the
laws....
Was it ambition, vanity, or spite
That prompted thee with Congress to
unite;
Or did all three within thy bosom roll,
Thou heart of hero with a traitor's soul?

Odell's poems not only boosted the morale of Loyalist readers, but also provided a model for future American writers of satiric verse.

freedom from Great Britain so they could pass their own local laws. Odell complained that they were failing in their loyalty to the mother country. Odell prospered and became a slave owner. He held a number of important government posts, including First Secretary of the province; he also held a seat on New Brunswick's executive council. Over the years, he became a highly respected figure in New Brunswick politics.

Odell continued to write poetry. He also wrote about poetry in *An essay on the elements, accents and prosody of the English language,* which was published in 1804.

In 1812 Odell retired at seventy-five, and his son, William Franklin Odell, became provincial secretary. Odell died in Fredericton, New Brunswick, on November 25, 1818.

For More Information

Boatner, Mark M., III. "Odell, Jonathan." *Encyclopedia of the American Revolution.* Mechanicsburg, PA: Stackpole Books, 1994, p. 813.

Boynton, Percy H. *American Poetry.* New York: Charles Scribners' Sons, 1918, p. 614.

Calhoon, Robert M. "Odell, Jonathan." *American National Biography,* Vol. 16. Edited by John A. Garraty and Mark C. Carnes. New York: Oxford University Press, 1999, pp. 618-19.

"Jonathan Odell." *American Writers Before 1800: A Biographical and Critical Dictionary.* Edited by James A. Levernier and Douglas R. Wilmes. Westport, CT: Greenwood Press, 1983.

"Odell, Jonathan." *National Cyclopaedia of American Biography,* Vol. 25. New York: James T. White & Co., 1936, pp. 212-13.

Purcell, L. Edward. "Odell, Jonathan." *Who Was Who in the American Revolution.* New York: Facts on File, 1993, pp. 355-56.

Randall, Willard Sterne. *Benedict Arnold: Patriot and Traitor.* New York: William Morrow and Co., Inc., 1990, pp. 458, 466-67.

Tyler, Moses Coit. "The Literary Warfare of the Loyalists Against American Independence: Jonathan Odell, Their Chief Satirist." *The Literary History of the American Revolution, 1763-1783.* New York: G. P. Putnam's Sons, 1897, pp. 97-129.

Vincent, Tom. "Odell, Jonathan." *The Oxford Companion to Canadian Literature.* Edited by Eugene Benson and William Toye. Toronto: Oxford University Press, 1997, pp. 878-79.

Thomas Paine

Born January 29, 1737
Thetford, England
Died June 8, 1809
New York, New York

American writer, political leader, reformer

Thomas Paine was one of the first writers to realize the power of the press in bringing about political reform. Paine's writings greatly influenced the American Revolution (1775–83) and the French Revolution (1789–99). In them he expressed his beliefs that man is rational and basically good but corrupted by society, that all men are equal, and that justice is dependent on a nation's economic system.

"It is always to be taken for granted, that those who oppose an equality of rights never mean the exclusion should take place on themselves."

Thomas Paine was born on January 29, 1737. His father, Joseph Pain (Thomas later added the final "e" to his last name) was a Quaker, a member of the Society of Friends. Quakers like young Paine's father distrusted both religious and governmental authority. Thomas's mother, Frances Cocke Pain, known for having been bad-tempered and a bit strange, was eleven years older than her husband.

His family was poor and young Thomas Paine received very limited schooling during his unhappy childhood. "Tom" Paine, as he was known, lived near the gallows where poor people were sometimes hanged for such offenses as stealing food to feed their families. On the other hand, wealthy people who committed serious crimes, such as murder, often went

Portrait: Thomas Paine. *Reproduced courtesy of the Library of Congress.*

Deism and Thomas Paine

The eighteenth century in France, England, and America, known as the Age of Enlightenment, provided new ways of thinking about the world, including the religious realm. Some Americans followed the lead of French thinkers who rejected traditional ideas about God as the source of all knowledge in the world, and turned instead to human reason. The religion of Deism flourished at the end of the Revolutionary War.

Deists adopted nature itself as a sort of impersonal god that served as the principle that organized all life. They rejected the idea that the Bible was the source of God's sacred word, as well as traditional images of God. Although the Deists were small in number, many members of traditional religions viewed them as a menace. They feared that a spread of Deism would mean losing the threat of divine punishment for sin, which might bring about the downfall of traditional religion and lead society into moral confusion or even chaos.

After Thomas Paine returned to America in 1802, the Deistical Society in New York, whose members shared his religious beliefs, hoped that he would stay with them and use his powers of writing to further their cause. Though he was happy occasionally to write for their journal, *The Prospect,* he desired to write for a larger audience. Near the end of his life, Paine was approached several times to reject the deistic beliefs that had caused him to suffer much scorn and embrace traditional Christianity, but he never did.

free; therefore, Paine came to learn that often there was one law for the rich and another for the poor.

At age thirteen, Paine went to work for his father, learning the difficult trade of making corsets, intricate undergarments of whalebone worn by wealthy women. Young Paine soon grew restless and went on to hold a variety of odd jobs. He went to sea at age nineteen. But after seeing what a hard life it was, he returned a few months later and went to work for a manufacturer in London, England.

In 1759, Paine wed Mary Lambert, who worked as a maid for a wealthy family. Little is known about the couple's marriage, but within a year Mary Paine died, leaving Paine a widower. Although some historians claim she and her baby died in childbirth, others point out that a great deal of mystery surrounded Mary Paine's death. Paine never wrote about this experience or about women in general.

Career failure, divorce, and the move to America

While working at various jobs, Paine read widely and educated himself in politics and science. He tried his hand at making a living by tracking down smugglers and trying to collect taxes from them. He lost this job when he published a paper arguing that higher wages for tax collectors would help stop corruption in the tax collecting service. For seventeen years he worked unsuccessfully at this and other jobs, including schoolteacher, tobacco shop worker, and grocer.

In 1771, Paine married Elizabeth Ollive, ten years his junior. He and Elizabeth separated three years later for reasons he never revealed, even to his friends. After that Paine had many close relationships with women but never remarried.

In 1774, the thirty-seven-year-old Paine met **Benjamin Franklin** (see entry), who was then representing America's interests in England, and the great patriot advised Paine to relocate to America. Franklin, who wrote of "the genius in his eyes," provided the young man with letters of recommendation to show to possible employers in the New World.

Paine's writings spur on American independence

In 1774, the tall, muscular Paine sailed for Philadelphia, Pennsylvania, where he found work as a journalist with the *Pennsylvania Magazine*. In 1775, he wrote a pamphlet criticizing slavery in America as unjust. In Philadelphia, he met the patriot **Benjamin Rush** (see entry), who suggested that he write a pamphlet urging America to declare its independence from England. On January 10, 1776, Paine published the fifty-page pamphlet *Common Sense*. Fearing what might happen to him if he became known as the author of the pamphlet, Paine published it anonymously (without his name). *Common Sense* included a number of statements that would make the British consider Paine a traitor, including his reference to King **George III** (see entry) as "the Royal brute of Great Britain."

At that time, Americans were split on the question of whether or not to declare independence. Paine wrote in an easy-to-understand style that England was overtaxing them, that the English form of government with the king at its head was corrupt, and that there was little sense in an island thousands of miles away governing the American continent.

Joins army, works for U.S. Congress

Common Sense, a call to action, became wildly popular almost immediately, selling half a million copies. Historian James Stokesbury pointed out in *A Short History of the American Revolution* that "It was an astonishingly successful piece of propaganda, not less so because it convinced those who were already half-convinced anyway." (Propaganda is material used to persuade people to support a particular point of view.) Continental army general **George Washington** (see entry) himself said it turned the tide in favor of independence.

When the Revolutionary War started to go badly for the Americans in 1776, Paine joined the ill-equipped Continental army and took part in the retreat of George Washington and his troops across New Jersey away from the British army. That year, Paine also published the first of sixteen *Crisis* papers, which appeared between 1776 and 1783. The papers encouraged the practice of patriotism so eloquently that George Washington ordered that they be read to every American soldier for inspiration.

The *Crisis* began with the challenging first line, "These are the times that try men's souls." Paine continued, "The summer soldier and the sunshine patriot [those who display their patriotism only in good times] will, in this crisis, shrink from the service of their country; but he that stands it *now,* deserves the love and thanks of man and woman. Tyranny [absolute power], like hell, is not easily conquered.... The heart that feels not now, is dead; the blood of his children will curse his cowardice, who shrinks back at a time when a little might have saved the whole ... he whose heart is firm, and whose conscience approves his conduct, will pursue his principles unto death."

In 1777, to give Paine some means of support, the U.S. Congress appointed him Secretary of the Committee of Foreign Affairs. He was forced to resign from the post in 1779 because he published some secret information.

Plagued by financial problems

For the next two years, Paine worked as a clerk of the Pennsylvania General Assembly, using part of his salary to start a fund to help provide for needy soldiers. He also published a number of writings. Over the years, Paine's writings sold very well. But he always refused to accept profits from them because he said it would cheapen their value, and he wound up living in poverty after the American Revolution ended in 1783. He applied to the U.S. Congress for financial help, but his enemies there buried the request.

Paine was appreciated by many Americans for his eloquence and for his devotion to the cause of independence, but he was also widely criticized for some of his political and religious writings. In his book about Paine entitled *Man of Reason,* writer A. Owen Aldridge described Paine as "vain, opinionated and hypersensitive," traits that did not add to his popularity. Because of the contributions Paine had made to the United States, the state of Pennsylvania gave him some money and the state of New York provided him with a farm in New Rochelle, New York.

Paine lived quietly on his farm for a few years, working on several inventions that interested him. In 1787, Paine visited England and France to raise funds to build in America an iron bridge he had designed. Although it was eventually built, as a financial venture the bridge was a failure for Paine.

Publishes *Rights of Man* in France

In 1789, a revolution broke out in France. Paine supported the cause of the French rebels against King **Louis XVI** (see entry), and he voiced that support in his book *The Rights of Man,* various editions of which were published in 1791 and 1792. Paine explained in his book the source of European discontent with their forms of government. He pointed out that they suffered from poverty, illiteracy (they were unable to read or write), unemployment, and frequent wars.

Rights was tremendously popular in England, France, and America, becoming one of the best-selling books of all time. It also enraged powerful people in England because it encouraged Englishmen to take up arms against their king. The British government put out a royal proclamation against Paine's writ-

Thomas Paine's book *The Rights of Man* encouraged Englishmen to take up arms against George III. Although it enraged British government officials, the book drew the attention of American, British, and French readers and became one of the best-selling books of all time.

ings, and a dummy of him was burned in London. Paine was charged with treason but he escaped imprisonment by fleeing to France in 1792.

The ups and downs of Paine's life in France

In 1792, when Paine arrived there, France was in the process of establishing a constitutional monarchy to limit the power of kings. Although he spoke no French, Paine was invited to take part in drawing up the new constitution. But then King Louis and Queen Marie-Antoinette tried to flee the country. They were arrested, tried for treason, and despite Paine's protests, beheaded.

Control of the French government then passed into the hands of Maximilien de Robespierre. Annoyed at Paine's protests over the execution of the king and queen, Robespierre had him imprisoned. He might have been executed himself, but future president James Monroe, then representing the United States in France, secured his release in late 1794 after Paine spent eleven months in prison. Paine was bitter that then-president George Washington had not gotten him released sooner, and he said so in a long *Letter to George Washington,* published in 1796.

Besides his interest in politics, Paine also had a strong interest in matters of religion. During his stay in prison, he began to write the book the *Age of Reason,* which defended religions that were based on rational thought (see box on p. 354). It was published in two parts in 1794 and 1796.

Unwelcome in America

In 1802, Paine returned to the United States at the invitation of patriots **Thomas Jefferson** (see entry) and James Monroe, both of whom admired him. Because of his writings, many Americans scorned Paine, holding him responsible for the period of large-scale murder that had occurred in France under Robespierre. History shows, however, that Paine had done his best to prevent the bloodbath.

Another matter in which Paine was misunderstood was in his religious beliefs. Although certain critics of his day blasted him for not believing in God, Thomas Paine was not an atheist, but a Deist, who celebrated man's reason, as were many leaders of the American independence movement, such as Thomas Jefferson and Benjamin Franklin.

When he returned to America, Paine discovered that some people had all but forgotten him, while many old friends, such as **Samuel Adams** and Benjamin Rush, had abandoned him because of his criticism of organized religion. He continued to write on politics and in opposition to religious superstition.

Comes to a sad end

In his final years, Thomas Paine, now poverty-stricken, in poor health, and treated as an outcast, wandered from place to place. He wore old, sometimes soiled clothing, and drank too much alcohol. He died in New York City on June 8, 1809, at the age of seventy-two.

Although Paine was to live in history as a hero of freedom-loving people everywhere, a statement written about him at the time of his death read, "He had lived long, did some good and much harm." Paine was buried at his farm in New Rochelle. Ten years later, journalist William Cobbitt brought Paine's remains back to England for burial but the remains later disappeared.

For More Information

Aldridge, A. Owen. *Man of Reason: the Life of Thomas Paine.* Philadelphia: J. B. Lippincott Co., 1959.

Boatner, Mark M, III. "Paine, Thomas." *Encyclopedia of the American Revolution.* Mechanicsburg, PA: Stackpole Books, 1994, pp. 825-28.

Coolidge, Olivia. *Tom Paine, Revolutionary.* New York: Charles Scribner's Sons, 1969, pp. 187, 194.

Hawke, David Freeman. *Paine.* New York: Harper & Row, 1974.

Meltzer, Milton. *Tom Paine: Voice of Revolution.* New York: Franklin Watts, 1996.

Stokesbury, James L. *A Short History of the American Revolution.* New York: William Morrow & Co., 1991, pp. 87, 115-16.

Vail, John. *Thomas Paine.* New York: Chelsea House Publishers, 1990.

Web Sites

Leemhuis, Benni. "A Biography of Thomas Paine." Based on *The American Revolution—an .HTML project.* [Online] Available http://odur.let.rug.nl/~usa/B/tpaine/paine.htm (accessed on 1/06/00).

William Pitt

Born November 15, 1708
London, England
Died May 11, 1778
Kent County, England

British prime minister, member of Parliament

"It is my opinion that this kingdom has no right to lay a tax upon the colonies. At the same time I assert the authority of this kingdom over the colonies to be sovereign and supreme in every circumstance of government and legislation whatsoever."

Portrait: William Pitt. *Reproduced courtesy of the Library of Congress.*

William Pitt was a politician of tremendous influence in Great Britain for more than forty years. He opposed the unfair taxation of the American colonies in the critical years leading up to the American Revolution (1775–83), and advised settling the quarrel with them so they would remain part of the British empire. As leader of the British government, Pitt led Britain to victory over France in the French and Indian War (1756–63), gaining Canada and the Mississippi Valley for the British empire. He was known as William Pitt the Elder because his son also served in British government.

William Pitt was born on November 15, 1708, on fashionable Piccadilly Street in London, England, where many rich and high-born people lived. He was the younger son of Robert Pitt, a wealthy country squire, and his wife, Harriet Villiers. His was a political family. His father was a member of Parliament (see box on p. 366), occupying a seat for the county of Cornwall in the House of Commons. His grandfather was Thomas Pitt, who had been governor of Madras, India (at this time, England was making India part of the British empire). Much of the family wealth came through Thomas Pitt's service in India.

William Pitt was educated at Eton, a famous boys' boarding school, and at Trinity College, a part of Oxford University. Pitt did not graduate because he began to suffer from gout, a hereditary (inherited) disease that caused painful swelling of the joints. Upon the advice of his doctor to seek out warmer climates, Pitt traveled to Italy and France. He then studied law at the University of Utrecht in the Netherlands.

Because Pitt was a younger son, he would not inherit the family estate in Cornwall. Instead, he needed to select a career to support himself. As a member of the upper class (a gentleman), only three choices were open to him: join the Anglican church as a minister, resume his studies to become a lawyer, or join the army. Upon his return to England, Pitt chose to join the British army. In 1731, at the age of twenty-three, he purchased a cornetcy (a low-level officer's rank) in a regiment known as Cobham's Horse. At this time, British army officers bought their commissions (military ranks) instead of training for them or being promoted because of battlefield bravery.

Enters Parliament

Pitt, however, was more interested in political life than the army. When his older brother, Thomas, decided not to run for reelection to the family seat in Parliament, William ran and won the election in 1735. Pitt had one of the longest and most famous political careers in British history.

In his early years, Pitt was a member of the House of Commons (only noblemen could sit in the House of Lords). In his first speech, he criticized King George II (1683–1760), a move that caused his dismissal from the army. Next, Pitt attacked the king's weak foreign policy, because he believed the king was too soft in his dealings with France, England's longtime enemy. George II had been born in Germany, spoke only German, and was more interested in his German lands than in England. He left much of the governing of England to Parliament.

The Prince of Wales supported Pitt and his political allies in openly opposing France. (The Prince of Wales is a title given to the king's heir, usually his oldest son). Pitt also earned the king's displeasure by criticizing the British crown's payment of foreign troops. (Remember that this family of British kings descended from a marriage with a prince from a German state called Hanover. It was this German connection that provided the German soldiers who were so hated during the American Revolution).

Pitt soon earned the name "The Great Commoner" for his criticism of the king and the wealthy upper classes. During the course of his long career, Pitt spoke out against financial support for the king's projects in Hanover and against taxation (of both British and American citizens). He spoke out for freedom of the press and for a strong army and navy. The poor and middle-class people of England felt that Pitt was looking after their interests instead of German interests, that he was protecting them from a French invasion, and that he was committed to bettering their lives by spending British tax dollars at home in England. Pitt often appealed to the people, whom he called the "voice of England," and with their support won political victories.

However, possibly because of his political ambitions, Pitt did not always oppose the king. In 1737, he voted to grant the Prince of Wales an annual allowance of 100,000 pounds (a large sum of money). The king showed his pleasure by naming Pitt a "groom of the bed chamber" to the Prince of Wales, an honorary title. Pitt later lost this post after he again displeased the king. This love-hate relationship between the crown and Pitt would last throughout Pitt's career, as would the gout that continued to plague him.

Pitt was reelected to the House of Commons in 1741. He soon showed a real ability for organizing and managing, and was asked to form a cabinet. (This means his political party was in power, and he was to head the government with cabinet ministers of his choice; see box on p. 366.) In 1746, he was named to his first major post, as paymaster general of the armed forces.

Marries into political family

Pitt married Lady Hester Grenville on November 16, 1754. She was the only daughter of a famous political family, which included Richard Grenville, later the Earl of Temple, and George Grenville, British prime minister in 1763. Pitt and his Grenville brothers-in-law did not always agree on politics. George Grenville, for instance, favored taxing the American colonies and had little patience for their claims of "no taxation without representation."

Pitt did have a happy marriage with Lady Hester, and their family included three sons and two daughters. Their second son, also named William, gained fame as the politician who successfully led the British government in its war against France under the Emperor Napoleon. One of their daughters was Lady Hester Lucy Stanhope, who was known for her travels in the Middle East.

The Pitt family had a home in St. James's Square in a fashionable area of London (for when Parliament was in session) and country estates in Somerset and Kent counties. The Kent home, called Hayes Place, was Pitt's favorite residence and he enjoyed gardening while at home.

Helps defeat the French

In 1756, Pitt was named secretary of state and became leader of the House of Commons. His Grenville brothers-in-law also received posts. Richard became first lord of the admiralty (he ran the navy) and George was named treasurer of the navy.

By 1757, England was losing a war against France, and Pitt was asked to organize Britain's defense as the secretary of war. In Europe, this war was known as the Seven Years' War (1756–63). Known in America as the French and Indian War, it was a struggle to see whether England or France would dominate the colonial world. Under Pitt's leadership, the French navy was destroyed, the French lost Quebec to General James Wolfe (one of the able young officers Pitt had promoted), and the French were driven from India. By 1761, England had won the war and controlled most of Canada, the Mississippi Valley, and the West Indies in the Caribbean Sea.

This war was typical of the ongoing struggle among the European powers to gain territory. The struggles often spilled over into their colonial possessions in the Americas, India, Africa, the oceans, and the rich islands in the Caribbean Sea, and these territories often changed hands.

Pitt's policy of promoting capable army and navy officers helped England win the war. He also realized the need for a strong army and navy, and found a better system for managing war supplies (food, uniforms, weapons, and so on). Pitt demonstrated strong leadership, a willingness to make decisions, and a talent for war strategy. Like many great men, he also suffered from pride and arrogance (a superior attitude). Because of his coldness, he had few political allies. Despite his genius, this inability to be a team player cost Pitt political victories throughout his career.

Loses royal favor

Pitt was convinced that the future of England, a small, island country, depended upon expanding and protecting her empire overseas. The empire provided England with money, raw materials, and other goods from all over the world. (The American colonies were the richest of Britain's many possessions). Under Pitt's leadership, England was a strong military power that discouraged other European nations from trying to conquer British territory. This policy changed when **George III** (1738–1820; see entry), the new king, ascended to the throne upon his grandfather's death in 1760. George III, who would rule for sixty years, was determined to show his kingdom (and Pitt) just who was in charge. George III was the first of the Hanoverian kings to be born and educated in England and he was much more interested in English affairs than George I or George II.

With his Tory (or Royalist) political party, George III would tax the American colonies into open rebellion against Great Britain. One of his first acts, however, was to disregard Pitt's advice to declare war on Spain in 1761. Pitt, convinced that Spain would soon attack England, resigned in protest. History then proved Pitt was right, as Spain declared war against England in 1762.

Although ill with gout between 1762 and 1764, Pitt reentered the House of Commons. There he managed to irritate the new king by supporting American complaints against the government. Parliament had passed the Sugar Act in 1764 and the Stamp Act in 1765, both designed to raise money by taxing the American colonists. The colonists reacted with violent protests, and Parliament responded by sending British

The British Parliament

Parliament, the name given to the British law-making body, is made up of three parts: the Crown, the House of Lords, and the House of Commons. The Crown refers to the ruling king or queen, who has the right to veto (overturn) votes in the House of Commons. The House of Lords is made up of noblemen (dukes, earls, and so on), who usually hold a seat that has been in their family for generations. The House of Lords had its beginnings in the councils of nobles and high church officials who used to advise the ancient kings of England.

The House of Commons has members who are elected by British subjects in England, Scotland, Wales, and Ireland. The House of Commons is the most powerful part of Parliament. It proposes the laws and then passes or rejects them. The prime minister (roughly equal to the U.S. president) is the head of the political party who wins the most votes in the election, and is always chosen from the House of Commons. When the new session of parliament opens following the election, the prime minister is asked to form a cabinet (or ministry). The cabinet is a group of advisers who look after certain areas such as defense, finance, or social conditions.

When a party loses an election, the prime minister and his cabinet must resign. The new officials are then chosen from the winning party and a new session of parliament begins.

troops to America to enforce the taxation. The rift between mother country and colonies grew more bitter.

The colonists claimed that the acts amounted to unfair taxation. Pitt agreed. The Americans and Pitt began to make distinctions between types of taxes. They approved of taxes that were put in place to help commerce (that is, taxes on goods imported into the colonies). But they objected to taxes whose only purpose was to raise money for the government. The Stamp Act was one such tax. Its purpose was to raise money to pay for the increase in government needed when Canada moved from French to English rule. Pitt, like the Americans, said that colonial assemblies (like the Continental Congress) should be the only government bodies able to pass tax laws in the colonies. Pitt's views summed up the split that existed in the British Parliament at this time. Some in government supported total control over the colonies, while others favored allowing the colonial governments some decision-making power. Pitt, however, never supported the American colonies breaking away from England.

By 1765, Pitt was suffering from the mental illness that would continue to plague him for the remainder of his life. Some historians believe this condition was manic-depression, a type of mental illness in which a person suffers severe and prolonged mood swings.

Raised to the peerage

After the next election in 1766, Pitt was again approached to form a cabinet, which he did. The same year, the king honored Pitt for his service to England by making him the first Earl of Chatham of Kent County and Viscount (pronounced VY-count) Pitt of Somerset County. Since Pitt was now a nobleman, he could not sit in the House of Commons and moved instead into the House of Lords. This move was very unpopular with the English people, who loudly criticized their former hero. This criticism hurt Pitt deeply. By early 1767, Pitt was suffering again from illness and retired from public life until the fall of 1768. While Pitt was ill, the Townshend Acts were passed, placing duties (taxes) on lead, paint, glass, paper, and tea going into the American colonies. These Acts were another major source of discontent in the colonies.

Pitt resigned from the ministry (the cabinet) in 1768, and returned to his seat in Parliament in 1770 and 1771. From 1772 through 1774, Pitt suffered again from illness and rarely took his seat in the House of Lords. In 1774, he did make a speech pleading for the government to "adopt a more gentle mode of governing America." The next year, Pitt introduced a bill to peaceably settle Britain's differences with America. Pitt's bill acknowledged the right of the colonists to tax themselves, allowed for a congress to meet in the American capital of Philadelphia, Pennsylvania, and proposed that the Americans, as good British subjects, help support the king by donating an annual sum of money. The bill was defeated in Parliament. Unfortunately Pitt, one of the few people in Parliament working for a peaceful solution to the American problem, fell ill and was again absent from public life throughout 1776. In mid-

1777, he again addressed the House of Lords, pleading with Parliament to end the war.

Attitude toward the American colonies

Pitt was regarded as a hero in the colonies. The Americans appreciated his speaking out against the Stamp Act in 1765. Pitt also opposed the "Intolerable Acts" passed by Parliament to punish the colonies for the Boston Tea Party, in which they destroyed tons of British tea, in 1773. The acts closed the port of Boston, took away self-government in Massachusetts, and forced the citizens of Boston to house the British soldiers stationed there.

Pitt also angered the king and pleased the Americans when he proposed that no taxes be levied without the consent of the American local governments (called assemblies). In 1775, he proposed that British troops be withdrawn from Boston. This further earned American gratitude, even though his motion failed to pass. In 1777, he spoke against the British practice of hiring Native Americans to fight against the colonials.

While Pitt supported the Americans' right to representation and fair taxes, he never believed in granting them their independence from England. He knew that Britain's strength rested on her colonial possessions, which provided much money for England.

Later years

On April 7, 1778, Pitt made his last speech in Parliament, rising to oppose the idea of independence for the American colonies. He suffered a seizure and collapsed. When he seemed to be recovering, Pitt was moved to his country home at Hayes Place. He lingered for several weeks, and died on May 11, 1778, at the age of sixty-nine. Pitt is buried in Westminster Abbey in London.

For More Information

Cockburn, J. S. "Pitt the Elder." *Encyclopedia of World Biography.* David Eggenberger, editor-in-chief. Palatine, IL: McGraw-Hill, 1973, pp. 464-66.

Lowe, William C. "Pitt, William, 1st Earl of Chatham. Known as the Elder Pitt." *The American Revolution 1775-1783. An Encyclopedia.* Vol. 2: M-

Z. Richard L. Blanco, ed. New York: Garland Publishing, 1993, pp. 1306-09.

Wilcoxen, Charlotte. "British Sympathy for America." *Daughters of the American Revolution Magazine*. Vol. 110, 1976, pp. 323-25.

Web Sites

Pitt's Speech on the Stamp Act. [Online] Available http://odur.let.rug....sa/D/1751-1775/stampact/sapitt.htm (accessed on April 14, 1999).

Zaagsma, Gerben. *Sugar Act and Stamp Act.* [Online] Available http://odur.let.rug.nl/~usa/E/sugar_stamp/act01.htm (accessed on April 14, 1999).

Casimir Pulaski

Born March 4, 1747
Winiary Estate near Warsaw, Poland
Died October 11, 1779
Savannah, Georgia

Military leader

"I came [to America], where freedom is being defended, to serve it, and to live or die for it."

Portrait: Casimir Pulaski. *Reproduced by permission of the U.S. Signal Corporation.*

Casimir Pulaski, freedom fighter, was a young man of outstanding bravery and energy. He fought to free his own country of Poland from domination by Russia. Falsely accused of trying to assassinate the king of Poland, he went into exile in France, where he heard talk of revolution in America. He offered his expertise to the cause and distinguished himself as a military instructor and soldier before his tragic death during the battle for Savannah, Georgia.

Casimir Pulaski was born in 1747 on his family's estate, about forty miles southwest of Poland's capital city of Warsaw. He was the second son and one of eight children born to Josef Pulaski, a lawyer, and Marjanna Zielinska Pulaski, an heiress. The Pulaskis were among the wealthiest of Poland's lesser nobility (a step below the upper ranks). All eight of the Pulaski children were healthy enough to survive to adulthood. The family was warm and loving, and the children remained close throughout their lives. They practiced the Roman Catholic religion.

According to biographer Clarence A. Manning, for the Pulaski boys, childhood "was an almost ideal existence ... the customs of the day prescribed that children should not be overburdened with discipline and education. There was plenty of good and active exercise in the open air, many objects of diversion around the one-storied manor house ... and nearby were the villages with the homes of the [servants] and the peasants." Casimir Pulaski learned to hunt and shoot, and "at a very early age was recognized in all manly sports as a natural leader."

Pulaski's father was educated in the classics (the literature of ancient Greece and Rome), and he passed this knowledge on to his son. Josef Pulaski served as a lawyer to Poland's richest men, preparing speeches for noblemen to deliver at government meetings. He became directly involved in politics when a grateful wealthy family arranged for him to become a mayor in 1732.

When Casimir Pulaski was twelve, his father sent him for more formal schooling in Warsaw. Apparently the boy was not much of a scholar; his father chose a school not known for high standards. There were no restrictions placed on young Pulaski; he could come and go as he pleased, and he could study whatever subjects he wished. He probably dabbled in the study of French, Italian, public speaking, dancing, and good manners—subjects considered suitable for a young gentleman of his time. When he had completed his studies, his father sent the fifteen-year-old youth to serve in the court of Prince Karl of Courland, son of King Augustus of Poland.

His duties during the six months he spent at Prince Karl's court were light. He took up pistol shooting, wrestling, and card playing and practiced stunts on horseback. He also became bewitched by Prince Karl's nineteen-year-old wife, and according to Clarence Manning, this "was the nearest to a love affair that he was ever to know."

Political situation in Poland

Pulaski grew up during a time of political upheaval in Polish history. Russia, Poland's much larger and aggressive neighbor, was gradually extending its control over Poland. As a boy, Pulaski often heard the story of how his grandfather had been killed in a battle against Russia. At the court of Prince Karl, he overheard more discussions of Russian domination.

Poland had a political system in which the king had little power and noblemen mismanaged the government. Josef

Pulaski had grown rich from the troubled system, but his feelings toward it changed after the 1763 death of King Augustus.

In the normal way, Prince Karl would have been elected the new king. However, Queen Catherine of Russia managed (partly by force and partly by trickery) to get her former lover, Stanislas August Poniatowski, placed on the throne. It was clear that he would be nothing but a puppet for Russia. Josef Pulaski and his sons were disgusted, and they talked seriously about going to war to rid Poland of the Russians.

In 1767 Russian troops entered Poland to force its lawmakers to end the privileged status of the Roman Catholic Church. For the Pulaskis, this was the last straw. Josef Pulaski helped form a resistance organization, and he was placed in charge of its military arm. On his twenty-first birthday, Casimir Pulaski was given the command of a military regiment. For the next three years, he learned the art of warfare and distinguished himself in military campaigns against Russian soldiers, fighting "For Faith and Freedom." He gained invaluable experience collecting supplies and recruiting men to the cause. For a time it seemed that Poland's army, once the butt of jokes, might actually rise up and win this struggle.

In October 1771, Casimir was falsely accused of kidnaping King Stanislas, and in 1772, he fled Poland, never to return. That same year, Russia, Prussia (a state in Germany), and Austria divided Poland among themselves. The fight for Poland's freedom had failed; Pulaski lost his father and a brother in the cause. King Stanislas spread the word that Pulaski was a murdering troublemaker, and Pulaski, briefly the idol of all Europe, was scorned and ridiculed.

Exile

Pulaski's experiences had been instructive. He developed a passion for the cause of liberty. He also developed some unpopular notions of what was due to an army fighting for liberty. He had seen his soldiers suffer because civilians were not patriotic enough to make sacrifices for them. He had allowed his men to go out into the countryside to take what they needed wherever they could find it. Despite howls of protest, he continued to believe that this behavior was proper during wartime.

Pulaski spent two years wandering through Europe, laying low to avoid the Russians. While he was away, in September 1773, a Warsaw court condemned him to death for supposedly trying to kill the king. He finally made his way to Paris, France, where he lived under a false name (though many knew who he was) and grew depressed from inactivity.

Then Pulaski heard that the country of Turkey had taken up arms against Russia. He grew excited and decided to go to Turkey to ask for help in liberating Poland. He convinced Polish patriots (including his own family members) to put up money for this venture. But the Turks were defeated by the Russians in June 1774, and Pulaski was forced to return to France.

Hears of revolution in America

King **Louis XVI** (see entry) granted the disgraced Pulaski his permission to remain in France, as long as he did so quietly and under an assumed name. Pulaski was humiliated. He also faced the problem of how to support himself. He was twenty-eight years old, had little education, expensive habits, and no job skills except for soldiering. Although he had a fine reputation as a soldier, and it was common for soldiers to serve in foreign armies, no army would take on a man who had been condemned as a regicide (pronounced REJ-i-SIDE; king killer). He took to gambling and fell deeper and deeper into debt. No one seemed willing to help, and he considered suicide, but his religion did not allow it. Matters reached a low point in 1775, when he was thrown into debtors' prison.

Finally, his friends rallied around the former hero, secured his release from prison, and paid his debts. But what was he to do next?

In the summer of 1776, Silas Deane of Connecticut arrived in France to discuss military assistance in America's struggle for independence from Great Britain. In October 1776, Pulaski wrote Deane, expressing "the zeal which I have to contribute in my particular way to the success of the cause of English America."

Pulaski's letter went unanswered. But, when **Benjamin Franklin** (see entry) arrived in France, he made inquiries among his many acquaintances in Paris. Franklin was told that Pulaski was an outstanding soldier. In fact, of all the men who applied to fight for American liberty, Pulaski was easily the most qualified. But to Franklin, there was a major hurdle in enlisting Pulaski. Franklin wanted the kings of Europe to see the American cause as a respectable one, and Pulaski, with a charge of regicide hanging over him, was looked upon with disfavor.

But Pulaski's friends, who believed he could salvage his tarnished reputation in America, spoke on his behalf to Franklin. Franklin promised nothing, but he did offer to pay for Pulaski's trip to America and to write a letter of introduction to General **George Washington** (see entry). After that, it would be Washington's and Congress's decision what to do with Pulaski.

Pulaski goes to America

For Pulaski, Franklin's offer opened up a prospect of a brighter future. He could fight for liberty with men who were willing to risk their own lives in a great cause. In the process he might clear his name.

Casimir Pulaski arrived in the New World in July 1777. As a nobleman (a count), he found American ideas of equality very strange. He realized he had a lot to learn.

Eager to get to work, Pulaski went immediately to Washington's headquarters near Philadelphia. In addition to Franklin's letter, Pulaski had brought with him a letter of introduction from the wife of the **Marquis de Lafayette** (see entry). Lafayette at once took him to see George Washington, who was very impressed by the serious Polish officer. It took a whole month, and Pulaski grew impatient at the delay, but on September 15, 1777, on Washington's recommendation, the Continental Congress created a new position, "Commander of the Horse," and appointed Pulaski a general in charge of the cavalry (troops who fight on horseback).

Pulaski trains and outfits his soldiers

Pulaski ran into trouble right away. He spoke no English and was often unable to understand what was being said to him. He was unwilling to take orders from Washington. The two men never grew close, yet Washington saw and appreciated Pulaski's leadership qualities.

It was obvious that Pulaski was willing and ready to help. He spent the winter of 1777 at Trenton, New Jersey, dazzling everyone with his trick riding skills and drilling soldiers in cavalry techniques. But he grew frustrated when he saw that the Americans did not look upon a cavalry in the same way he did. His vision was to use the cavalry as a fighting force of swordsmen who could take independent action without having to wait for orders from above. The Americans had learned how to fight on the frontier, where horses were often more of a hindrance than a help, and guns were their weapon of choice. They did not see a cavalry as a superior unit, but just one of several types of fighting forces.

Frustrated, Pulaski resigned from his position and asked that he be allowed to form a special unit. On March 28, 1778, Pulaski received permission, and over the next five months he formed the unit that earned him the title "father of the American cavalry." His new unit consisted of Americans, Frenchmen, Poles, Irishmen, German deserters from the British army, and prisoners of war.

Pulaski faced problems getting supplies and paychecks for his men, the same kind of problems General Washington endured throughout the war. Congress had to approve everything, and Congress was several days' journey away. Pulaski was exasperated at the huge amount of paperwork involved in getting the most minor supplies. Sometimes he used his own money; other times he allowed his men to go out into the countryside and take what they needed. Citizens complained, and so did Congress. Washington sent several warning letters, but no doubt he sympathized with Pulaski. Pulaski remained unfazed: the needs of his men were foremost, and he expected all patriotic Americans to feel the same way.

Pulaski's unit is battle tested

By late summer of 1778, Pulaski's Legion was finally ready, and he was enormously proud of it. In August, the Legion passed inspection by an impressed Congress in Philadelphia. But still there were delays, and Pulaski grew irritable.

Finally, on October 4, 1778, General Washington ordered Pulaski to Little Egg Harbor, New Jersey, a few miles north of modern Atlantic City. The harbor was a haven for

The American siege of Savannah was no surprise to the British: a deserter informed the British of the American army's plan. The battle ensued, and as a result, Pulaski was shot and killed by the well-prepared British forces. *Reproduced by permission of Archive Photos.*

American privateers, which were ships owned by private citizens that attacked and captured enemy vessels. British soldiers were on their way to raid Little Egg Harbor and Pulaski's Legion was supposed to thwart this attack. Unfortunately, one of Pulaski's German deserters betrayed him by warning the British. The encounter was a disaster for the Americans; fifty officers and men were killed, including one of Pulaski's commanders.

Pulaski took a great deal of criticism over the battle losses. His personality had earned him enemies, who revived the old charges of regicide. They complained that after all the money spent on the Legion, it had proved useless. Pulaski wrote a long letter to Congress defending the honor of his men. He said he was the victim of prejudice against foreigners. He reminded them that he had funded the Legion out of his own money. He seriously considered returning to Europe.

Joins war in the South

General Washington did not know what to do with Pulaski and his Legion. He offered to let Pulaski spend the winter of 1778–79 on the frontier (upstate New York), where American settlements were being raided by combined British-Indian war parties. Pulaski went, but he soon realized that the frontier was not the place for his type of fighting unit. Men who were trained to fight with swords on horseback were no match for the occasional surprise Indian-style attack. After only two weeks, Pulaski wrote to Washington that he was leaving that place "where there is nothing but bears to fight," and returning to Poland.

But Pulaski changed his mind. It seemed he could not stand to leave America with the war unfinished; he wanted one last chance to prove that his theories of warfare were sound.

The war shifted to the South in late 1778. In December the British captured Savannah, Georgia, then turned their attention to South Carolina. Pulaski and his Legion reached Charleston, South Carolina, on May 8, 1779. The city, one of the largest in the southern states, had been under siege for some time and morale was at a low point. Pulaski was just in time to prevent the surrender of Charleston to the British. In the fighting that followed, the Americans prevailed over a greater number of British soldiers. The victory was a big boost for the Americans, proving to anyone who doubted that they would fight for their cause.

But many lives were lost, including forty of Pulaski's foot soldiers. Still, he was hailed as a hero, and he was pleased when Southern military leaders sought him out and asked for his advice. After all the personal attacks he had experienced in the North, and all the bickering with Congress over money matters, Pulaski finally felt appreciated in the refined atmosphere of Charleston.

The British abandoned South Carolina and retreated to their heavily fortified stronghold at Savannah, Georgia. The American siege of Savannah began on September 3, 1779, and it went on for more than a month. The odds favored the Americans, whose force of 1,500 was assisted by 4,000 French soldiers. A major assault was planned for October 9. Pulaski's orders were to position his 200 cavalry behind the French foot soldiers and wait for the proper moment to attack. But once again, a deserter informed the British of the American plan. Surprised by heavy British fire, the French soldiers panicked. In the chaos, Pulaski charged forward and was shot. Wounded, he fell from his horse. The British held their fire while the dying general was carried from the battlefield. The siege ended on October 28 with Savannah still in British hands.

Pulaski was carried to an American ship, the *Wasp*, where he died on October 11 at the age of thirty-two. His body was buried at sea. News of the death of the gallant soldier was greeted with sadness. King Stanislas of Poland said: "Pulaski has died as he lived—a hero—but an enemy of kings." Today, Casimir Pulaski is especially revered among Polish Americans, who have set aside a special day to celebrate his memory.

For More Information

Boatner, Mark M, III. "Pulaski, Casimir." *Encyclopedia of the American Revolution.* Mechanicsburg, PA: Stackpole Books, 1994, pp. 320-22,638, 900-01.

Collins, David R. *Casimir Pulaski: Soldier on Horseback.* New York: Pelican, 1995.

Manning, Clarence A. *Soldier of Liberty, Casimir Pulaski.* New York: Philosophical Library, 1945.

Web Sites

Kulczycki, John J. "Casimir Pulaski 1747-1779: A Short Biography." Published by the Polish Museum of America. [Online] Available http://cpl.lib.uic.edu/003cpl/pulaskibiog.html (accessed on 10/8/99).

David Ramsay

Born April 2, 1749
Lancaster County, Pennsylvania
Died May 8, 1815
Charleston, South Carolina

Physician, politician, historian

"[American colonists believed that] all government was a political institution between men naturally equal, not for [increasing the power] of one, or a few, but for the general happiness of the whole community."

David Ramsay was a man of many talents. He was born into humble circumstances and lacked family connections. But he became a wealthy and successful physician in an America that had freed itself from the type of European social system in which this would not have been possible. Ramsay became the foremost American historian of Revolutionary times and a spokesman for the revolutionary generation's politicians and thinkers.

David Ramsay was born in Drumore Township, Lancaster County, Pennsylvania. His parents had come to America from Ireland and were the owners of a small farm. Ramsay's older brother, Nathaniel, went on to become an officer in the Continental army (formed during the American Revolution) and a Maryland politician.

David Ramsay graduated from what is now Princeton University in New Jersey in 1765. After teaching for a short time, he went on to receive a medical degree in 1772 from what is now the University of Pennsylvania in Philadelphia. There he studied under the esteemed physician **Benjamin Rush** (see entry).

Portrait: David Ramsay. *Reproduced by permission of Archive Photos, Inc.*

Ramsay was a very ambitious young man. After he completed his education, he worked as a doctor for one year in Maryland, near the home of his brother. Then in 1773 Ramsay moved to Charleston, South Carolina, where he was to remain for the rest of his life.

The Charleston in which Ramsay arrived was a thriving community that provided a fine opportunity for a young physician to make his mark. Ramsay found success there within a mere two years. Physician Benjamin Rush had given the young doctor a recommendation that referred to Ramsay as "far superior to any person we ever graduated at our college." Ramsay became a respected member of an important local church, gained election to the state legislature (where laws are made), and started a medical practice that soon began to flourish.

Marries, begins political career

In 1775 Ramsay married his first wife, Sabina Ellis, the daughter of a wealthy family of merchants. But the young woman died within a year, after giving birth to the couple's daughter. The money Ramsay inherited from his wife, coupled with his earnings as a physician, made him a wealthy man.

Beginning in his college years, Ramsay had opposed policies of Great Britain that seemed to him unfair to the colonists. He developed a belief in extreme republicanism. This is a system in which voters hold the power and carry out government policies through elected representatives. Ramsay expressed his political beliefs to his fellow colonists by way of pamphlets and public speeches and through his involvement in government service and the military.

While continuing his medical practice, Ramsay began a political career in Charleston in 1776, near the start of the Revolutionary War (1775–83). He was elected as a representative to the South Carolina legislature, where he was to serve on and off for twenty-one years.

Serves militia, joins Congress, remarries

During the middle of the Revolutionary War, when the British threatened to attack Charleston, Ramsay served as surgeon in the Charleston militia (a volunteer group of soldiers.) He was captured by the British and held for eleven months at a military prison in St. Augustine, Florida, until his release in June 1781.

From 1782 to 1786 Ramsay was a member of the South Carolina delegation to the Continental Congress, then America's governing body. At the Congress, Ramsay was an early supporter of a strong central government, rather than a type of government in which the individual states held greater power. He also became known for supporting a move to allow black men to join the American militia.

In 1783 Ramsay, age thirty-four, married for the second time, to Frances Witherspoon, the twenty-four-year-old daughter of John Witherspoon, a signer of the Declaration of Independence. Her father was the president of Princeton University, and although he was not wealthy, he was well known. The marriage brought Ramsay a lot of attention in the community, but he soon faced heartache once again when his second wife and infant son died fifteen months after the wedding.

Developments in political and personal life

From 1784 to 1790 Ramsay again served in the South Carolina House of Representatives. He was elected to the temporary position of Chairman of the Continental Congress in 1775 and held the position until Congress chose a permanent president in 1786.

In 1787 Ramsay took as his third wife Martha Laurens, daughter of Henry Laurens, one of the wealthiest merchants in South Carolina and president of the Continental Congress. The marriage introduced Ramsay into Charleston high society. Now he had both wealth and social position. It was also a love match; Martha Ramsay once wrote in her diary that her husband was "the spring of all my earthly happiness." Over sixteen years, the Ramsays produced eleven children; all but two survived to adulthood. The couple enjoyed a happy marriage until Martha Ramsay's death in 1811 at age fifty-one.

In 1788 Ramsay lost his bid to be elected to the U.S. House of Representatives. South Carolina voters suspected him of favoring the abolition of slavery, and the state's economy depended on slave labor. He was also known to have connections with northern abolitionists, such as Benjamin Rush. Abolitionists wanted to see the end of slavery in the United States. Ramsay was defeated in the election by a pro-slavery candidate.

Ramsay remained active in state and national politics, and took an active role in Charleston's cultural, charitable, and medical affairs. He helped form the Medical Society of South Carolina in 1789 and served as its first treasurer.

Faces political ups and downs

In 1792 Ramsay began serving the first of his three two-year terms in the South Carolina Senate; each time he was also elected president of the Senate. As a senator, Ramsay favored the state's wealthy class. During his time in office, he voted against sympathetic treatment toward people in debt, but he opposed the importation of black slaves. The voters and his fellow legislators recognized him as being honest and able.

In 1794 Ramsay failed in his run for a U.S. Senate seat. Historians say he lost the election primarily because of his anti-slavery stand.

History as a writer

Ramsay was a multitalented man who is best remembered for his contributions as a writer of history. He wrote some excellent articles on the history of medicine, and his two-volume *History of the Revolution of South Carolina* was published in 1785.

Ramsay is most widely recognized for his *History of the American Revolution,* a two-volume set published in 1789. Like many other American historians of his time, Ramsay borrowed heavily from the writings of British historian **Edmund Burke** (see entry).

With the publication of his *History,* Ramsay became the most respected historian in America and one of its best known writers. Six editions of his *History* were published between 1789 and 1865; several foreign-language editions were also published.

While his knowledgeable interpretations of events of his time are very valuable, history has shown that Ramsay was not always careful to write the entire truth. But for nearly one hundred years after the publication of his *History*, he remained the only historian to discuss the many different motives that led people to support the Revolution and the American Constitution. It was Ramsay's idea that a group of strong-minded men brought about American independence, changed the existing social structure, and made the most of the young nation's expanding economy.

Later life

In 1807 Ramsay published *The Life of George Washington,* a popular early study of the life of the first U.S. president. After the death of his third wife in 1811, Ramsay published *Memoirs of the Life of Martha Laurens Ramsay,* a tribute to the spouse he greatly missed.

In Ramsay's later years, he became the "grand old man" of Charleston thinkers, and prominent people often came to visit him. He also enjoyed frequent contact with his large, close family.

In his 1815 memoirs, Ramsay's friend Robert Y. Hayne wrote: Ramsay "was a most agreeable companion; his memory was stored with an infinite fund of interesting or amusing anecdotes, which gave great sprightliness and zest to his conversation. He never assumed any superiority over those with whom he conversed, and always took ... pleasure in the society of young men of intelligence or [loyalty to their principles]."

Throughout his life, Ramsay faced constant financial problems. His writings earned little money and he proved to be a poor businessman. Ramsay made a disastrous investment when he bought land in hopes of reselling it for a profit. He lost so much money that he could not pay his debts, despite his thriving medical practice.

Ramsay was forced into bankruptcy in 1798 and struggled with major debts for the rest of his life. It is interesting to note that throughout his career as a lawmaker, Ramsay had shown no sympathy for the plight of people in debt.

Final work published after death

Ramsay met a violent death. On the afternoon of May 6, 1815, he was walking home from downtown Charleston when he passed by William Linnen, a tailor. Some time before, Ramsay had testified in a courtroom case that Linnen showed signs of insanity. On this occasion, Linnen shot Ramsay in the back with a large pistol. Ramsay was carried home by friends, but the wounds were fatal.

On his deathbed, Ramsay said he was not afraid to die. He declared, "I call on all present to bear witness, that I consider the unfortunate perpetrator [doer] of this deed a lunatic, and free from guilt." After two days of suffering, Ramsay died at the age of sixty-six. He was buried on the grounds of his beloved Congregational Church.

A few years after Ramsay's death, his ambitious nine-volume *Universal History Americanized* was published through the efforts of his friends and family. The book received mixed reviews and did not sell well. But Ramsay's reputation had already been well established, especially by the second volume of his *History of the United States*. About that book, historian and reviewer Abiel Holmes said in 1818, "[It] will always hold a distinguished rank in the historical productions of our country."

History student James K. Polk (1795–1849), who served as the eleventh president of the United States, once compared David Ramsay to Tacitus, a famous historian of ancient Rome. Polk described Ramsay as transmitting to those who followed in the New World "in the unpolished language of truth, the spirit of liberty which [called to action] the first founders of the republic."

For More Information

Boatner, Mark M., III. "Ramsay, David." *Encyclopedia of the American Revolution*. Mechanicsburg, PA: Stackpole Books, 1994, pp. 911-12.

Bourgoin, Suzanne M. and Paula K. Byers, eds. "Ramsay, David." *Encyclopedia of World Biography*. Detroit, MI: Gale, 1999, vol. 13, p. 21.

Dolan, J.P. "Ramsay, David." *Dictionary of American Medical Biography*. Martin Kaufman, Stuart Galishoff, and Todd L. Savitt, eds. Westport, CT: Greenwood Press, 1984, vol. 2, pp. 622-23.

Dolan, J.P. *To Be an American: David Ramsay and the Making of the American Consciousness*. Columbia, SC: University of South Carolina Press, 1991.

Purcell, L. Edward. "Ramsay, David." *Who Was Who in the American Revolution*. New York: Facts on File, 1993, p. 398.

Whitney, David C. "David Ramsay." *The Colonial Spirit of '76: The People of the Revolution*. Broadview, IL: J.G. Ferguson Publishing Co., 1974, p. 343.

Esther De Berdt Reed

Born October 22, 1746
London, England
Died September 18, 1780
Philadelphia, Pennsylvania

Organization leader

"If these great affairs must be brought to a crisis and decided, it had better be in our time than our children's."

Portrait: Esther De Berdt Reed. *Reproduced by permission of Archive Photos, Inc.*

Esther De Berdt Reed was a patriot and the head of a women's group that provided goods needed by the soldiers of the Continental army during the Revolutionary War (1775–83). Her involvement in public affairs and her often-criticized efforts to involve women in patriotic activities broadened the role of women in the new country.

Esther De Berdt, born in 1746 in London, England, was one of two children of Martha Symon De Berdt and Dennys De Berdt, an English businessman who traded with colonists in Delaware and Massachusetts. The fair-haired, attractive young Esther was a lively talker and a lover of books. Whether or not "Hette" or "Hettie," as she was known to her family, received any formal schooling outside her home is unknown.

In 1763, when Esther De Berdt was seventeen, she and Joseph Reed, an American from New Jersey, fell in love. Reed was in England studying law and tending to his family's business interests. Due to the young man's desire to build up his business in America and Dennys De Berdt's opposition to the match (he believed Reed was not worthy of his daughter), the couple did not marry until May 31, 1770.

Joseph Reed's friend Stephen Sayre wrote about Dennys De Berdt's opposition to the marriage: "You have one material comfort that the old codger must soon pop off and leave his fortune." But Sayre was mistaken. De Berdt did die shortly before the wedding but left his family with serious financial problems. In order to help Esther's mother escape public shame, the young couple brought her with them across the Atlantic Ocean and settled in Philadelphia, Pennsylvania.

Hosts patriots, flees war-torn Philadelphia

In time, Joseph Reed gained success as a lawyer and a businessman. He also became one of the leaders of the cause of American independence. He was a member of the First Continental Congress, a meeting of representatives of the American colonies that met in Philadelphia in the fall of 1774 to decide what to do about America's ongoing problems with England. During the congress the Reeds entertained its representatives, including **George Washington, John Adams** (see entries), and Silas Deane, who wrote to his wife about Esther Reed, that she had "a most elegant figure and countenance" (face), and that she was "a Daughter of Liberty."

The Reeds had six children; five lived to adulthood. Esther Reed took care of them on her own from July 1775 to January 1777, while her husband served as George Washington's military aide.

From 1777 through 1778 Joseph Reed served in the Continental Congress. On three occasions during the revolutionary turmoil, his wife and children were forced to flee Philadelphia to escape the fighting in the streets. From September 1777 to January 1778 they lived in Norristown, Pennsylvania, and Flemington, New Jersey. Perhaps because she was British, Esther Reed's life there was made miserable by British soldiers and roving bands of Loyalists (colonists who remained loyal to England). In February 1778, while living in Pennsylvania near Washington's headquarters, Reed described her situation in a letter to her close friend, Mrs. John Cox. "I am easiest [most relaxed] when [my husband] is [away] from home, as his being here brings danger with it. There are so many disloyal to the cause of this country, that they lay in wait for those who are active in it."

Starts fund raising campaign

Joseph Reed was elected president of the Pennsylvania government, and he held the position from December 1778 until 1781. At that time, the Reed family once again settled in Philadelphia, and Esther De Berdt Reed was known as "Mrs. President."

By 1780, the fifth year of the Revolutionary War, the soldiers of General George Washington's Continental army were living under horrible conditions. Their clothing was ragged, and their shoes and boots were full of holes. Food supplied them was scarce and sometimes not fit to eat, and they suffered from a variety of diseases. At the same time, Esther Reed was having her own problems dealing with smallpox, a contagious disease that causes fever, vomiting, skin eruptions, and sometimes death. Upon her recovery, she came up with an idea to help the suffering Continental soldiers. Reed began the Association of Philadelphia, then the largest women's organization in America. Reed's organization began a campaign among the women of the Philadelphia area to raise funds to help the soldiers of the Continental army.

Because it was uncommon for women of that time to assert themselves in money matters, Reed was very careful as to how she went about the campaign. First, she published a large poster explaining why women should help the army. She stressed that in difficult times true patriots—both male and female—should help the American soldiers in their time of need. She ended by asking for money for her cause.

Reed and her group seek support

Reed helped write "Sentiments of an American Woman," a well-thought-out argument about why women should participate in public affairs. In the essay, the authors cited numerous examples of women throughout history who had done so and called on colonial women to sacrifice any luxuries and contribute their money to the Continental army.

The essay was distributed door to door by members of Reed's organization as they went about contacting every household in Philadelphia. The women, disregarding normal rules of polite behavior, asked for money not only from middle- and upper-class people; they also approached immi-

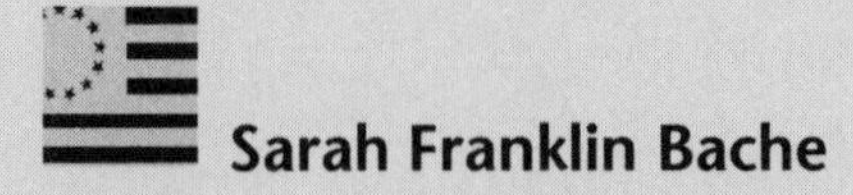

Sarah Franklin Bache

Sarah Franklin Bache (pronounced BEECH; 1743–1808) was the daughter of **Benjamin Franklin** and **Deborah Read Franklin** (see entries). In 1767 she married Richard Bache, an English-born merchant who served on the Pennsylvania Board of War during the American Revolution. The couple had eight children. As a young married woman, Bache worked closely with Esther De Berdt Reed as a member of the Association of Philadelphia, an organization of thirty-eight women who went door to door to the homes of Philadelphia colonists asking them to contribute money to help the Continental soldiers.

Esther Reed died in 1780, just when the group had purchased enough cloth to sew 2,000 shirts for the soldiers camped at Valley Forge. Bache took over as leader of the Association of Philadelphia. Much of the cutting of the cloth for the shirts was done at her house. Bache not only continued to raise funds and do volunteer work with injured soldiers but also supervised the sewing of the shirts.

Like Reed, Bache hoped that colonial women would follow the example of the Philadelphians and make some effort to help the American army. She and other group members wrote letters to friends to help spread the movement. In the end, similar committees of women were set up in New Jersey and Maryland as well as in other Pennsylvania towns.

grants, the poor, and servants to collect even the smallest of contributions. The women hoped the gift of money would show how dedicated American women were to the cause of patriotism.

Reed cleverly made sure that the wives of influential men were asked to be part of the effort. These included Sally McKean, wife of the chief justice of Pennsylvania, and Benjamin Franklin's daughter, Sarah Franklin Bache, the wife of a well-known businessman.

Not all the people of Philadelphia supported Reed's efforts. Many Loyalist women found the whole campaign disgusting. Women were not expected to have any concern about financial matters, and the Loyalists thought the women involved in Reed's campaign were very rude. Loyalist Anna Rawle wrote: "Of all absurdities [foolish acts], the ladies going about for money exceeded everything; they were so [annoyingly persistent] that people were obliged to give them something to get rid of them."

Campaign succeeds, women make shirts

By July 4, 1780, Reed and her thirty-eight female helpers were able to raise thousands of dollars for the cause. Esther Reed wrote to George Washington that the women wished to give each Continental soldier $2 "to be entirely at his own disposal." Reed said: "The money ... will be as proof of our [devotion] for the great Cause of America, and of our Esteem and Gratitude for those who so bravely defend it."

Washington feared that some men would use the money to gamble or buy liquor and asked that it be used to produce linen shirts for the soldiers. So Reed's group purchased enough cloth to sew more than 2,000 shirts.

Reed's work continues after her death

In September 1780, only two weeks after the linen was purchased, Esther De Berdt Reed died unexpectedly in Philadelphia at age thirty-three of an intestinal disease. She was buried at Philadelphia's Second Presbyterian Church. Joseph Reed's sister came to live with him to help raise the couple's five children. After Reed's death, George Washington wrote to her husband that he regretted "the loss of your amiable [pleasant] lady."

Sarah Franklin Bache (see box) carried forward the work of the Association of Philadelphia. Due to the efforts of Reed, Bache, and other women, fund-raising groups were begun in a number of Pennsylvania, Maryland, and New Jersey towns, though none was as productive as the Philadelphia campaign.

In a tribute written about Reed after her death, she was honored as being "received into the paradise of female patriotism with [great] distinction.... She sacrificed her ease, her health, and it may be her life, for her country." In 1868 the remains of Reed and her husband were removed to Philadelphia's Laurel Hill Cemetery.

For More Information

Alden, John. *Stephen Sayre, American Revolutionary Adventurer.* Baton Rouge: Louisiana State University Press, 1983, pp. 9–13, 16–17, 19, 20–25, 28.

Allison, Robert J. *American Eras: The Revolutionary Era, 1754–1783.* Detroit: Gale, 1998, pp. 257–58.

Claghorn, Charles E. *Women Patriots of the American Revolution.* Metuchen, NJ: Scarecrow Press, 1991, pp. 160–61.

Kerber, Linda K. *Women of the Republic: Intellect & Ideology in Revolutionary America.* Chapel Hill: University of North Carolina Press, 1980, pp. 99, 102, 278.

Meyer, Edith Patterson. *Petticoat Patriots of the American Revolution.* New York: Vanguard Press, 1976, pp. 133–35.

Roche, John F. *Joseph Reed: A Moderate in the American Revolution.* New York: AMS Press, 1968, p. 127.

Roche, John F. "Reed, Esther De Berdt."*Notable American Women 1607–1950, A Biographical Dictionary,* Vol.3. Edited by Edward T. James. Cambridge, MA: Belknap Press of Harvard University Press, 1971, pp. 123–24.

Ward, Harry M. "Reed, Esther De Berdt." *American National Biography.* New York: Oxford University Press, 1999, pp. 263–65.

Zeinert, Karen. *Those Remarkable Women of the American Revolution.* Brookfield, CT: Millbrook Press, 1996, pp. 50–55.

Paul Revere

Born January 1, 1735
Boston, Massachusetts
Died May 10, 1818
Boston, Massachusetts

Silversmith, industrialist, political leader, courier, soldier

"I alarmed the Captain of the Minute Men, and after that I alarmed almost every house till I got to Lexington ... [crying] 'The Regulars [British soldiers] are out! The Regulars are out!'"

Portrait: Paul Revere. *Reproduced by permission of Archive Photos, Inc.*

Paul Revere, one of colonial Boston's leading silver artisans, was accomplished in several fields. This creative and versatile man was an innovator in the processing of copper and bronze and an important political organizer in Revolutionary Boston. He is best known as the subject of a famous poem by Henry Wadsworth Longfellow titled *Paul Revere's Ride.*

Paul Revere's father was a man of French descent named Apollos De Rivoire (pronounced ah-po-LOW duh ruh-VWAR), who later changed his last name to the simpler Revere. He came as a boy to Boston from the British Isle of Guernsey and learned the silversmith trade, which included the crafting and repair of silver articles. Paul was the third of thirteen children born to Apollos and his wife, Deborah Hichborn Revere.

Young Paul was educated at the North Writing School in Boston and learned from his father how to create elegant silver and gold objects. Apollos Revere died when Paul was nineteen, leaving his son with the major financial responsibility for the large family. The young man now had to pay the rent for the house and fully equipped silver shop, either with money he earned or with the items he crafted. In time, the shop

Revere operated for nearly forty years provided him with a very comfortable living.

Revere employed a number of assistants in his shop to produce his designs for items ranging from spoons and forks to entire tea sets. His bowls and pitchers were especially prized. His work remains among the outstanding achievements in American decorative arts.

Revere also branched out into other crafts, including engraving copper printing plates. His shop produced business cards, songbooks, certificates, magazine illustrations, and menus for taverns. He would later engrave the printing plates for the state of Massachusetts's first money and design the official seal for the State of Massachusetts, which remains in use today.

Military service, marriage, business expansion

In 1754 France and her Indian allies were fighting the British in the American colonies in a conflict known as the French and Indian War (1754–63). The war was part of a larger global conflict. In 1756, when Massachusetts asked for volunteers to fight, Paul Revere served as a second lieutenant (pronounced lew-TEN-ant) in the colonial artillery (the gunners' group). He took part in an unsuccessful expedition to capture Crown Point in New York. But before the next winter set in, he returned to Boston and went back to running his shop. At that time, armies did not continue to fight in the winter.

In 1757 Revere married Sarah Orne. When she died in childbirth in 1773, Revere married Rachel Walker. Revere had sixteen children, eight by each wife; five died in infancy.

As the nation prepared for war and Revere approached middle age, he helped in the war effort and also expanded his business activities. From 1768 to 1775 Revere ran his silversmithing business, produced surgical instruments, and worked repairing teeth and wiring in false teeth made from walrus ivory or animal teeth. He also made engravings of political cartoons that reached a wide audience.

Political involvement

It was through his contacts with businessmen and members of Boston organizations that Revere became involved in politics. Revere was a member of the Masons, a secret society that promoted charity and mutual aid. As a result of his membership in the Masonic Lodge of St. Andrew from 1760 to 1809, he became friends with revolutionary activists such as James Otis and Joseph Warren (see **Mercy Otis Warren** entry). As an old man Revere said that the period he served as the grand master of the Massachusetts Grand Lodge of Masons (from 1795 to 1797) brought him the "greatest happiness" of his life. During the 1760s and 1770s, as the political situation in America heated up, Revere spent most of his free time on revolutionary activities.

In 1765 Revere became a member of the Sons of Liberty, a radical political organization. Radicals desire extreme change in the political system or social structure. In 1768 Revere fashioned one of the most famous pieces of colonial silver, the Liberty Bowl. It had been ordered by the Sons of Liberty to honor the members of the Massachusetts House of Representatives who stood up to their British rulers by protesting the Townshend Acts. The Townshend Acts imposed taxes on the colonists for such items as glass, paints, paper, and tea.

Revere's most famous engraving was an image of the Boston Massacre, an encounter between a group of American patriots and British soldiers that took place on March 5, 1770. The violent street encounter left four men dead and eight wounded. Revere's engraving of colonists being shot by British soldiers stirred up Americans to oppose British rule and made him one of the best-known producers of anti-British propaganda. Propaganda is information and argument designed to influence public opinion about political matters.

In 1770 Revere bought an old but roomy brown house at Boston's North Square. This home is preserved as a memorial to the renowned patriot and remains one of the biggest tourist draws in Boston.

Helps plan Boston Tea Party

Revere observed the movements of British soldiers in and around Boston and reported them to his fellow revolutionaries. He frequently delivered messages on horseback for the Boston Committee of Correspondence and the Massachusetts Committee of Safety. The committees of correspondence were groups in the various colonies that shared information, coordinated the activities of colonial agitators, and organized public opinion against the British government. The Massachusetts Committee of Safety was one of many committees in different locales that had the authority to call up militias, groups of volunteer soldiers.

Along with other members of the Sons of Liberty, Revere took an active part in planning and carrying out the 1773 Boston Tea Party, a political action in which Boston citizens threw hundreds of crates of tea into Boston Harbor to protest British taxation practices.

Gains fame as courier

Revere was one of the most respected couriers of the American Revolution. Couriers are messengers who deliver information, usually in haste. It was an important strategy on the part of the Sons of Liberty to make sure every British action against the colonists was well publicized, in order to rile up Americans against their British rulers and prepare them to go to war.

After the Boston Tea Party, Revere spread the word about the event to the cities of New York and Philadelphia. He made the seven-hundred-mile winter trip in a mere eleven days, faster than anyone thought possible. Revere then became the official courier of the Massachusetts provincial assembly to the First Continental Congress, the revolutionary government that met in Philadelphia, Pennsylvania, in 1774.

The First Continental Congress met to discuss what the colonies should do about their worsening relations with the British government. Revere brought Congress news of events in Boston (where British soldiers were stationed) and carried copies of Congressional documents to the colonies. Revere became so well known that he was mentioned by name in England's newspapers.

Paul Revere's most famous ride was carried out on April 18, 1775. Revere and two men went from Boston to Lexington and Concord, Massachusetts, to warn the revolutionaries there about the coming of British troops. In fact, Revere was prevented by British troops from getting the message through, but one of his companions succeeded in doing so (see box).

Paul Revere's Famous Ride

Around the time of the beginning of the Revolutionary War, Paul Revere was a silversmith with a flourishing business in colonial Boston. He designed and crafted beautiful teapots, silverware, and platters from silver and pewter (a less expensive mix of tin and lead). Although he could have lost his business and his life, Revere was a rebel. Today we would call him a patriot, one of the first to object to British tyranny and rise in the fight for liberty.

Like most of the rebels, Revere at first wanted the British to recognize the Americans' rights to make some decisions for themselves. Soon, however, the rebels wanted more. They wanted complete freedom from England.

As part of the rebel spy network in Boston, Revere had watched the British seize the American war supplies at the nearby towns of Jamaica Plains, Salem, and Marshfield. He knew that the British would be marching again and, this time, the Americans planned to be prepared. But the rebels didn't know exactly where the British would head and whether they would make their move by ship, up the Charles River, or by land. The rebels' goal was to learn more about the British plan and then send out messengers to warn the America militiamen throughout the countryside.

Then on the night of April 18, 1775, a signal came from the Old North Church in Boston. From the bell tower, high above the town, the light of two lanterns gleamed into the darkness. Revere and William Dawes, waiting below, now knew that the British were crossing the Charles River to march overland to the American arsenal at Concord, a town about twenty miles west of Boston. Revere managed to warn the Americans in several towns before being detained for questioning by the British, but Dawes continued his ride through the night.

The Americans were warned and on the morning of April 19, their militia (citizen soldiers) formed up at Lexington, on the road from Boston. When the British attempted to march through, the Americans blocked their path. The British ordered them to desist, the Americans refused, the British gave the order to fire, and there came "the shot that was heard 'round the world." It was the beginning of the American Revolutionary War.

Paul Revere's midnight ride and the battles at Lexington and Concord are celebrated in a famous poem called *Paul Revere's Ride* by Henry Wadsworth Longfellow. The poem somewhat distorted events as they happened, but made Revere's name one of the best known in the popular history of the American Revolution.

Paul Revere's ride from Boston to Lexington and Concord to warn revolutionaries about approaching British troops was immortalized in a poem by Henry Wadsworth Longfellow. *Reproduced by permission of the National Archives and Records Administration.*

Wartime activities

After the Revolutionary War broke out in 1775, Revere served as a lieutenant colonel in a Massachusetts artillery unit. From 1778 to 1779, he was commander of Castle Island in Boston Harbor. Revere and his soldiers did not see much action at this post. However, they did take part in minor expeditions to Newport, Rhode Island, and to Worcester (pronounced WUSS-ter) Massachusetts.

Revere's military career was undistinguished and ended under a black cloud because of the failure of the Penobscot Expedition of 1779. Revere had been ordered to keep himself and one hundred men in a state of readiness, so that with one hour's notice they could leave their camp and attack the enemy at Penobscot, Maine.

But Revere ran into trouble with two of the leaders of the Penobscot Expedition, who were plagued by indecision and confusion. Their lack of leadership allowed time for the enemy to organize a relief expedition. The Americans were forced to retreat.

Court-martialed, found not guilty

After the defeat at Penobscot, Revere was accused of disobedience, cowardly behavior, and unsoldierly conduct. He lost his command at Castle Island on September 6, 1779. Revere demanded a court-martial, a trial in a court made up of military personnel. Three years later he was found not guilty of any wrongdoing.

Starts new businesses

The fighting ended in 1781 and Revere returned to his silver shop. Before long he was leaving more and more of the shop's business in the hands of his oldest son while he branched out into other business ventures. In 1783 Revere began importing goods from Great Britain to stock a small hardware store, where for the next six years, he sold such items as eyeglasses, cloth, wallpaper, playing cards, and sealing wax.

As American manufacturing industries took off at the end of the eighteenth century, Revere saw that the United States was importing all of its sheet copper from England. He became the first man in the United States to learn how to roll sheet copper. He set up a foundry and began producing copper goods at Canton, Massachusetts, where he also opened a gunpowder mill. Canton was a village outside of Boston where Revere could get the water power he needed to turn copper rolls and press metal flat. He supplied nails, bolts, and spikes to Boston's developing shipyards.

Expands business operations

In time Revere expanded his business to produce cannons and cast bells. Finally his foundry replaced his silversmithing. The foundry eventually became the Revere Copper and Brass Company, which is still operating today. One of his bells can still be heard ringing in Boston's famous King's Chapel.

Copper sheeting he produced was used on the hull of the U.S.S. *Constitution* and on the dome of the Massachusetts State House. Revere worked with inventor Robert Fulton in 1808 and 1809 to develop copper boilers for steamboats.

By the turn of the nineteenth century, Paul Revere was a rich man. No one in America was a more skilled artist with silver, and his bell casting operation produced more than four hundred bells for churches throughout the new nation. The Reveres moved into a handsome yellow-painted brick house. Revere sent his sons to be educated in Europe and bought luxurious clothing for his daughters. He bought himself a fine horse.

Community involvement

Throughout his lifetime, Revere was involved in many community and social groups. He was very active in working for the passage of the Constitution of the United States (1789). Revere was the first president of the Massachusetts Charitable Mechanics Association, an organization founded in 1794 and made up of artisans, laborers, and businessmen. Its aim was to improve working conditions for laborers and aid members who fell on hard times. He was also a member of the Massachusetts Charitable Fire Society and the Boston Library Society.

From 1795 until 1802 Revere served as the coroner of Suffolk County. A coroner is a public official whose chief duty is to determine the causes of any deaths that are not obviously due to natural causes. He also helped to create Boston's first board of health, and he held the position of its president for two years, begining in 1799.

Later years

Paul Revere continued his work in the metal trade until his retirement at the age of seventy-six. In 1804 he formally made his son, Joseph Warren Revere, his business partner. A few years later, he turned over his successful copper business to be run by his sons and grandsons. He was grief-stricken by the deaths of his wife Rachel and his son Paul in 1813. He lived for five more years until his death at the age of eighty-three on May 10, 1818.

After his death, his obituary in the *Boston Intelligence* newspaper stated, "seldom has the tomb closed upon a life so honorable and useful." Paul Revere was buried at Boston's Granary Burying Ground, alongside several other patriots.

For More Information

Boatner, Mark M., III. "Revere, Paul." *Encyclopedia of the American Revolution*. Mechanicsburg, PA: Stackpole Books, 1996, pp. 930-32.

Bourgoin, Suzanne M,. and Paula K. Byers, eds. "Revere, Paul." *Encyclopedia of World Biography*. Detroit: Gale Research, 1998, vol. 13, pp. 110-11.

Forbes, Esther. *America's Paul Revere*. Boston, MA: Houghton Mifflin Co., 1946, renewed 1974.

Rinaldi, Ann. *The Secret of Sarah Revere*. New York: Harcourt Brace, 1995.

Web Sites

"Boston Society of Mechanics History." [Online] Available http://www.mindstorm.com/mechanics/history.html (accessed on 10/15/99).

"Paul Revere: A Brief Biography." Paul Revere Memorial Association, 1997. [Online] Available http://www.paulreverehouse.org/theman/bio.html (accessed on 10/15/99).

Frederika von Riedesel

Born July 11, 1746
Germany
Died March 29, 1808
Berlin, Germany

Baroness, camp follower

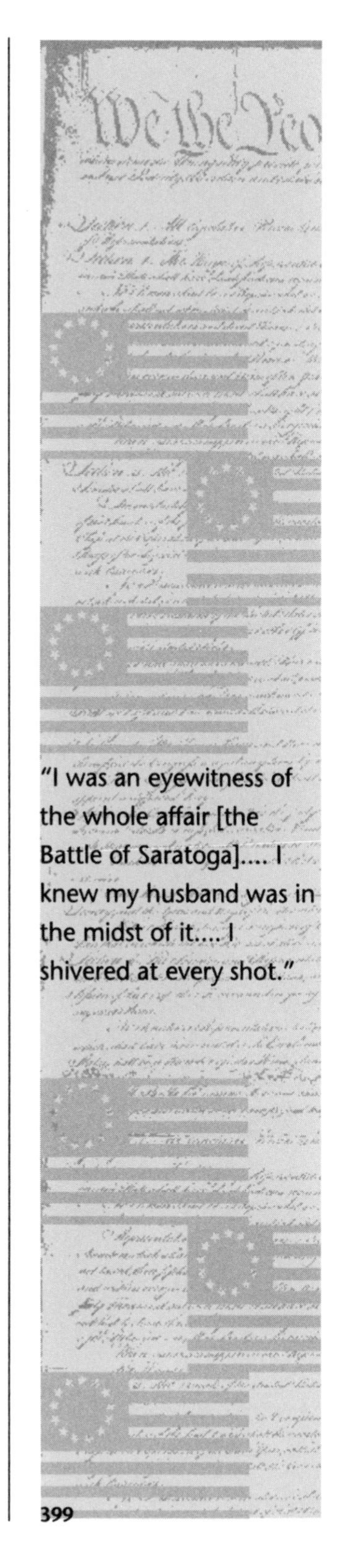

Frederika von Riedesel was a German noblewoman who spent six years living in America during the time of the Revolutionary War (1775–83). She saw battles, was taken prisoner, nursed her children through illnesses, and maintained a brave and optimistic outlook. A book comprising the letters she wrote during that time offers a vivid picture of that eventful period in American history.

Frederika Charlotte Luisa von Massow (later von Riedesel) was born into a wealthy German family in 1746. The baroness, as she was most often referred to in adulthood, was the daughter of Count Massow, head of an army formed by the German King Frederick William II (1744–1797).

Count Massow had his family come and live with him near the various battle sites where he was posted. During times of peace the family lived in their permanent home. As the von Riedesel daughters grew up, they became beauties, and young soldiers were drawn to their home.

In 1762, at age seventeen, "Fritschen," as young Frederika was nicknamed, married twenty-one-year-old Friederich

Adolphus von Riedesel (pronounced REE-day-zel), a young captain in the German cavalry (a unit of soldiers on horseback). Their wedding was a fancy affair attended by many members of the nobility. By the time of the birth of their first child in 1766, the couple owned their own home in Berlin. They experienced great sorrow, though, when both of their first two children died in infancy.

Husband sent to fight American colonists

By the age of thirty-seven, Captain von Riedesel was an army officer in service to the Duke of Brunswick and lived with his growing family in a fine home in Wolfenbüttel, Germany. In the mid-1770s, the duke made an agreement with King **George III** (see entry) of England to send more than 4,000 German soldiers to America to fight against the American colonists who were rebelling against England. Von Riedesel was promoted to general and made commander of the first group of German soldiers to go. In 1776 he and his troops traveled across the Atlantic Ocean and reached Quebec, Canada.

A year earlier, in 1775, America had failed in its attempt to invade Canada (a British possession) and make it a fourteenth American colony, and Canada had remained under British control. Von Riedesel and his men served in Canada alongside British army troops under the command of British Major-General **John Burgoyne** (see entry).

Baroness journeys to America

The military sometimes allowed a small number of women to accompany their husbands who were in active military service so they could nurse the wounded, wash the soldiers' clothes, and help boost the men's morale. The baroness did not accompany her husband when he left for Canada, however, because she was about to give birth. She stayed in Germany for a year taking care of her children before setting off with them to join General von Riedesel in Canada.

Baroness von Riedesel had a special carriage built in Germany to carry her family and their supplies on their seventy-five-day journey through Belgium and to the coast of France. The overland part of their trip through those countries was marked with difficulties. On one gruesome occasion, the baroness was looking out of the carriage when she was struck through the open window by an object hanging from a tree—the object turned out to be the body of a hanged man. She was relieved to arrive at the French coast, where they left the coach behind, crossed the English Channel by boat, and took a stagecoach the rest of the way to London, where they then boarded a ship and proceeded to Quebec, Canada.

Baroness von Riedesel was thirty-one years old in 1777 when she and her three young daughters joined her husband in Quebec. An attractive and cheerful woman, she had dark hair and bright blue eyes. In her diary the baroness mentioned that many friends warned her against coming to North America, where the people "lived upon horseflesh and cats." Her chief concern was that she was not able to understand English. As the war moved into the colonies the family's comfortable existence in Canada was soon to be replaced by the discomforts of traveling through the wilderness.

Tide turns after early victory

General John Burgoyne wanted to gain control of New York (where most people were still loyal to Great Britain) and use it as a base of operations. If he controlled the Hudson River and Lake Champlain valleys in northern New York, he could prevent the movement of American military supplies and soldiers across the Hudson River. Historians have named this attempt Burgoyne's Offensive; it was carried out from June to October 1777.

On July 5, 1777, Burgoyne's soldiers easily captured New York's Fort Ticonderoga on Lake Champlain. Along with General von Riedesel and his German troops, he then headed south to Fort Edward and Fort George on their way to Albany, New York. Baroness von Riedesel traveled with them on the slow journey through unfamiliar wilderness, during which many of the travelers became sick.

The 185-mile journey from Quebec to Fort Edward on the Hudson River left Burgoyne dangerously short of supplies. He ordered General von Riedesel to lead German troops through the New York countryside to seize cattle, horses, and carriages. Von Riedesel protested that the plan was too dangerous, and he urged his wife to stay at Fort Edward for her

The Baroness's Account of the Retreat from Saratoga

Baroness von Riedesel's account of the retreat from Saratoga is recounted in *America Rebels: Narratives of the Patriots*: "The whole army clamored for a retreat, and my husband promised to make it possible, provided only that no time was lost. But General Burgoyne, to whom an [honorary title] had been promised if he brought about a junction with the army of General Howe, could not determine upon this course, and lost everything by his loitering. About two o'clock in the afternoon, the firing of cannon and small arms was again heard, and all was alarm and confusion. My husband sent me a message telling me to [go] to a house, which was not far from there. I seated myself in the calash [carriage] with my children, and had scarcely driven up to the house when I saw, on the opposite side of the Hudson River, five or six men with guns aimed at us. Almost involuntarily, I threw the children on the bottom of the calash and myself over them. At the same instant the [rude peasants] fired, and shattered the arm of a poor English soldier behind us, who was already wounded, and was also on the point of retreating into the house. Immediately after our arrival a frightful [cannon attack] began, principally directed against the house in which we had sought shelter, probably because the enemy believed, for seeing so many people flocking around it, that all the generals made it their headquarters. Alas! It harbored [only] wounded soldiers or women! We were finally obliged to take refuge in a cellar, in which I laid myself down in a corner not far from the door. My children laid down on the earth with their heads upon my lap, and in this manner we passed the entire night. [The cellar had been used as a lavatory by the people fearful of going outdoors.] A horrible stench, the cries of the children, and yet more than all this, my own anguish, prevented me from closing my eyes."

own safety. But the baroness insisted on accompanying the other wives who were going to follow the army. The expedition met with disastrous defeat at Bennington, Vermont, in August 1777.

A few months later, at Saratoga, New York, the campaign went terribly wrong for the British once again. In October 1777, 6,000 British and German troops were defeated by the forces of the American general Horatio Gates. On October 17, 1777, Generals Burgoyne and von Riedesel, outnumbered and surrounded, went to the camp of General Gates and surrendered their troops. This was the first great victory of the Americans and probably the decisive battle of the Revolution. Later, the baroness wrote that she believed General Burgoyne had acted wisely in surrendering to the Americans. The Americans told her that had the British not surrendered "we all would have been massacred."

After the surrender

History has shown that the failure of the invasion was in no way the fault of General von Riedesel. In fact, the general had trained his troops to fight in the American style, spreading out and keeping their movements flexible so they could react at once to changes in the battle. On two occasions his troops actually were responsible for British victories in battle.

After the British surrendered to Gates, von Riedesel, his wife, and his troops became prisoners of war. The baroness was very concerned about how the American soldiers would treat her and her children. She wrote in her journal: "While riding through the American camp, I was comforted to notice that nobody glanced at us insultingly, that they all bowed to me, and some of them even looked with pity to see a woman with small children there. I confess that I was afraid to go to the enemy as [becoming a war prisoner] was an entirely new experience for me."

The baroness recorded interesting accounts of meeting many influential people, including Lord Germain, the British secretary of state for the colonies; General **William Howe**, the commander-in-chief of the British in Boston; John Burgoyne, the British general who was her husband's boss; and **George Washington** (see entries), who would later become the first U.S. president.

Life in Cambridge and on the journey south

After the British surrender at Saratoga, the baroness and her children were invited to Albany, New York, as guests of General Philip Schuyler of the Continental army. Following a short stay there, the family traveled on to Cambridge, Massachusetts. They were to remain prisoners of war for two years. But because General von Riedesel held an important position in the British

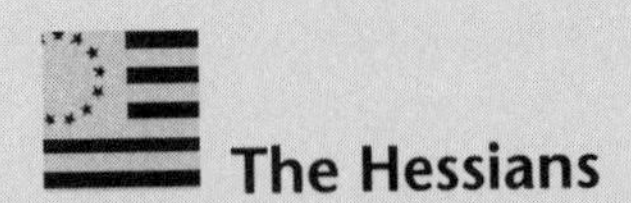

The Hessians

At the time of the American Revolution (1775–83), Germany was made up of more than three hundred tiny areas called principalities. Many of them supplied soldiers to the British army in its battle against the American colonists. The largest group came from Hesse-Cassel. As a result, all of the Germans fighting with the British were inaccurately referred to as "Hessians" (pronounced HESS-shuns).

King George III of England did not have enough soldiers in his own army to supply the needs of his commanders in America. The war was not popular in England, and not enough Englishmen volunteered. He was forced to give money for the services of German mercenaries (paid soldiers), who had served in this way for many years. But though they were called mercenaries, most of the German soldiers were not paid. They simply received their daily food rations. It was Frederick II, the Prince of Hesse-Cassel, who greatly profited when he sold the services of 12,000 mercenaries to the English king for a large amount of money.

A total of 30,000 German soldiers fought in North America for the British. Many of the German soldiers deserted the British army to stay in a new country full of possibilities. Americans actually offered free land to the mercenaries if they would switch sides against the British and support the cause of American independence. As many as 5,000 German soldiers may have stayed in America when their fellow countrymen returned home after the fighting. More than 7,700 German soldiers died in America from diseases and battle wounds.

military, he and his family were treated well by the patriots. The von Riedesels were given quarters by the Loyalists (colonists loyal to England) and spent their time in the Boston area pleasantly, sometimes attending dinner parties and balls.

Life in Virginia

In November 1778 the von Riedesels were given a carriage and an escort and, as prisoners of war, were told by the Americans to set off for Virginia The Americans in Boston were running into food shortages and did not have enough for the captured British officers and their troops. In addition, George Washington feared that they might rise up and try to rescue their comrades in Newport, Rhode Island.

During their trip southward, food was in short supply, and the von Riedesel family was constantly hungry. They also had to deal with the perils of traveling in heavy snow, ice, and mud. Often the Americans who were obliged to take them in treated them with rudeness and suspicion. The baroness gracefully handled these hardships, remaining optimistic. This was in contrast to her husband, who often became quite depressed during his years in America.

The von Riedesels arrived in Virginia in January 1779 and stayed for nearly a year on an estate near Charlottesville. The general enjoyed gardening there, and the Baroness sang and played a piano bought for her by her husband. Their children were also happy living on the plantation. The general and the baroness were dinner guests of **Thomas Jefferson** (see entry), the newly elected governor of Virginia, who appreciated their company despite the fact that they fought on opposite sides in the war.

Family spends time in New York and Quebec

From Virginia, the von Riedesels, still prisoners of war, obeyed the command of the Americans to travel to New York City, where the General was to be exchanged for an American prisoner. Events unfolded slowly and the general and his family were detained for a year. During their stay, the baroness and the children were vaccinated against the outbreak of smallpox, a highly infectious disease that was rapidly spreading at the time.

In New York the von Riedesels lived in an elegant house with carpeting and mahogany furniture. The wealthy English families in the area competed with one another in making them as comfortable as possible during their confinement. Finally, in 1779, the American officials exchanged two of their prisoners, General von Riedesel and another officer, for American general Benjamin Lincoln.

During the winter of 1780–81 the British placed the newly freed General von Riedesel in charge of troops on Long Island, New York. While there, the baroness gave birth to a daughter, whom she named Amerika. Then, in the summer of 1781, the general was ordered back to Quebec, Canada, and he and his family made the journey northward. They stayed in

Canada until the signing of the 1783 treaty that ended the Revolutionary War.

Returning home

When General von Riedesel was released from service to the British army, he and his family began to make their way back to Germany. While in England they had tea with the British royal family. The baroness was happy to entertain Queen Charlotte Sophia and her daughters, the royal princesses, with her interesting tales of America.

The von Riedesels then returned to Brunswick. Of the 4,000 German troops that had gone to Canada with the general, only 2,800 returned. For six years von Riedesel served as commander of the Brunswick troops in the southern provinces of the country of Holland. He then retired to his castle at Lauterbach, later becoming an official of the city of Brunswick.

The couple tell their story

The baroness had written many details about her stay in America in letters to her mother. After the family returned to Germany, her letters were edited and made into a book that remains one of the best eyewitness accounts of the Revolutionary War.

The general also prepared a book, arranging his notes and papers and working with a young writer, Max von Eelking, to put his autobiography into print. Unfortunately, by the time the book was published, the general had passed away.

General von Riedesel died in his sleep on January 7, 1800. Through careful management of his fortune, von Riedesel was able to leave his wife and each of his five daughters a substantial income after his death.

Baroness's book makes its mark; her final years

Baroness von Riedesel survived her husband by eight years. She was happy to visit with her daughters and grandchildren but remained lonely without her mate of thirty-seven years. Having sold some of her property and possessions, she went to live at her castle at Lauterbach. In Germany, the book that was produced from her letters was called *Extracts from Let-*

ters and Papers of General, Baron von Riedesel and His Wife nee [formerly] Massow, Concerning Their Common Voyage to America and Their Sojourn in That Country. A reference was made to the general in the title for fear that the baroness would disgrace her gender and her rank in society by being known as a female author. The title page noted that the book was printed as a manuscript for the family.

The book proved very popular and sold widely. In 1827 it was published in English under the title *Letters and Memoirs Relating to the War of American Independence, and the Capture of the German Troops at Saratoga* and sold well in America. A more complete translation was made in 1867, titled *Letters and Journals Relating to the War of the American Revolution.*

During the early 1800s, the baroness spent much of her time visiting with her family and enjoying parties and court life in Berlin. In the spring of 1808 Baroness von Riedesel, then in Berlin, was planning to make a visit to the family castle at Lauterbach, but she died suddenly on March 29. At her request, her body was laid beside that of her husband in the family vault at Lauterbach.

For More Information

Anticaglia, Elizabeth. *Heroines of '76.* New York: Walker and Company, 1975.

Boatner, Mark M. "Riedesel, Baron Friederich Adolphus." *Encyclopedia of the American Revolution.* New York: David McKay, 1966, pp. 932–34.

Dorson, Richard N., ed. *America Rebels: Narratives of the Patriots.* New York: Pantheon, 1953.

Lunt, James. *John Burgoyne of Saratoga.* New York: Harcourt, Brace, Jovanovich, 1975.

Meyer, Edith Patterson. *Petticoat Patriots of the American Revolution.* New York: The Vanguard Press, 1976.

Riedesel, Baroness von. *Journal and Correspondence of a Tour of Duty 1776–1783.* Translated by Marvin L. Brown Jr. and Marta Huth. Chapel Hill: University of North Carolina Press 1965.

Riedesel, Mrs. General. *Letters and Journals Relating to the War of the American Revolution and the Capture of the German Troops at Saratoga.* Translated by William L. Stone. Albany: Joel Munsell, 1867.

Tharp, Louise Hall. *The Baroness and the General.* Boston: Little, Brown, 1962.

Zeinert, Karen. *Those Remarkable Women of the American Revolution.* Brookfield, CT: Millbrook Press, 1996.

James Rivington

Born 1724
London, England
Died July 4, 1802
New York, New York

Publisher, printer, bookseller, spy

"[I have] always meant honestly and openly to do [my] duty as a servant of the public... [and my press] has always been open and free to all parties."

Portrait: James Rivington. *Reproduced by permission of Archive Photos, Inc.*

James Rivington, born in London to a family of publishers, was named by the king of England as the Royal Printer of New York during the Revolutionary War (1775–83). His *Royal Gazette* became one of the best-selling newspapers in the colonies, and it is considered the first daily newspaper to be published in the United States. He began the war as a Tory or Loyalist—someone who wanted to remain loyal to and keep the American colonies a part of England—but in 1781 he began to work as a spy for General **George Washington** (1732–1799; see entry). Rivington's work for the patriot cause was not known during his lifetime, however, and he died poor and unrecognized.

James Rivington was born in England in 1724, the sixth son of Charles Rivington and Eleanor Pease. His early life was spent in Derbyshire, but in the 1740s, he entered into his family's publishing business in London. In 1752, he married Elizabeth Minshull, but she died young. Their only child died in infancy.

Rivington and his brother John ran the family operation until Rivington left in 1756 to open his own publishing business with James Fletcher, Jr. This partnership proved immensely profitable because of their success in publishing *History of England,* a book by Tobias Smollett (1721–1771), a major British author.

According to people who knew Rivington at this time, he liked to spend money and live well. He was known for his fine clothing and for the vast amounts of money he spent at the race track in Newmarket. However, Rivington soon gambled his earnings away and declared bankruptcy. Bankruptcy is the practice by which a person legally declares himself unable to pay his debts and gives to the people he owes the right to divide his belongings and take them in payment of his debts.

Threatened with debtor's prison, Rivington decided to begin a new life in the American colonies. (At this time in England, many of the people in prison were there because they were unable to pay their bills. Legally, they could be kept in prison until they, or their family, paid off those debts.) Rivington immigrated to the United States and settled in Philadelphia, Pennsylvania, in 1760.

Begins new life in America

In America, Rivington made his living as a bookseller, and he again became successful. Upon his arrival in 1760, he opened a book shop on Market Street in Philadelphia. Then, in September 1760, he opened a second store in Hanover Square in New York City. He advertised himself as the only "London book seller in America" and offered to supply the public libraries with books. He opened a third bookstore on King Street in Boston, Massachusetts, in 1762. The stores also sold other merchandise, such as paintings.

Thus Rivington had created a chain of bookstores that captured a large part of the book trade in three of the colonies' largest cities: Boston in New England, and New York and Philadelphia in what were known as the "Middle Colonies." In 1765, Rivington concentrated his business at the New York City location, possibly in part because he had his eye on another money-making venture. In 1766, while living in Annapolis, Maryland, he offered people shares in his "Maryland Lottery." This was a scheme to sell people land at a profit. However, the scheme failed and Rivington again declared bankruptcy.

Once again, Rivington overcame adversity. In November 1768, he opened a book-selling business as J. Rivington &

Co. in the Wall Street business district of New York City. He again reaped success through a wise choice of authors to publish. In 1768, he published the poems of Charles Churchill, an English writer known for his satirical works poking fun at people or ideas. By 1769, Rivington was well enough established in New York City society that he was able to win the hand of Elizabeth Van Horne, who belonged to a prominent family. The couple had two sons and a daughter.

Rivington's second marriage seems to have steadied him. His book-selling business continued to prosper, and in 1773, he expanded to include a print shop that did pamphlets and handbills (printed advertisements) as well as books. Accounts from the time describe Rivington as an elegant dresser, well mannered, interested in theater, and fond of high living (good food and parties).

Begins publishing *New-York Gazetteer*

In the spring of 1773, Rivington began a new venture. He issued free copies of a new newspaper that was eventually to be called *Rivington's New-York Gazetteer; or the Connecticut, New Jersey, Hudson's River, and Quebec Weekly Advertiser*. Most readers soon shortened the name to the *New-York Gazetteer*. Deciding to publish a newspaper was a costly business in colonial America. First, a printing press, an expensive investment, had to be shipped from England. Rivington also had to purchase printing plates and other supplies. He even had to arrange for the purchase of paper from England, since few paper mills existed in the colonies. At this time, paper was made from cotton rags, and it was expensive.

Colonial papers were unlike modern newspapers, which are typeset with computers and printed on computerized presses. Rivington's paper had to be typeset by hand, by a typesetter who selected each letter and placed it in a large wooden tray. Then the letters were inked, loaded onto the printed press, and pressed over sheets of paper, one page at a time, by a pressman. When enough of a particular page had been printed, the letters were unloaded from the printed plate, cleaned, stored, and then reused to typeset the next page. It was a time-consuming, dirty task but one that demanded great attention and some artistry.

Rivington had different goals in mind when he began publishing the paper. Most newspapers of the time were openly biased, in favor of one point of view. No one used on-site correspondents to report local news, so the typical colonial paper was full of sensational stories and rumors. These papers were also very repetitive, because they reprinted stories from each other.

Rivington wanted to use his *New-York Gazetteer* to publish both sides of the argument as to whether the American colonies should rebel against England. He also proposed to include more international news than other American papers. The happenings in other parts of the world were important to Americans because if they declared war against England, the colonists wanted to know whether they could expect support from England's enemies in Europe (namely, France and Spain).

His background in book publishing helped Rivington make the *New-York Gazetteer* a quality publication. It appealed to readers because of its attractive layout, good quality paper, and easy-to-read typefaces. By 1774, the *New-York Gazetteer* claimed a readership of more than 3,600 people. This was a huge audience for a colonial newspaper, and it made Rivington's one of the largest and best-read papers in America. Rivington himself claimed that his paper was sold throughout the colonies, in the West Indies, England, France, Ireland, and the Mediterranean countries in Europe.

The Sons of Liberty have a political agenda

While modern readers can appreciate Rivington's attempt to report the news in an unbiased way, those who lived during his time did not. The patriots relied on the newspapers to print stories that would make their readers angry with the British and eager to break away from England. As the patriots stirred up rebellion against England, Rivington responded by printing more stories that gave reasons why the American colonies should remain tied to England.

The Sons of Liberty openly challenged Rivington as a traitor to the cause of freedom. The Sons of Liberty was the name given to groups of patriots who formed to protest the passage of the Stamp Act in 1765. The Stamp Act imposed a fee on all printed material. The Sons of Liberty knew that putting a fee on newspapers and pamphlets would interfere with their ability to get their message of rebellion to the colonists. Later the Sons openly promoted armed rebellion against England, and used violence to persuade others to this viewpoint. Rivington, a good businessman, knew when to back down. He signed a form supporting the group and promised to print stories and editorials that fit the patriot agenda.

Printshop destroyed by patriot mob

The Sons of Liberty, however, were not convinced of Rivington's change of heart. In 1774, Isaac Sears (1730–1786), one of the patriots openly criticized in the *New-York Gazetteer,* decided that Rivington needed a lesson. Sears led a mob of supporters who ransacked Rivington's print shop and damaged his printing plates. Rivington himself was arrested and brought before the Continental Congress (the local patriot government), questioned, and then released. His newspaper continued to be closely watched by the Sons of Liberty.

In November 1775, the Sons of Liberty were fed up. Rivington had continued to print Loyalist stories and editorials, so this time the patriot mob that attacked Rivington's shop burned it to the ground. They destroyed the printing press and, according to legend, took away the printing plates to melt down into bullets for the patriot cause.

Named Royal Printer of New York

The incident not only ruined Rivington's livelihood, it probably frightened him. He left for England in January 1776. During his year in England, he was appointed the Royal Printer of New York by King **George III** (see entry). This honor meant that Rivington could print the King's royal coat of arms symbol on his newspapers. Thus readers would know that Rivington had the king's favor.

Meanwhile, back in America, the Revolutionary War had heated up. It looked like the British were going to win the war because they had more and better trained soldiers and a navy to ship troops and supplies. By January 1777, British general William Howe's army occupied New York City. Rivington's fears of the patriots' vengeance lessened, and he returned to New York later in 1777 with a new printing press and type. He reopened his print shop in October and resumed publication of his newspaper, now calling it *Rivington's New York Loyal Gazetteer*. In December, he renamed the newspaper *The Royal Gazette.*

Patriots denounce *The Royal Gazette*

Whether Rivington was responding to his role as the King's voice in New York, or whether Rivington was angry about his treatment at the hands of the Sons of Liberty, his commitment to reporting both sides of the news changed. *The Royal Gazette* now printed stories that clearly favored the British. He printed poems, letters, and essays that made fun of patriot leaders, including General Washington. He poked fun at the continuing American losses in the battlefield, and tried to weaken the public's enthusiasm for the war.

The American Loyalists and the British troops stationed in New York eagerly supported *The Royal Gazette,* but his British bias earned Rivington ongoing criticism and threats from the patriot leaders and the general public. However, while the British army was in New York City, the patriots could not move against Rivington or his printing operation. Among themselves, the patriots called Rivington's paper "The Lying Gazette."

Nevertheless, Rivington's newspaper was the most important Tory newspaper in the colonies during the Revolutionary War. When wartime shortages of paper and ink threatened to stop publication, other Tory publishers were willing to help Rivington keep *The Royal Gazette* going. With their help, *The Royal Gazette* continuously published, at least five days each week, from the summer of 1778 until the summer of 1783, when the war ended. For this reason, many historians consider *The Royal Gazette* the first daily newspaper in the United States.

Changes allegiance to work for rebel cause

About 1781, Rivington had a change of heart and began passing information about British plans to General Washington. The reason for this change is unknown. However, Rivington may have sensed that victory now lay within America's grasp and decided to side with the expected victors. The

The Role of the Press in Colonial America

The earliest American newspaper on record was published in the South in 1638. By the time of the American Revolutionary War (1775–83), there were forty-two newspapers being printed in the colonies, with the New England, Middle, and Southern colonies evenly represented. About a third of the newspapers were Tory or Loyalist in tone (they favored remaining part of Britain). The majority of the colonial newspapers were issued weekly, and were purchased by subscription by several hundred people. Many more, however, actually heard the news, which was read aloud in coffeehouses and taverns.

Sharing the news by reading it aloud in public places served two purposes. It made the news available to those unable to pay for a paper. And it informed those unable to read (at the time of the Revolution, almost half the male population was illiterate).

Colonial newspapers carried different information from modern papers. A typical colonial paper was four pages (a large sheet folded in half and printed as four pages). The front page was filled with advertisements. The other pages carried reprints of news stories from other papers and the text of speeches and sermons. The papers also offered poetry, letters, essays, and editorials. Many editorials were unsigned, so that the authorities could not find and punish the colonial authors who urged the colonists to rebel against English rule.

In Colonial America there weren't any telephones, computers, faxes, e-mails, cars, or trains. Information was shared by people traveling by horseback, on foot, or by ship. News arrived slowly and was eagerly awaited. The newspapers were one way for patriots to share their messages of the benefits of declaring the American colonies' independence from England. At this time, each colony considered itself a separate entity. By showing the colonists that they had something in common (their grievances against England), the newspapers helped forge a sense of community among the colonies. This sense of being one nation was vital to the colonies' success in gaining their freedom from England.

Americans had won battles at Saratoga, New York, and Trenton, New Jersey, and the British suffered from lack of supplies and soldiers to replace those killed in battle.

Whatever the reason, Rivington was admirably placed to collect and deliver military information to Washington.

Like many newspaper publishers, Rivington's shop also functioned as a gathering place. It was here that subscribers picked up their latest edition of the newspaper, and some lingered to read it aloud for the benefit of the illiterate in the audience (those who could not read or write). Rivington had only to be in his shop to hear British officers and Loyalist supporters discussing the news.

Rivington's work as a patriot spy was rumored for many years among historians. It was finally considered proved with the printing of "The Tory and the Spy: The Double Life of James Rivington," written by Catherine Snell Crary, and published in a historical magazine in 1959. Among other evidence offered by Crary was the fact that in 1781, Rivington passed along a set of British naval signals to the French admiral patrolling the American coast (France had agreed to support the American cause). The signals helped this French ally intercept messages between British ships, so the French admiral could then plan counter moves against the British.

Rivington's readers and the general public, however, did not know of his new patriot sympathies. They saw only his newspaper stories, which continued to support the British. This Loyalist cover helped Rivington in his role as double agent, spying for both sides.

When the British left New York City in 1783 at the end of the war, General Washington sent American officers and troops to Rivington's home to protect him from the wrath of the jubilant Americans. Washington himself is said to have visited the Rivington house. This protection seems to have puzzled Rivington's neighbors. Why would the patriot general protect the Tory whose newspaper worked to damage Washington's cause? Only the passage of time would reveal Rivington's part in the British withdrawal from New York City.

Again faces bankruptcy

With the American army occupying New York City, Rivington tried to keep his newspaper going. He renamed it *Rivington's New York Gazette and Universal Advertiser* and removed the royal arms. However, Isaac Sears and some of his friends visited Rivington and shut down the paper, ending Rivington's career as a newspaper editor-publisher. After the war ended in 1783, Rivington tried to mend his fortunes by setting up as a bookseller and stationer (supplier of writing supplies). His business did not flourish, perhaps because many Americans did not patronize his shop because they were still bitter about his Loyalist leanings during the war. Rivington died in poverty in New York City in 1802.

Today, Rivington's dual role in the war is known, and a street in New York City is named for him.

For More Information

Blanco, Richard L., ed. *The American Revolution, 1775-1783*. Vol. 1. New York: Garland Publishing, 1993, pp. 843-49.

Crary, Catherine Snell. "The Tory and the Spy: The Double Life of James Rivington." *William and Mary Quarterly,* 16 (1959): 61-72.

Duyckinck, Evert A., and George L. Duyckinck. *Cyclopaedia of American Literature: Embracing Personal and Critical Notices of Authors, and Selections from Their Writings, From the Earliest Period to the Present Day; With Portraits, Autographs, and Other Illustrations*. Vol. 1. Philadelphia: Wm. Rutter Co., 1875, reprinted, 1965, pp. 217, 290-95, 456, 472-74, 478.

Purcell, L. Edward. "James Rivington." *Who Was Who in the American Revolution*. New York: Facts on File, 1993, p. 408.

Web Sites

Pennsylvania Historical Society, 1300 Locust St., Philadelphia, PA 19107. Tel: (215) 732-6200. Fax: (215) 732-2680. [Online] Available http://www.libertynet.org/~pahist (accessed on 7/19/99).

Betsy Ross

Born January 1, 1752
Philadelphia, Pennsylvania
Died January 30, 1836
Philadelphia, Pennsylvania

Shop manager, upholsterer, seamstress

"I remember having heard my mother ... say frequently that she, with her own hands ... made the first Star Spangled Banner that ever was made."

Rachel Fletcher, daughter of Betsy Ross

Betsy Ross is widely believed to have made the first American flag. Widowed three times, she had seven daughters, lived through the American Revolution, and for sixty-two years ran her own small business. This spirited, independent woman lived a remarkable life that was very much tied up with the events of the Revolution.

Elizabeth "Betsy" Griscom Ross Ashburn Claypoole, who will be called here by her more popular name, Betsy Ross, was born on January 1, 1752, in Philadelphia, Pennsylvania. Ross was the eighth of seventeen children born to Rebecca and Samuel Griscom, who ran a construction business. Young Ross was an attractive girl with thick brown hair and blue eyes who showed strong skills with a needle and thread. Until age twelve she attended a school run by the Religious Society of Friends, whose members were called Quakers.

Learns upholstery trade, marries, is widowed

In 1764 Ross began working for John Webster to learn the trade of upholstering, which in colonial times involved

Portrait: Betsy Ross. *Reproduced by permission of AP/Wide World Photos.*

more than covering furniture: Upholsterers also hung wallpaper and made carpets, umbrellas, mattresses, draperies, tablecloths, blankets, flags, tents, furniture for ships, and other items.

While working at Webster's shop, the young girl met and fell in love with her fellow shop worker, John Ross, the son of an Episcopal minister. Ross's Quaker parents were upset by the relationship and insisted that she end it. They feared that the Quaker community might reject the entire family if Ross married outside her religion. But the strong-willed young woman would not be swayed from her decision. In 1773 John and Betsy ran away and were married. Just as her parents had feared, the Quakers disowned Ross, but her parents were permitted to remain members of the church. Back in Philadelphia, the couple rented a small house, using part of it for a new upholstery business and living in the other rooms.

In 1775 relations between the American colonies and Great Britain, the mother country, were tense. John Ross was a member of a volunteer force of American patriots who had promised to defend the citizens of Philadelphia if British soldiers attacked the city. In December 1775 he was guarding a store of gunpowder when it exploded. Friends brought him home to his wife, who nursed him until he died on January 21, 1776.

Sews the Stars and Stripes

On June 14, 1777, America's Second Continental Congress passed a resolution approving the design of a flag to represent the newly formed United States of America. The short document said: "Resolved that the Flag of the United States be made of thirteen stripes, alternate red and white; that the Union be thirteen stars white in a blue field, representing a new constellation."

According to Betsy Ross's grandson, William Canby, who sent a paper to the Pennsylvania Historical Society in March 1870, in late 1776 Betsy Ross was visited at her shop by **George Washington** (see entry), head of the Continental army; George Ross, her late husband's uncle; and Robert Morris, a wealthy landowner. They had brought her a sketch of a new American flag and asked her to make one. She suggested using the more easily made five-pointed stars instead of the six-pointed stars on the sketch. The men liked and approved

Did Betsy Ross Sew the First Stars and Stripes?

Historical proof exists that Betsy Ross made a flag called the Cambridge flag, or Continental colors, the flag of America's Continental army. But there is no real proof that Ross sewed the first Stars and Stripes flag. Her daughter Clarissa, her niece Margaret, and other relatives did sign statements swearing to the fact that she told them she had made the flag. In addition, George Washington was in Philadelphia in late May and early June of 1776, and it is known that he had shown concern about the design of a new national flag.

Still, some historians doubt that Betsy Ross made the first American flag. They cite the fact that there are no written documents to support the claim and point out that no eyewitnesses came forward to verify it. But the public loved and accepted the flag story. In 1887 Ross's rented home, where she was said to have sewn the first flag, became a national historic site run by the Betsy Ross Memorial Association.

In 1925 Samuel Wetherill, a Quaker minister and descendant of Ross, found a paper pattern for a five-pointed star in a long-sealed safe. It had been signed by Ross's daughter Clarissa. There is a possibility it was Ross's original star pattern and had been put there for safekeeping.

her design, and she sewed the flag in her back parlor. Canby's story was repeated in *Harper's Monthly* magazine and other publications, including history books.

Takes over business, remarries

The young widow continued to run the upholstery business on her own. In 1776 Ross was reintroduced to Joseph Ashburn, who had once been her schoolmate. Ashburn commanded a ship called the *Swallow,* which he sailed to the West Indies. While there, he loaded his ship with items such as sugar, molasses, and tobacco to sell back home. When war started between America and Great Britain in 1775, the *Swallow* became a privateer, a privately owned ship that had permission from the American government to attack and capture British ships, especially those carrying trade items.

Privateering was very dangerous, because British patrols were on the lookout for American ships. By 1777 the

According to Betsy Ross's grandson, the seamstress (far right) was visited at her shop by George Washington, George Ross, and Robert Morris in late 1776. The three men brought with them a sketch proposal for the new American flag. *Reproduced by permission of the National Archives and Records Administration.*

British had made it almost impossible for the *Swallow* and ships like it to leave Philadelphia. Captain Ashburn laid low for a while, using his free time to court Betsy Ross, who finally agreed to marry him. On June 15, 1777, family and friends witnessed their wedding at a Lutheran Church near Philadelphia. After the wedding, Ross continued to work in the shop, and Ashburn resumed his trips to the West Indies. In August 1777 he returned from there with supplies for the two American forts that guarded Philadelphia.

Life in war-torn Philadelphia

In mid-1777 it appeared that a British attack on Philadelphia would soon occur. Joseph Ashburn, fearing he would be taken prisoner, left the city. The British attempt to seize Philadelphia began in September. Some Americans responded by fighting in the streets, but most citizens, including Betsy Ross, stayed inside their homes. Warfare in and around Philadelphia resulted in many injuries and deaths. Ross helped nurse both British and American soldiers and waited to hear word about her missing husband.

Life in Philadelphia grew difficult. Food and supplies were scarce for both the Americans and the British. The British decided to destroy Philadelphia's forts, where American soldiers were preventing them from bringing their supplies down the Delaware River into Philadelphia. Their efforts succeeded, and in October 1777 both forts fell to the British. A worried Ross finally learned that her husband was safe and had been hiding the *Swallow* in nearby New Jersey to prevent its capture by the British.

Hard times reverse when British leave city

In the winter of 1777–78 the Delaware River was once again open to the British, who brought supplies into Philadelphia, including cloth. An unhappy but uncomplaining Ross made dresses for Loyalist women (those who had remained loyal to England) and repaired the uniforms of British soldiers. But along with other Philadelphians she secretly sent badly needed food, medicine, and clothing to American soldiers at nearby Valley Forge.

In early 1778 the colonists of Philadelphia had a hard time finding food and firewood, while British officers occupying the city were enjoying fine meals and blazing fireplaces. The situation changed on June 18, 1778, when the British and the Loyalists suddenly abandoned Philadelphia. The British authorities had ordered them to New York after Congress had rejected new British terms for peace. Ross and other Americans celebrated in the streets as once again American flags flew over the city.

In the summer of 1778 Ashburn returned to Philadelphia, a city in turmoil. A British blockade of the port had shut off water routes, so American ships could not dock there. What supplies citizens could get were expensive.

Gives birth to two daughters; war ends

At summer's end Ashburn braved the British blockade and set off for the West Indies to obtain trade goods. He repeated the trip a number of times over the next year. During that time Ross continued sewing and helped the war effort by loading ammunition into containers for the Continental army.

With the profit from Ashburn's blockade runs, and the improvement of Ross's business, she was able to take some time off from work to care for the couple's first child, Lucilla, born on September 15, 1779. Assistants were able to take over some of Ross's work duties.

In October 1780 Ashburn set sail for the West Indies for the last time. In late November Ross learned from other sailors that the British had tightened their blockade and were taking over many American ships. With prices sky high and food in shorter supply than ever, times were very tough. Ross gave birth to her second child, Eliza, on February 25, 1781; she remained worried when no word came from her husband. In October 1781 Ross rejoiced when word reached Philadelphia that the Revolutionary War was at an end with the surrender of the British at Yorktown, Pennsylvania. Ross could resume her regular work in peace.

On August 15, 1782, John Claypoole, an old friend, came to visit Ross and carried with him sad news. Claypoole told her that he and Joseph Ashburn had been captured at sea by the British navy and sent to a prison in England. In March Joseph had become ill and died at the prison. Ross, now widowed for the second time, was heartbroken.

Claypoole, who had known Ross since childhood, made frequent visits to her home. Over time their affection for one another grew. He told Ross that he had decided to resume sailing a privateer and asked her to marry him. Ross made it clear that she would never again marry a sailor. Claypoole decided to give up life on the sea and find work in Philadelphia.

The couple wed on May 8, 1783, at Philadelphia's Christ Church, and began working together at the upholstery shop. John used his experience as a soldier and sailor to produce and repair tents, cots, knapsacks, and other items for the army and to make and repair ship furniture and mattresses.

Joys and sorrows

In 1782 the Claypooles and their daughters joined the Society of Free Quakers, a new group for Quakers who had been disowned during the Revolution for breaking church rules. In the new church women were considered equal partners to men, an unusual arrangement for the time.

After the United States signed a peace treaty with Britain in 1783, goods and fabrics were imported into America in large quantities. With more work than ever before, the Claypoole family prospered. In April 1785 Ross gave birth to a third daughter, Clarissa Sidney; a fourth daughter, Susan, was born in November 1786. The Claypooles decided to move their family to a larger house while keeping their business going at their old address. In 1786 the family suffered the loss of their oldest daughter, Lucilla, and Sarah Donaldson, Ross's sister, to illness.

The Claypoole family grew to eight with the births of Rachel in 1789 and Jane in 1792. The next year Philadelphia was struck with an outbreak of the deadly, infectious disease called yellow fever. Ross's immediate family was spared, but she lost her mother, father, and oldest sister, Deborah. With the coming of the winter frost, the outbreak finally ended. Deborah's daughter came to live with the family, and they decided to move to an even larger house, where they lived happily for several years.

Business prospers, family grows

The flag-making part of the Claypooles' business picked up in 1795 when the design of the American flag underwent its first change. The addition of two new states, Vermont and Kentucky, meant that two more stars had to be added, and many new flags were ordered.

That same year, Ross gave birth to her seventh daughter, Harriet, who died at the age of ten months. Soon the household grew by one more when Ross's niece Margaret came to live with them after the deaths of her parents, husband, and son.

Later years

In the late 1700s John Claypoole took a job with the U.S. government while his wife continued to run the upholstery business. Then in 1800 Claypoole's failing health forced him to give up his job. Ross turned over many of her work duties to assistants and spent most of her time caring for her husband. The marriages of their daughters and the birth of several grandchildren brightened these difficult times.

The outbreak of the War of 1812 (1812–15) between the United States and Great Britain caused the upholstery business to greatly increase as merchants, shipping companies, and military groups ordered flags. The conflict ended in an American victory.

Ross was stunned by the loss of her third husband, John, who died on August 3, 1817, but continued to manage her business for ten more years, before finally retiring in 1827. She spent her final years living at the homes of her daughters in different Pennsylvania towns. She loved to have her family gather around and listen as she told stories. The children's favorite was her tale of how George Washington came to her shop and together they drew up plans for the Stars and Stripes.

Near the end of her life Ross became blind and was unable to leave her home. But relatives made frequent visits, and she was kept as comfortable as possible until she died peacefully on January 30, 1836. Ross was buried next to John Claypoole at Mount Mariah, Philadelphia's Quaker cemetery.

Flag story is popularized

More than forty years after her death, Betsy Ross was publicly credited with sewing the first American Stars and Stripes flag, though even today there are questions about whether or not she actually did. The story of her making the flag gained wide acceptance over the years, and in 1952 the U.S. government issued a postage stamp in her honor on the two-hundredth anniversary of her birth. The stamp bears a reproduction of a famous painting by C. H. Weisgerber that depicts Betsy Ross in her living room with George Washington and other patriots, discussing the design of the first American flag.

For More Information

Bourgoin, Suzanne M., and Paula Byers, eds. "Betsy Ross" in *Encyclopedia of World Biography,* 2nd ed. Detroit: Gale, 1998, pp. 297–98.

Boatner, Mark M., III. "Flag, American." *Encyclopedia of the American Revolution.* New York David McKay, 1966, pp. 369–70.

DeBarr, Candice M., and Jack A. Bonkowske. *Saga of the American Flag: An Illustrated History.* Tucson: Harbinger House, 1990, p. 23.

St. George, Judith. *Betsy Ross: Patriot of Philadelphia.* New York: Henry Holt, 1997.

Thompson, Ray. *Betsy Ross: Last of Philadelphia's Free Quakers.* Fort Washington, PA: The Bicentennial Press, 1972.

Wallner, Alexandra. *Betsy Ross.* New York: Holiday House, 1994.

Zeinert, Karen. *Those Remarkable Women of the Revolution.* Brookfield, CT: Millbrook Press, 1996, pp. 62–63.

Web Sites

"Point–Counterpoint: Betsy Ross and the Flag." [Online] Available http://www.libertynet.org/ iha/betsy/flagpcp.html (accessed on 3/23/99).

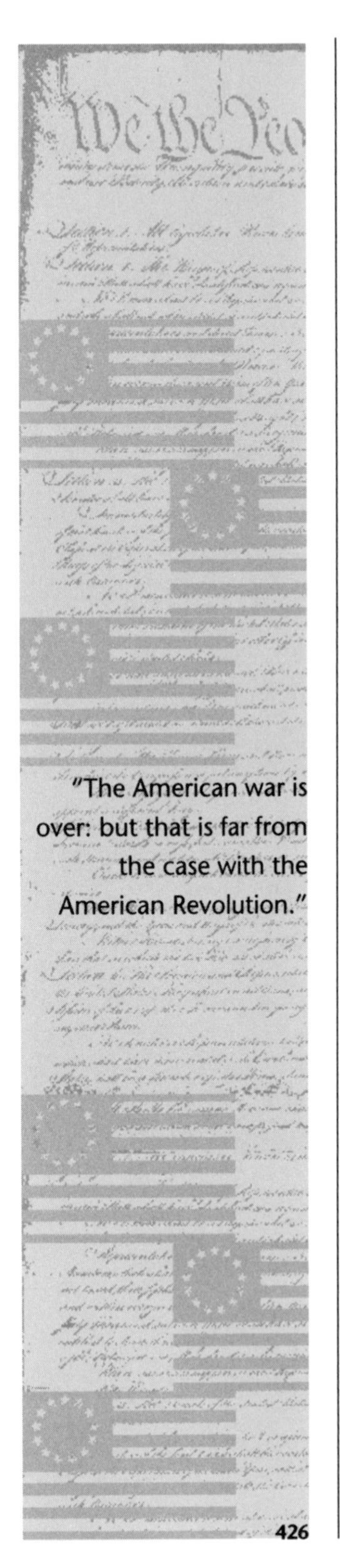

Benjamin Rush

Born December 24, 1745
Byberry, Pennsylvania
Died April 19, 1813
Philadelphia, Pennsylvania

Physician, educator, writer, reformer, political leader

A signer of the Declaration of Independence, Benjamin Rush was the best known medical man of his day and the first to also gain a reputation as a writer. A driving force in the fields of American politics and education, he was a vigorous enemy of slavery and capital punishment and was also noted for his enlightened treatment of the mentally ill.

Born in Pennsylvania in late 1745, Benjamin Rush was only six years old when his father died. His mother then opened a grocery store to support her seven children. At age eight, Rush studied at a school in Maryland run by his uncle, Samuel Finley. The boy made such rapid progress that he entered college only five years later.

In 1760, at age fifteen, Rush graduated from the College of New Jersey (now Princeton University). Samuel Finley urged his nephew to become a medical doctor. In 1761, Rush went to Philadelphia, Pennsylvania, and for six years studied medicine with Dr. John Redmond. Next he traveled to Edinburgh, Scotland, then the world's leading center of medical knowledge, where he earned a medical degree from the University of Edinburgh in 1768.

Rush then worked in hospitals in London, England, and Paris, France. He was a well-dressed young man of medium height and build, with piercing blue eyes, a hooked nose, and a broad forehead. An energetic, confident person, he attracted people to him. In Europe, he met and became friends with the American statesman **Benjamin Franklin** (see entry) and many well-known British writers and thinkers of the time. Rush became known for his interest in what is today called social science, the study of society and how people relate to it.

In his book *Revolutionary Doctor,* Carl Binger, M.D., pointed out that early in Rush's life he determined to devote himself to the good of mankind. Binger described the physician as "an unusually [handsome] man with energy and charm, a little deficient in humor and a little vain, but with warmth and affection and a capacity for sincere relationships."

Early in his life Benjamin Rush determined to devote himself to the good of mankind. *Reproduced courtesy of the Library of Congress.*

Writes textbook, marries, attends Continental Congress

In 1769, at age twenty-three, Rush returned to America and accepted an appointment at what is now the University of Pennsylvania as the first chemistry professor in the United States. In 1770, he published the first American chemistry textbook.

In 1775, while visiting in Princeton, New Jersey, Rush met sixteen-year-old Julia Stockton. A year later, the two began their thirty-seven-year marriage that produced thirteen children, though only nine survived to adulthood. The couple was devoted to one another, and Rush frequently shared his personal and professional problems with his calm and loyal wife. Their son, Richard Rush, was later to serve as an advisor and ambassador for four U.S. presidents.

Within several months of his 1776 marriage, the thirty-year-old physician was appointed a representative from Pennsylvania to the Continental Congress in Philadelphia. There, men from the American colonies met to decide their country's future after years of objecting to British taxation policies. Benjamin Rush had become well known for his 1775 essay, *On Patriotism,* in which he protested the Tea Act. This act was passed by England to provide cheap tea for the colonists in exchange for America's acceptance of England's right to place new taxes on the colonies.

About this situation, Rush had written that if the English were permitted to sell the cheap tea in the colonies, "Then farewell American liberty!" He warned that the chests of tea to be sold "contain something worse than death—the seed of SLAVERY. Remember, my countrymen, the present era ... will fix the constitution of America forever. Think of your ancestors."

While serving in the Congress, Rush became friends with patriots **John Adams, Thomas Jefferson,** and **Thomas Paine** (see entries). At Rush's urging, Paine wrote the famous pamphlet *Common Sense* to encourage Americans to declare their independence from England. Rush signed the Declaration of Independence, which was adopted by Congress in Philadelphia in 1776.

Resigns army position

In 1777 and 1778, Rush served as a Surgeon General in the Continental army. But before long he had a dispute with his superior and former professor, Dr. William Shippen. Rush was angry about the dreadful conditions that existed in army hospitals at the time. When the problem did not improve over time, he sent a letter to General **George Washington** (see entry), accusing Dr. Shippen of poor management. Washington passed the letter on to Congress, which investigated the matter and ruled in favor of Shippen. The infuriated Rush then resigned his surgeon general position in April 1778.

Rush also was part of the Conway Cabal, part of a secret plot to replace George Washington as head of the Continental army. After visiting Washington's military camp shortly after the beginning of the Revolutionary War (1775–83), Rush wrote an unsigned letter to patriot **Patrick**

Henry in which he stated that Washington was a weak general and should be replaced by American General **Horatio Gates** or Major General Thomas Conway. Also taking part in the efforts to have Washington removed from office were **Samuel Adams** (see entries), Richard Henry Lee, and Thomas Mifflin. Rush's letter was sent on to George Washington, who confronted the physician after recognizing his fine handwriting. Almost at once, Rush resigned from the military.

In later years, Rush expressed his regret for his involvement in the plot, and he supported Washington's being elected the first president of the United States in 1789. However, according to historian David Freeman Hawke in *Benjamin Rush, Revolutionary Gadfly,* within the first year of Washington's presidency, Rush feared that "the principles of the revolution were being plowed under" and that a strong central government was becoming controlled by wealthy Americans to further their own interests. Discouraged by politics, Rush concentrated in the latter part of his life on medicine and matters of social reform.

A busy career

In 1780, Rush began lecturing to college students and returned to working as a physician. He set up his own medical practice and served on the part-time medical staff of Pennsylvania Hospital for the rest of his life. He was dedicated to both teaching his students in lecture class and providing one-on-one training to a much smaller group that attended him as he treated his patients at the hospital. There, in 1786, he founded the first free medical clinic in the United States for the relief of poor people, and he worked at the facility for many years without pay.

In 1789, Rush was appointed head of the department of the Theory and Practice of Medicine at the College of Philadelphia. Two years later, when the institution became the University of Pennsylvania, the physician-patriot helped organize its medical school, where he taught for many years.

Studies yellow fever; serves U.S. government

Rush wielded great influence in the medical community during and after revolutionary times, but he embraced

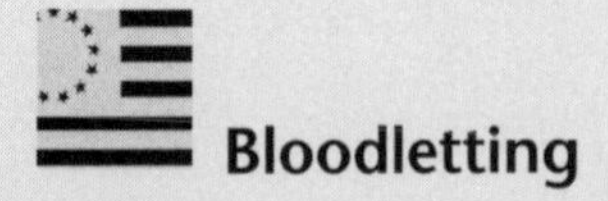

Bloodletting

Benjamin Rush learned about and began practicing bloodletting while in medical school in Scotland. Bloodletting is a process by which blood is drained from the body of a medical patient. From the fifth century through the mid-nineteenth century, many surgeons and barbers, who often served as medical men in the absence of doctors, routinely used bloodletting as a treatment to help cure patients of certain ailments. The method was commonly used for fevers, infections, and, strangely enough, even for excess bleeding.

Blood was drained from the patient's body using leeches (bloodsucking worms), medical instruments, or both. Doctors affixed leeches to the body by turning a wineglass full of the worms upside down on the affected part of the body. After the leech attached itself by biting, it could fill itself with half an ounce to an ounce of blood.

Blood could also be drained by making a number of incisions, or cuts, into the body. Blood was then caught in a shallow bowl. The procedure was stopped when the patient began to feel faint. From the seventeenth to the nineteenth centuries, blood was caught in heated little glass cups. The warm air created a vacuum and made the blood flow into the cup. Rush sometimes tried to cure his patients by draining up to 80 percent of their blood.

Former president George Washington died from a throat infection in 1799, after a great deal of his blood had been drained from his body in less than twenty-four hours. Although bloodletting is no longer widely practiced today, leeches are still sometimes used to relieve blood congestion during certain operations.

some ideas that caused much disagreement. He believed that all diseases were caused by the "excitability of blood vessels" and could be cured by bloodletting, a process by which the blood was drained from the patient's body (see box).

In the second half of the eighteenth century, there were frequent outbreaks of diseases, such as yellow fever, in the eastern United States. From 1793 to 1805, dangerous epidemics plagued Philadelphia. Rush worked heroically with the victims when most other people had fled to the safety of the countryside. Unfortunately, bloodletting, his treatment of choice, proved to be very ineffective in helping his patients.

But Rush also had some good ideas for treating patients, which he described in his book published in 1794, *An Account of the Bilious Remitting Yellow Fever.* Rush went against the medical thinking of his time by proposing the advanced idea that unsanitary conditions had largely contributed to the spread of yellow fever. Rush is credited for his innovations in a number of other fields as well, including the study of dental decay and veterinary training (the study of the medical treatment of animals).

In 1797, President John Adams appointed Rush Treasurer of the United States Mint, a post in which he served part-time until his death in 1813. President Thomas Jefferson later appointed him a scientific advisor for the famous Lewis and Clark Expedition (1804–06), in which Americans Meriwether Lewis and William Clark explored the country's western lands.

Promotes education, supports social reforms

Rush had a strong interest in education. He helped with the founding of Dickinson College and helped to manage the affairs of what became Franklin and Marshall College, both in the state of Pennsylvania. A believer in education for women, he was also a strong supporter of the Young Ladies Academy in Philadelphia, a school for girls. He also supported a system of free public schools, as well as promoting the idea of a national university for the United States that would teach only subjects connected to the study of government, including law, the principles of business, matters of war, and economics. But the idea was never put into action.

Rush also made efforts to help people he thought were discriminated against. Biographer Carl Binger wrote of him: "When [Rush] saw what he conceived to be an evil, he had to shout it down from the housetops, always with the hope—even the expectation—of its being immediately eradicated" or done away with.

As a social reformer, Rush wrote pamphlets attacking slavery, capital punishment (death administered by the state as punishment), war, and the use of tobacco and alcohol. In 1774, he helped found the Pennsylvania Society for Promoting the Abolition of Slavery, the first U.S. antislavery society. He also served as its president.

Rush is known for his enlightened approach to the treatment of mental illness, from which his eldest and favorite son, John, suffered. Rush was before his time in realizing and teaching that some mental illnesses have physical causes. He spent many years working with mentally handicapped individuals, treating them with kindness and compassion. He helped to improve their living conditions and did away with the use of chains to keep them immobilized. He encouraged mental patients to listen to music, sew, garden, and exercise every day. In 1812, Rush published the first American book about the treatment of the mentally ill, *Medical Inquiries and Observations upon Diseases of the Mind.*

Remembered after death

Rush lived out his final years recognized as one of the most accomplished Americans of his day. He died in Philadelphia on April 13, 1813, probably of pneumonia. He was buried at the city's Christ Church Burial Ground beside his mother and father and next to the future gravesite of his wife, who outlived him by more than thirty years. Shortly after Rush's death, Thomas Jefferson wrote of him in a letter to **John Adams** (see entry): "a better man than Rush could not have left us, more benevolent [generous], more learned, of finer genius, or more honest."

In the centuries after his death, the contributions of Benjamin Rush to America's medical community were not forgotten. In 1837, several of Rush's former students founded Rush Medical College in Chicago, Illinois, naming it in his honor. In Philadelphia in 1965, the American Psychiatric Association placed a bronze plaque at his gravesite, honoring him as the "Father of American Psychiatry."

For More Information

Binger, Carl, M.D. *Revolutionary Doctor: Benjamin Rush, 1746-1813.* New York: W.W. Norton & Co., Inc., 1966.

Boatner, Mark M., III. "Rush, Benjamin." *Encyclopedia of the American Revolution.* Mechanicsburg, PA: Stackpole Books, 1994, pp. 951-52.

D'Elia, Donald J. "Rush, Benjamin." *Encyclopedia of American Biography,* 2nd ed. Edited by John A. Garraty and Jerome L. Sternstein. New York: HarperCollins Publishers, 1996, pp. 969-70.

Hawke, David Freeman. *Benjamin Rush, Revolutionary Gadfly.* Indianapolis: The Bobbs-Merrill Co., Inc., 1971.

Web Sites

Ford, Graham. "Phlebotomy: The Ancient Art of Bloodletting." Museum of Questionable Medical Devices [Online] Available http://www.mtn.org/quack/devices/phlebo.htm (accessed on 1/6/00).

Leitch, Alexander. *A Princeton Companion.* Princeton, NJ: Princeton University Press, 1978. [Online] Available http://mondrian.princeton.edu/CampusWWW (accessed on 6/8/99).

"Rush, Benjamin." AND Reference Data Ltd. and *The Cambridge Dictionary of American Biography.* Edited by J. S. Bowmen. Oxford, UK: Cambridge University Press, 1995. [Online] Available http://search.biography.com/print_record.pl?id=19094 (accessed on 1/6/00).

Deborah Sampson

Born December 17, 1760
Plympton, Massachusetts
Died April 29, 1827
Sharon, Massachusetts

Farmer, soldier, public speaker

"Wrought upon ... by an enthusiasm and frenzy ... did I throw off the soft [clothing] of my sex, and assume those of the warrior."

Portrait: Deborah Sampson. *Reproduced by permission of the Rhode Island Historical Society/Women in Military Service Memorial Foundation.*

Disguised as a man, Deborah Sampson served admirably as a soldier in the Continental army during the American Revolutionary War (1775–83) and later gave speeches about her time in the military. She established a public presence for women that went far beyond the normal cultural limits of her time. The former soldier then went on to become a wife and mother. She asked for and received a military pension (money benefits) from the U.S. government, also unheard of for a woman of her time.

Deborah Sampson was born on December 17, 1760, to a poor family in Plympton, Massachusetts (located near Plymouth, Massachusetts). Her father, Jonathan Sampson Jr., deserted his family to go to sea. His wife, Deborah Bradford Sampson, a descendant of esteemed Massachusetts governor William Bradford, was later informed that her husband had perished in a shipwreck.

When Sampson was only five her mother became ill. No longer able to care for her children, Deborah Bradford Sampson gave them up to live with other families. After being shuffled from family to family, eight-year-old Deborah was sent to the farm of a church assistant, Deacon Thomas, near Middleborough, Massachusetts. There she entered into a legal agreement to work for the family for several years in exchange for food and lodging.

The farmer's family treated Sampson kindly. While living with them, the strong-willed young woman developed skills as a farmhand and an appreciation of nature. She plowed the fields, spread fertilizer, milked cows, stacked hay, and became a skilled carpenter. The deacon believed strongly in the importance of education—even for girls—and allowed Sampson to attend classes with his boys.

Posing as a man, Sampson enlists

In 1778, at the age of eighteen, Sampson was released by law from serving the Thomases and began working at other farms in the area. She borrowed newspapers and learned about the American Revolution, which was then in progress. At age twenty the young woman took a position as a part-time teacher at the Middleborough School, where she insisted that the girls learn as much as the boys. Although released from service to the Thomases, she continued to live at their home, doing chores part time, raising her own sheep and chickens, and selling cloth she had woven.

Sampson was patriotic and loved adventure. About five feet, eight inches tall, she was a heavy-boned young woman with a long, narrow face, blonde hair, and blue eyes. In 1782 twenty-one-year-old Sampson decided to do something very unusual. One story says that with twelve dollars she had saved she bought fabric and fashioned for herself a man's suit. Another says that she had a local tailor make a suit for a man in her size. In any event, she left her teaching job, claiming she was going to accept a better position.

In March 1782 the British Parliament voted to put an end to the fighting in America. British soldiers remained in America, however, and the Continental army was ordered to stay together until a peace treaty was signed (it was signed on September 3, 1783). Young men were hesitant to join the army because there was no guarantee they would be paid their wages on a regular basis. Immediate cash payments, called bounties, were sometimes offered to entice them to join. Some men signed up, waited until they were paid the bounty, then abandoned their positions. Then they signed up again in another location, to receive yet another bounty.

In the spring of 1782, Sampson dressed in male clothing, cut her hair to shoulder length, and tied it back in the fashion of men of that time. Near Middleborough, she went to an army recruiting office, where men signed up for military duty. But it was not long before her act of deception was discovered. According to one version of the story, she was leaving a tavern with a group of soldiers when a local woman recognized her despite the uniform. Sampson was forced to return the unused part of the bounty she had been paid, and was forbidden ever to re-enter the local recruiting office. Women then had not been granted the right to serve in the military.

Repeats the deception

But Sampson, who had enjoyed the freedom of her experience of passing as a man, did not abandon her plan to join the army. In May 1782 she traveled to Bellingham, Massachusetts. Using the first and middle name of her oldest brother (who had died before her birth), Robert Shurtliff, Sampson enlisted in the Fourth Massachusetts Regiment. Apparently the young woman's appearance caused no suspicion, and she was sent to Worcester, Massachusetts, along with several other recruits.

Determined to continue the military career she had come to love, Sampson altered her uniform and her body shape. She flattened her chest by wrapping it tightly with cloth. When a fellow soldier saw her and questioned why a man knew how to sew, she claimed that she had learned the skill because there were no girls in her family. Since she had no whiskers, Sampson was nicknamed "Molly" or "the blooming boy." Her lack of a beard was not considered unusual, as many soldiers in the Revolutionary War were too young to shave.

In the early summer of 1782, Sampson's military unit was sent to West Point, New York, to fight as foot soldiers and flush out Tories in nearby East Chester, New York. Tories were colonists who stayed loyal to Great Britain during the time of the American Revolution. Unwilling to admit that their cause had been lost, the Tories were still causing trouble in New York.

In the spring of 1782, General **George Washington** (see entry) had established his headquarters at Newburgh, New York, fourteen miles north of West Point. In nearby New Windsor, the main force of the Continental army, 9,000 strong, was stationed.

Deborah Sampson—disguised as a man—served in several military units, including the Light Infantry Division. *Reproduced by permission of Archive Photos, Inc.*

Makes her mark as a soldier

As Robert Shurtliff, Sampson drilled and marched. Her sturdy body allowed her to do the hard physical labor of setting up camp and rigging defenses. The young woman was an excellent shot and was assigned to a special group in the Light Infantry Division called the Rangers, light infantry soldiers who fought on foot. The Rangers sometimes acted as spies and brought back information on enemy activities.

As part of her duties Sampson was sent on scouting and raiding expeditions. She slept on a wooden bunk in a tent with five other soldiers. To avoid having her gender detected, she changed her clothes in the dark and saved her trips to the outdoor toilet for nighttime. During one clash with the Tories, Sampson received two shots through the coat and one through the cap. Another time she was slashed on the left side of her face with a sword, but she behaved as though the wound was a mere scratch so she could avoid being examined by a doctor.

Survives ambush attack

To keep up her deception, Sampson avoided making close friends. But she was very attractive, and several young women who visited her military camp fell in love with the young soldier. Sampson was careful to politely reject such interest.

In the summer of 1782, Sampson was wounded in the thigh by a musket ball and carried to an aid station for medical help. Fearing the surgeon who came to examine her would penetrate her disguise, she said that her only wound was a slight scratch on the head. He treated her for that and released her.

When safely alone, Sampson used a penknife to probe her thigh for the musket ball that had injured her. It is not known whether or not she was able to remove it, but the young woman suffered terribly and returned to duty before she had fully recovered. The wound bothered her for the rest of her life.

Becomes general's aide

In November 1782 Sampson went with her company to Fort Ticonderoga, New York, where she fought against some Native Americans who were fighting in support of the Tories. The natives thought the Tories would later help them keep their traditional lands out of the hands of American colonists. Impressed with her energetic attitude, General John Paterson made Sampson his personal assistant. The young soldier now had a small room of her own and slept in a feather bed. Each day she cleaned the general's boots, polished his swords, arranged his clothing, prepared food for him, and went on errands.

On April 19, 1783, American soldiers were elated to hear General George Washington's announcement of "the cessation of hostilities between the United States of America and the King of Great Britain." When Sampson heard the news, she had mixed feelings. She knew that America's final victory would mean her return to her former life.

Catches malaria; doctor discovers her secret

At war's end, Sampson went with her military unit to Philadelphia. While exploring in the area, she caught the infectious disease malaria. Suffering with a fever, she drifted in and out of consciousness. At one point, funeral planners were discussing where to take her body. Fortunately, Dr. Barnabas Binney was then attending the young soldier. When he saw his patient struggling to regain consciousness, he told the funeral workers to leave.

Dr. Binney soon discovered his patient was not male but female. He said nothing of his discovery to Sampson, thinking perhaps that because she was barely conscious, she did not realize he knew. He revealed her secret only to a woman who helped with the treatment of patients, asking her not to reveal the soldier's gender. When Sampson's condition improved, Dr. Binney had her moved to his own home, where she was nursed back to health by Dr. Binney's niece.

Travels west then returns to Philadelphia

After recovering, Sampson returned to her army duties, joining a group of soldiers for a journey to survey rocks and minerals in a remote region of Virginia. After arriving there she suffered a relapse of her illness and spent some time with a group of friendly Indians while her comrades continued their journey. When she recovered, Sampson returned to Philadelphia to say goodbye to Dr. Binney. Sampson departed Philadelphia and headed to West Point where her regiment, the Fourth Massachusetts, was to be disbanded.

Military career ends; resumes civilian life

There are conflicting stories concerning Sampson's visit with Dr. Binney and what happened afterward. In one version of the story, Dr. Binney did not reveal to Sampson that he knew her gender, but asked her to carry a letter for him to her West Point commander, Major General John Paterson. All accounts seem to agree that during her trip to West Point, a violent storm capsized the boat on which Sampson was a passenger. Her trunk full of clothing, along with her diary, landed at the bottom of the Hudson River. Sampson survived and continued her journey.

The story then goes on to say that the letter from Dr. Binney to General Paterson praised Sampson's intelligence and morals and revealed the fact that she was a woman. General Paterson sent the young woman, still in men's clothing, with a letter to deliver to General George Washington. Washington gave Sampson a copy of papers showing that she had served in the military with honor but was now discharged.

Whatever version is true, Deborah Sampson's career in the Continental army came to an end in October 1783. Sampson journeyed toward Boston, stopping at her uncle's farm in Stoughton, Massachusetts. She worked there as a farmhand, wearing men's clothing, including part of her uniform. In the spring of 1784 she began to wear skirts again.

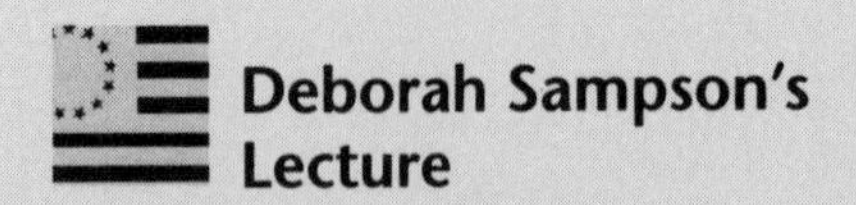

Deborah Sampson's Lecture

The lengthy speech Deborah Sampson gave as she traveled about New England told little about her military experiences. But it was full of admiration for George Washington and the cause of American independence. She said it was her enthusiasm that led her to join the army.

During the presentation, Sampson said she placed a high value on the traditional role played by women in American life and apologized for her deception in posing as a man. Her performance was full of contradictions as she celebrated women's traditional roles while at the same time showing by her story that she had rejected their limitations.

During her presentation Sampson appeared in a blue-and-white military costume and performed a military exercise with firearms. Then in her forties, Sampson recorded in her diary the audience's disbelief that a woman who looked so young had served in the Revolutionary Army. "Some of them, which I happened to overhear, swore that I was a lad of not more than eighteen years of age," she wrote.

Receives pension from State of Massachusetts

In April 1784 Sampson married Benjamin Gannett, a farmer from Sharon, Massachusetts, whom she met while working at her uncle's farm. The couple had two daughters and a son who, like his mother, became a soldier. Because Sampson's war wound began to act up, she could only do limited farm work.

When Sampson's story leaked out, she got a variety of reactions. Some people respected her for her exploits; others thought her behavior outrageous. For the rest of her life, she wore her uniform during veterans' parades (veterans are ex-soldiers).

In January 1792 Sampson petitioned the government of Massachusetts for back pay that she had never received from the army. Her petition was approved and signed by **John Hancock** (see entry), the governor of Massachusetts. According to a document issued by the General Court of Massachusetts, Sampson "did actually perform the duty of a soldier in the late army of the United States ... for which she has received no compensation ... [she] exhibited an extraordinary instance of female heroism by discharging the duties of a faithful gallant soldier, and at the same time preserving the virtue and chastity of her sex unsuspected and unblemished."

Seeks payment from federal government

Despite her pay from the state of Massachusetts, the Gannett family went on struggling and living the life of the poor. In 1797 the story of Sampson's life was published under the title *The Female Review.* In 1802 Sampson hired a writer to compose a speech about her life. She traveled about New England giving the speech, hoping to use the publicity from the lectures to help gain a soldier's pension from the U.S. government.

In the early 1800s Sampson met patriot **Paul Revere** (see entry), by then an old man. Revere had become famous in 1775 for riding his horse from Boston to Lexington and Concord, Massachusetts, to warn the patriots of the coming of British soldiers. Revere told Sampson he would use his influence to try and get her a government pension. In 1804 Revere wrote a letter to a Massachusetts congressman in which he commended Sampson as "a woman of handsome talents, good morals, a dutiful wife, and an affectionate parent." He also mentioned that she was not in good health.

In response, in 1805 the U.S. Congress granted Sampson a monthly pension of $4 for being injured in the performance of a soldier's duties. The pension allowed the Gannetts to buy a house on their farmland and do some landscaping of the property. The pension was doubled in 1818.

Remembered after death

Sampson died in 1827 and was buried near her home. Four years later her husband Benjamin, then in poor health, appealed to the U.S. Congress for the continuance of his wife's pension for himself. But at that time there was no law giving pensions to army widows, much less widowers. Gannett reapplied in 1836 after Congress passed such an act. He submitted a bill of six hundred dollars as evidence of the medical bills his wife's war wounds had cost the family. By then, Benjamin was very poor, and his two daughters had to depend on charity for their support.

Seven years later the U.S. government paid Sampson's heirs $466.66, as Benjamin Gannett had died eleven months earlier. In granting the money, the Committee on Revolutionary Pensions stated: "The whole history of the American Revolution records no case like this, and furnishes no other similar example of female heroism, fidelity, and courage." The committee writers added "there cannot be a parallel case in all time."

Many versions of Sampson's story have appeared in the more than two centuries since the war's end. But the basic facts of her life are well documented, and she continues to be recognized for her assertiveness and courage. Sampson was paid a special honor during World War II (1939–45) when a warship was christened the *Deborah Sampson Gannett* and launched at Baltimore, Maryland, on April 10, 1944. It was dedicated to "the sole female soldier of the American Revolution."

For More Information

Cheney, Cora. *The Incredible Deborah.* New York: Charles Scribner & Sons, 1967.

DePauw, Linda G. *Founding Mothers: Women of America in the Revolutionary Era.* Boston: Houghton Mifflin, 1975.

Evans, Elizabeth. *Weathering the Storm: Women of the American Revolution.* New York: Charles Scribner's Sons, 1975.

Freeman, Lucy, and Alma Halbert Bond. *America's First Woman Warrior: The Courage of Deborah Sampson.* New York: Paragon House, 1992.

Henretta, James A. "Unruly Women: Jemima Wilkinson and Deborah Sampson Gannett." *America's History.* 2nd ed. New York: Worth Publishers, 1997.

Meyer, Edith Patterson. *Petticoat Patriots of the American Revolution.* New York: The Vanguard Press, 1976.

Simister, Florence Parker. *Girl With a Musket.* New York: Hastings House, 1959.

Wachs, Eleanor. *Deborah Sampson Gannett, America's First Woman Soldier: A Source Booklet.* Boston: The Commonwealth Museum at Columbia Point, 1990.

Daniel Shays

Born c. 1747
Hopkinton, Massachusetts
Died September 29, 1825
Sparta, New York

Farmer, soldier, political leader, insurrectionist

"I am by occupation a farmer and [because of] age and ... wounds rec'd [received] in the [Continental] army I am unable to perform but little or no manual labor."

Petition for Pension by Daniel Shays, aged seventy-one

During the American Revolution (1775–83), Daniel Shays served with distinction in the American army, earning battlefield promotions for bravery. He later gained notoriety as the leader of the Shays Rebellion of 1786. Like those who began the war, Shays and his followers were protesting what they considered unfair taxation. The rebellion was suppressed, Shays and the other rebels were pardoned, and the event led political leaders to press for a strong federal government.

Not much is known about Daniel Shays's life before he enlisted as a soldier in the American army during the Revolutionary War. He was the second of six children born to Patrick Shays and Margaret Dempsey, who married in 1744 and lived in Hopkinton, Massachusetts. It is believed that, like his Irish immigrant parents, Shays was a farmer before the war.

In 1772, Shays and Abigail Gilbert declared their intention of marriage. Abigail was born in 1760, the daughter of Jonathan Gilbert and Abigail Olds. Whether Shays and Abigail actually married in 1772 or sometime later is not known. Historical records show that their first child was born in 1773. In

Portrait: Daniel Shays. *Reproduced by permission of the Granger Collection, New York.*

1772, Shays did purchase sixty-eight acres of farmland in Shutesbury, Massachusetts.

Minute Men respond at Lexington

By 1773, as a man of about twenty-six, Shays was active in the local town militia (a group of citizen soldiers). He drilled his neighbors in marching in formation, and attained the rank of sergeant in the Minute Men. The Minute Men were American militia members who were prepared to respond to a call to arms at a minute's notice.

Shays, his father, and his brother, James, responded to such an alarm on April 19, 1775, when the British marched on Lexington, Massachusetts, to capture rebel leaders **John Hancock** (1737–1793) and **Samuel Adams** (1722–1803; see entries). The British planned to continue on to Concord to capture the rebel arsenal (stockpile of weapons). With other militia men, the Shayses faced the British soldiers at Lexington and then at Concord. These battles were the "shot heard 'round the world," and the beginning of the American Revolutionary War. Shays served as a militia man for eleven days at this time, and then responded to the call to join the newly organized American army at Boston. The state militias made up this new army.

Shays served as an ensign (the lowest rank of officer) in the Battle of Bunker Hill in June 1775. Shays was promoted to lieutenant (pronounced loo-TEN-ant) in 1776. He received his captain's commission on January 1, 1777, and served in the Fifth Massachusetts regiment of the Continental army.

Wounded and recognized for bravery

Shays also saw action in the campaign at Saratoga, New York, where British General **John Burgoyne** (see entry) and 5,000 British soldiers surrendered in October 1777. Many historians consider this battle a turning point in the Revolution because it proved that the American army could defeat the British. The British army at this time was considered the best in the world. However, their defeat at Saratoga convinced the French and then the Spanish to lend their support to the new American nation.

These bloody battles led to the need for more American soldiers, so Shays went on a recruiting mission. In 1778, he returned to the American army with twenty new recruits from the Shutesbury, Massachusetts, area. In 1778, while on leave from the army, Shays purchased 107 acres of land in Pelham, Massachusetts. At the same time, he sold his holdings in Shutesbury.

In July 1779, Shays served under General Anthony Wayne at the Battle of Stony Point, New York. It was at this battle that Wayne earned his nickname of "Mad Anthony Wayne" for his fearless bayonet charge of this British stronghold. (A bayonet is a knife that is attached to the shooting end of a gun.)

By 1780, Shays was serving under the **Marquis de Lafayette**, the French nobleman who joined the American army because of his admiration for **George Washington** (see entries) and the cause of liberty. Lafayette, a beloved leader, presented each of his officers with a sword. Shays, who needed the money, sold his sword. Many historians call Shays a man without honor because of this sale. However, most Continental soldiers were not paid on a regular basis, so Shays most likely needed money at the time.

Shays was probably not well educated, because his family had been so poor. However, like Lafayette, Shays did have some gift for leading men. In general, Shays was regarded as a good officer, one who cared for the men serving under him. He was praised several times for his bravery during battles, and was wounded in action at least once.

Return to civilian life

Shays received an honorable discharge from the American army at Newark, New Jersey, in October 1780. He returned to Pelham to take up farming. Before long, his neighbors were urging Shays to run for public office. In colonial times, every town had several posts that were held by leading citizens. In 1781, Shays served the town of Pelham on the Committee of Safety and in 1782 as a member of a committee that tried to decide the amount of money that Pelham should contribute to the American war effort. He was also reappointed to the Committee of Safety in 1782.

The Background of the Shays Rebellion

After the Revolutionary War ended in 1783, the United States faced the enormous task of setting up a central system (a federal government) that would run the states (the former thirteen colonies) as a single country. The leaders of the new country knew it was only a matter of time before the United States would have to defend itself from either foreign or domestic attack. The Shays Rebellion (1786–87) was the first real test of whether the new United States government would hold together in the face of armed rebellion. The rebellion had its roots in how the government was organized following the war.

When the war ended in 1783, the federal government had to establish laws and courts, issue money, and so on. The government also had to pay for the cost of the war against England. One of the ways it did this was to tax each state, including Massachusetts. The states were not allowed to pay their share by using the paper money issued during the war. Nor was any private business allowed to be done using paper money. Instead, the government wanted every debt or sale to be paid in gold coin, which very few people had.

These conditions helped create an economic depression (downturn), in which the paper money issued by the government steadily lost its value. Many people grew poor, as they could purchase less with their money and found fewer markets for any goods they produced. The problem was made worse because many American soldiers were still waiting for the new U.S. government to pay them for their wartime services. Unable to pay their bills, they lost their farms, land, and other belongings.

There were other sources of unhappiness. Many ordinary citizens thought that lawyers were paid too much for their services. These same lawyers were the ones who argued against them in the new courts of law. The common citizens also believed that their local government

Captain Shays, as he was known to his neighbors, was respected because of his military service during the war. Many people believed that he was a good town leader, and that he would take care of them in their dealings with the state and federal governments. Many colonists had learned to distrust government from the British mishandling of their complaints before the war. Now, the Americans transferred this distrust to their new American government, which they thought was run by rich men in faraway New York City (then the nation's capital).

officials acted superior toward them and were paid too high a salary. These citizens also felt the justice system had let them down. They did not believe that the courts would protect their interests, but would instead side with the wealthier people who owned property.

Men who owned property could vote in the young United States; those who did not own property could not. Poorer people purchased property by taking out a loan from the bank or from a wealthy person. If the new property owner could not repay the debt, he had to forfeit the land (a process called foreclosure). Once a farmer lost his property, he forfeited his right to vote. Thus, he had no say in who represented him in the government. This led many to once again cry out (as they had before the American Revolution), "No taxation without representation."

This series of problems led to a sense of injustice and disappointment that the Revolution had not gained them the liberties promised. Many poorer Americans felt bitter and disappointed in their new government.

While many poorer people throughout the new country felt the economic pinch, an active group of rebels began to meet in western Massachusetts. They challenged the local state militia, shut down the court system for a while, and faced a force of federal soldiers before giving up. The rebellion failed, but the U.S. government remembered its cause. New laws allowed debts to be paid in paper money. The Shays Rebellion also underlined the need for a stronger federal government, one that issued money that was worth something, one that had fair laws, and one that had the ability to respond to local armed conflicts "to ensure domestic tranquility" (calm). The stronger federal government was outlined in the U.S. Constitution, which was ratified (passed into law) in 1789.

Shays and neighbors unhappy with new American government

Shays's leadership ability was tested even before the war was officially over, when the citizens of Pelham and other western Massachusetts towns began to complain bitterly against the new U.S. government. For the most part, they were poor people who believed the government was letting them down. These people had high hopes after the Revolutionary War, and believed that a time of great prosperity was upon

A blacksmith is served a writ of attachment for debt. After the Revolutionary War, many citizens became disenchanted with the new U.S. government's debt collection enforcement policy. *Reproduced by permission of the Corbis Corporation (Bellevue).*

them. Instead, the war brought poverty and confusion as systems of the federal government were being established. Shays himself was charged several times with owing money (debts) and lost some land because of his inability to make payments on it.

Shays's neighbors began to lose their property because they could not pay their loans. Once they lost their property, they lost the right to vote and so could not choose who spoke for them in government decision making. They were taxed to pay for the war, but few had any money. Many joined mobs, which marched on the local town and state governments demanding relief from their economic problems.

By 1785, Shays had formed a town militia, which drilled in front of the town tavern in Pelham. Shays and his neighbors believed that they would once again have to fight an oppressive government (this time, the U.S. government) to gain the right to vote and to be taxed fairly. Other towns nearby also began to arm themselves. By August, Shays had been officially appointed to head this force of militia men. While Shays was the military leader, Luke Day of Springfield, Massachusetts, was making speeches to stir up popular support for what would soon become a full-scale rebellion.

Citizens take action against government

Shays's group of about 1,000 militia men marched on Springfield in September 1785 to prevent the court from meeting. The court was unpopular because it heard cases against debtors and sent some to prison. Shays and his men were met by Major General William Shepard, who commanded a force of about 1,000 Massachusetts state militia men. Shays agreed to allow the court to begin its session, provided that no debt cases would be tried and no debtors put into prison. An agreement was reached and the court session began.

However, by December, Shays and his band were disgusted because the courts and the government had made no progress toward fixing the economic situation. Shays and his men marched to Worcester (pronounced WUSS-ter), Massachusetts, and from there to Rutland, Vermont. In January 1787, Shays's army marched back to Springfield, with the intention of capturing the federal arsenal there (an arsenal is a stockpile of weapons). Tensions mounted.

In the meantime, the federal government appointed General Benjamin Lincoln to head a force of between 4,000 and 5,000 federal troops to suppress what had become an armed rebellion against the United States. People throughout the country began calling it "The Shays Rebellion" and the followers Shaysites. While Shays had much popular support, the government and wealthy citizens considered him and his followers traitors to the United States.

In January 1787, Lincoln and his troops marched from Boston to confront Shays's army, which by now numbered about 1,200 men. Shays did not wait for the federal troops to appear, and attacked the Springfield arsenal on January 25. The state militia under General Shepard opened fire, killing two Shaysites and wounding a third. Shays responded by retreating ten miles.

General Lincoln's federal force pursued Shays and his army from town to town across western Massachusetts. During this time, Lincoln offered the rebels a chance to surrender and be pardoned. Shays declined, saying that their grievances were real and that until they were addressed, the rebellion would continue. Finally, on February 3, Lincoln led his men thirty miles through a snowstorm to catch up with Shays at Petersham, Massachusetts. Lincoln's troops captured 150 rebels and sent the rest home. Thus ended what history now calls "The Shays Rebellion."

The aftermath of the Shays Rebellion

The federal government could not tolerate its citizens taking arms and rising against it. Shays and the other leaders of the rebellion were sentenced to death by hanging. The other rebels were warned sternly and then pardoned. Shays petitioned for a pardon in February 1788, and it was granted that June.

After the rebellion, Shays lived in West Sandgate, Vermont, until 1790. After the death of his wife, Abigail, Shays moved to New York, eventually settling in Preston Hollow. Historical records show that Shays married a second time, in April 1815, to Rhoda Coller Havens, a widow, in Hungerford, New York. In 1818, he petitioned the federal government for an army pension for his service in the Revolutionary War. After receiving a pension of twenty dollars per month, Shays purchased twelve acres of farm land in Sparta, New York, in 1820. He died there in 1825 at the age of seventy-eight. A marker near Union Cemetery in Livingston County, New York, records that Daniel Shays served in the Revolution and was the leader of the Shays Rebellion.

For More Information

Boatner, Mark M., III. "Shays, Daniel" and "Shays's Rebellion." *Encyclopedia of the American Revolution.* Mechanicsburg, PA: Stackpole Books, 1994, pp. 999-1001.

Feer, Robert A. *Shay's Rebellion.* New York: Garland Publishing, 1988, pp. 216-23.

Holland, Josiah Gilbert. *History of Western Massachusetts: The Counties of Hampden, Hampshire, Franklin, and Berkshire.* Vol. 1. Springfield, MA: Samuel Bowles and Company, 1855, pp. 292-95.

Nicholson, Mary Ann, ed. *The Family of Daniel Shays (excerpted from Descendants of Daniel Shays, November 1934 by Elmer S. Smail).* Boston: The New England Genealogical Society, 1987, pp. 4-9.

Parmenter, C. O. "Captain Daniel Shays." *History of Pelham, Massachusetts from 1738 to 1898, Including the Early History of Prescott.* Amherst, MA: Press of Carpenter & Morehouse, 1898, pp. 390-94.

Paulin, Michael. *The Ballad of Daniel Shays.* Athol, MA: The Transcript Press, 1986, pp. 100-07.

Purcell, L. Edward. "Shays, Daniel." *Who Was Who in the American Revolution.* New York: Facts on File, 1993, p. 438.

Charles Townshend

Born August 27, 1725
Norfolk, England
Died September 4, 1767
London, England

Member of Parliament

Charles Townshend was a brilliant and witty man, and a member of the British Parliament who strove to please those he thought could do him the most good. He is mostly remembered for the Townshend Acts of 1767, which taxed and angered the American colonies to revolt. The acts had a huge and fatal impact on relations between the colonies and Great Britain, and for this reason Townshend will always be remembered as the man who did so much to bring on the American Revolution.

"I shall never be governed in any action by any authority but that of my own free judgement, independent equally of the favor of Court and the censure of an Opposition."

Charles Townshend was born on August 27, 1725, to Charles Townshend and his wife, Audrey, daughter and heiress of Edward Harrison. Charles was their second son and one of five children. His siblings were George; Edward, who died in infancy; Roger, who was killed in a war in America in 1759; and Audrey.

Although the Townshends lived in England, the oldest son of the family held an Irish aristocratic title, Viscount (pronounced VY-count) Townshend. Charles's father was the third Viscount Townshend. Charles's older brother, George, inherited the title to become the fourth viscount.

Portrait: Charles Townshend. *Reproduced by permission of Archive Photos, Inc.*

The Townshends were related to several noble families and important men in British politics. Audrey Harrison Townshend's father was a director of the prosperous East India Company, whose tea would be dumped in protest into Boston, Massachusetts, Harbor in 1773 in a pre-Revolutionary War incident called the Boston Tea Party.

Despite his family's wealth and connections, Charles had an unhappy childhood, according to his biographers, Lewis Namier and John Brooke. His father, though intelligent, had a forceful and suspicious personality. His mother was intelligent but very free with her affections. The couple separated when Charles was fifteen; for the rest of his life Townshend senior remained bitter towards his wife. Charles went to live with his father, claiming an affection for him that he really did not feel. He also claimed to despise his mother and was not close to his siblings. His biographers described young Townshend as suffering from "poverty of heart."

Boyhood

Most of what is known about young Townshend's personal life comes from the letters he wrote to his father and the letters he received in return. Townshend was a sickly boy, and after reaching puberty he began to suffer from seizures that would plague him for the rest of his rather short life. Townshend may have had epilepsy, a disorder of the brain. The seizures left Townshend shaken and weak, but according to Namier and Brook, "with incredible ... drive he struggled on, giving his life a brilliant and amusing appearance. The tragic side was usually overlooked."

Perhaps because of his ill health, Townshend did not attend the same elite school his brother went to. He was educated somehow, and then attended Cambridge University. The years there, before he graduated in 1745, were marked by frequent bouts of sickness and disagreements with his father over money.

Young manhood

The pattern of poor health and constant criticisms from his father continued through Townshend's study of law at Leyden University in Holland (1746–47). His father would write long letters offering advice and complaining about the young Townshend's spending habits and about his mother. The young man would respond with long letters describing his poor health, asking for money, and thanking his father in flowery phrases for his wise and excellent advice. Townshend's strained relationship with his father may have contributed to Townshend's poor attitude towards all authority figures. He gradually learned how to get the better of his father by sweetly threatening to reconcile with his mother. His later political career would be marked by a tendency to favor whatever side of an issue pleased those in power the most and promised him the most benefit.

At Leyden, Townshend became well-known among his classmates (including **John Wilkes**; see entry) for his good humor, his wit, and his talent for mimicry.

Begins career in politics

In 1747 Townshend returned to England to complete his legal studies. The next year, he ran for and won a seat in the lower house of Parliament (Great Britain's lawmaking body). Both his legal studies and his run for Parliament cost money, which Townshend's father grudgingly paid. Townshend continued to suffer from bouts of ill health and soon gave up his law practice.

Townshend applied for various committee posts as part of his Parliamentary activities. In 1749, at his father's urging, he became a member of the Board of Trade. He held that position until 1754, when he became a member of the Board of Admiralty, the government department in charge of naval affairs (his own preference). In these positions he learned a great deal about trade issues between Great Britain and the American colonies.

Before Townshend's time, Great Britain had not interfered much in colonial affairs. Townshend believed that the British government should assert its powers to tax and control the colonies. He was now in a position to make recommendations about British policy toward the colonies. One of his first moves was to make the governor of New York financially independent of the New York Assembly (its lawmaking body). That is, the governor's salary—and his actions—would no longer depend on the will of the Assembly. Under Townshend's plan, the British-appointed royal governor would from then on take orders from England, not from a group of New Yorkers.

Gradually Townshend began to impress his peers in the government with his quick way of studying and understanding complicated issues. They applauded his long, witty speeches in Parliament. But Townshend made enemies too. Sometimes he would vigorously defend an issue he did not believe in, wait for others to join in the defense, then go over to the opposing side and laugh heartily at the defenders.

Marries; gains notice in political circles

In early 1753 Townshend sought permission from his father to marry. Because he was earning very little at the time, he asked that his father provide an annual sum to add to his own income. His father refused, writing: This "scheme and project ... is your own and I will have nothing to do with it." Charles Townshend was so upset that he spoke out forcefully when the Clandestine Marriage Bill was introduced in Parliament. (Clandestine is another word for hidden or concealed.) The bill gave parents more power than before over the marriages of their children.

Townshend's eloquent speech was much admired. **Horace Walpole** (1717–1797; see entry), a well-known historian and letter writer of the era, described Townshend at that time as "a young man of unbounded ambition.... His figure was tall..., his action [forceful], his voice loud, his laugh louder. He had art enough to disguise anything but his vanity." In their biography of Townshend, Namier and Brooke went on to describe Walpole's impression: "Walpole thought him marked by nature for leadership (wherein he was wrong); he had 'quickness of genius,' foresaw himself 'equal to anything,' had no passion but ambition."

On September 18, 1755, Townshend married Lady Caroline, a woman of considerable wealth who had a young son from a previous marriage. Her titles were Dowager Countess of Dalkeith, later Baroness Greenwich and the Duchess of Argyll. Lord Townshend once again complained bitterly about his son's request for money to marry. He was not invited to the wedding, and any pretense of friendly relations between father

Excerpts From Townshend Letters

In late 1745 and early 1746, twenty-year-old Charles Townshend was in Holland studying law at Leyden University. Over the winter he exchanged several letters with his father, Lord Townshend, in which the young man was forced to beg for money and his father complained about it in return. Below are excerpts from their correspondence after Lord Townshend wrote on March 3, 1746, ordering his son to return to England. Charles Townshend had written back that he would miss out on some important lessons if he returned early. His father replied:

"You now know clearly what my orders are: that you should return to England in the first week of May next or towards the later end of May at furthest, but you must be here before May is over. These are my final orders and therefore I do expect they should be obeyed without further argument."

Charles replied on June 5:

"I have had five convulsive fits, severe and of a long continuance, and [I am in such a poor state of health], which, if neglected, may have bad consequences and for which, therefore, with your permission, I will go through one course of [treatment] before I begin my journey. This will delay me but one fortnight [fourteen days] at most, and I hope as it is so necessary to my health it will have your approbation."

In fact, Townshend was delayed for more than a month. He wrote his father on July 2:

"At the latter end of next week I hope to arrive [home], where I shall endeavour by the dutiful behaviour I shall observe and by my constant attention to your will, to remove what objections you have to my conduct and to deserve your affection and your esteem."

and son came to an end with the marriage. Horace Walpole commented in a letter to a friend that with his newfound wealth and independence, Townshend was now set free. "I propose [that we will enjoy] great entertainment from him," wrote Walpole.

According to Namier and Brooke, Townshend's marriage was more a matter of convenience than love. His wife, who was eight years older than Townshend, had extensive connections with powerful members of the nobility who could help Townshend in his career. The couple seemed contented enough. Lady Dalkeith bore Townshend three children: a daughter, Anne, and two sons who died young. After his marriage, Townshend became good friends with his mother, with whom he had much in common. As Namier and Brooke put it: "Both were intelligent, witty, and malicious; not burdened with a conscience or a faith; and both disliked Lord Townshend."

Involved in colonial affairs

Townshend continued to use his powerful connections to get important jobs. He seemed to feel no loyalty toward anyone. He gained a reputation for changing his allegiances from one powerful person to another to further his own desire for money and power. In 1761 and 1762 he served as secretary-at-war. From 1763 to 1765 he served as president of the Board of Trade. By then he was well-known as a financial genius.

In 1763 the French and Indian War in the American colonies ended with a British victory. That war had pitted Great Britain against its longtime enemy, France, and France's Indian allies in a struggle over who would control North America. The British believed they had done most of the work of that war. They had protected the American colonists against the French and Indians, and they believed they were now entitled to tax the colonies to help pay off huge war debts. Charles Townshend was in complete agreement with that reasoning.

The first major tax on the colonies was the Stamp Act of 1765. It required that certain documents and other items ranging from newspapers to dice had to have stamps attached to them. The stamps had to be bought from official stamp agents, who would be appointed by Parliament. Townshend gave a lively and eloquent speech before Parliament supporting the stamp tax. According to a letter quoted by Namier, Townshend's speech ended with these words: "And now will these Americans, children planted by our care, nourished up by our indulgence until they are grown to a degree of strength and [luxury], and protected by our [weapons], will they grudge to contribute their mite [little bit of money] to relieve us from the heavy weight of that burden which we lie under?"

The Stamp Act was to go into effect in November 1765. Throughout the fall of 1765, talk of colonial riots and disturbances over the act was on every British politician's lips. In

December 1765, government official George Grenville stood up in Parliament and began the debate on the question of whether or not to declare the colonies in a state of rebellion. To the surprise of many, Townshend spoke against Grenville's motion. He knew that Grenville had fallen out of favor with King **George III** (see entry). Less than six months after the Stamp Act went into effect, it was repealed, and George Grenville was dismissed from his government office.

In July 1766 Prime Minister **William Pitt** (see entry) named Townshend Chancellor of the Exchequer, in charge of the collection and care of the British government's operating expenses.

Shortly after appointing Townshend to this powerful position, Pitt became seriously ill. Townshend became his unofficial successor in one of the most important positions in the British government. He was now chief adviser to King George III, who grew increasingly determined to force the American colonists into tax-paying submission.

One day in May 1767, Townshend stood up in Parliament and gave a long, rambling speech. Horace Walpole was there and wrote a description of it. He said: "It lasted an hour, with torrents of wit, ridicule, vanity, lies, and beautiful language." Townshend insulted and ridiculed other members of Parliament and King George. Many people who were present believed he must have been drunk, and from this speech Townshend earned the nickname "Champagne Charlie."

Townshend Acts are passed

Still, King George found Townshend to be clever and witty, loud and amusing; he liked Townshend very much. Townshend informed King George that he had figured out a way to tax the colonies without their objecting. Not only would his proposals raise money, he said, they would also demonstrate Parliament's power over the colonies.

King George listened and gave Townshend his support. Parliament passed the Townshend Acts on June 29, 1767. They included a Quartering Act, which ordered the colonies to house British troops, and a Revenue Act, which called for taxes on lead, glass, paint, tea, and other necessary items. (A revenue is money collected to pay for the expenses of government.)

The acts also took away certain elements of colonial self-government. The colonies had grown used to running their own affairs, but Townshend sought through his acts to assert royal authority.

By Townshend's prediction, the acts would probably not raise very much money in the colonies, but the colonies would certainly know who was in charge. He seemed to have no idea how the acts would be received in America. Other people knew how strongly Americans would object to the acts and predicted that they would lead to the British Empire's loss of the colonies.

Throughout the summer of 1767, Townshend suffered from a fever, which he neglected. It turned out to be typhus, an infectious disease caused by being bitten by lice or fleas. Within months after the acts that bore his name went into effect, Townshend died suddenly on September 4, 1767, at the young age of forty-two. He did not live to witness the American Revolution (1775–83) and American independence.

Biographers Namier and Brooke summed up Townshend as "a brilliant failure." Treated cruelly by a bully of a father, Townshend "grew up into a self-damaging type." He was, however, kind to his children.

For More Information

Namier, Louis, and John Brooke. *Charles Townshend.* New York: St. Martin's Press, 1964.

Web Sites

"To Tax or Not to Tax: The Rights and Justification of Parliament in Question: The Townshend Acts of 1767." [Online] Available http://odur.let.rug.nl~usa/E/tax/davis04.htm (accessed on September 29, 1999).

"Townshend, Charles, 1725-1767." [Online] Available http://www.clements.umich.edu/Webguides/T/TownsndC.html (accessed on September 29, 1999).

Horace Walpole

Born September 24, 1717
London, England
Died March 2, 1797
London, England

Writer, historian, politician

"I am what I always was, a [fervent supporter of] liberty in every part of the globe, and consequently ... I most heartily wish success to the Americans."

Horace Walpole was a brilliant eighteenth-century man of letters. An accomplished writer of essays, Walpole was also an expert in the fields of history, art history (particularly painting), and gardens. His *Memoirs,* which he wrote secretly from about 1751 to 1791, is one of the greatest sources of information about the political history of his time.

Horace Walpole, born in London, England, on September 24, 1717, was the fourth child and youngest son of the great British prime minister Sir Robert Walpole, First Earl of Orford, and Catherine Shorter Walpole. The child was christened Horatio, but he disliked the name, preferring to be called Horace.

Young Walpole enjoyed the advantages of wealth and family influence. After his early schooling, in 1727 Walpole went on to attend the highly respected Eton College. There he began a long friendship with Thomas Gray, who later became a famous poet. After leaving Eton in 1734, Walpole attended King's College at Cambridge, England. While at Cambridge, he took a leave of absence to spend time with his sick mother, who died in 1737.

Portrait: Horace Walpole. *Reproduced by permission of Archive Photos, Inc.*

The next year, Walpole published *Verses in Memory of King Henry VI: the Founder of King's College, Cambridge.* The poems are notable for Walpole's expression of hostility toward the Roman Catholic Church and for foreshadowing his later commitment to the style of writing known as Gothic. Gothic writing uses medieval settings (from the Middle Ages) to produce an effect of horror and mystery.

Comes into money, tours Europe

In the summer of 1738, Walpole's father gave him a substantial source of income in the form of sinecures (pronounced SIN-uh-cures), titles or positions that provide profit without involving much work or responsibility, which lasted throughout his lifetime. Walpole used some of his newly gained fortune to indulge his love for building things and collecting art objects. He also enjoyed gambling.

Walpole was a man of average height for the times, about five-feet-seven, thin, with pale skin and very bright eyes. His personality was lively, he dressed elegantly, and he spoke with a pleasant, though somewhat high-pitched voice. He was a brilliant and sensitive person; although he enjoyed conversing with people of all ages and backgrounds, he required the approval and affections of only a few people very close to him. He was honest and generous, and enjoyed surrounding himself with beautiful objects. He once said, "I would buy the Coliseum [of Rome] if I could."

In 1739 Walpole embarked with his friend Thomas Gray (the poet) on a grand tour of Europe. Personality differences caused them to quarrel during the trip, but the two men remained lifelong friends.

Begins correspondence, writes poem

The year 1739 was also when Walpole began writing the letters for which he became famous. Throughout his life, Walpole wrote thousands of letters in which he made observations on politics, literature, major events that took place throughout Europe and America, and the gossip of his day. Specialists use his letters as an important reference on the eighteenth century. The letters commented on such diverse subjects as the discovery of the planet Uranus, Benjamin

Franklin's experiments with electricity, ballooning, prison reform, and social customs, to name just a few topics. In them Walpole also analyzed the chief figures of British politics.

The people with whom Walpole mainly corresponded, besides his friend Thomas Gray, were Horace Mann, the American educator; various noblemen and noblewomen; poets, biographers, and friends from college; his close friend in his later years, Mary Berry; and Madame du Deffand, a witty Parisian woman who was sixty-nine years old when they began their fourteen-year exchange of letters. More than 4,000 of Walpole's letters have been printed.

In 1740 Walpole wrote *An Epistle to Mr. Ashtron from Florence*. This poem was a piece of satirical writing that reflected his deeply held political and religious commitment to Protestantism and to the Hanovers, the family that ruled England from 1714 until 1901. Satirical writing ridicules individuals or groups by pointing out their stupidities or abuses.

Walpole in Parliament

In 1742 Walpole became a Member of Parliament (the English law-making body) for the Borough of Callington in the section of England known as Cornwall. He kept that post until 1754, but he would remain in Parliament for fifteen more years. While in Parliament Walpole fought oppression and injustice, speaking out against the black slave trade as well as restrictions on the freedoms of colonists in America.

Walpole's primary concern in Parliament, though, was helping to promote the career of his first cousin and closest friend, Henry Seymour Conway. Conway was to become a field marshal in the military, a British secretary of state, and leader of the House of Commons, the lower house of Parliament. Because of Conway's painstaking efforts at getting the hated Stamp Act of 1765 repealed, the towns of Conway in New Hampshire and Massachusetts were named after him. The Stamp Act forced American colonists to pay taxes to England on a variety of papers and documents, including newspapers, so the British government could raise funds to pay off its war debts. It was the first direct tax ever imposed by Great Britain on the Americans, who rioted in opposition. Walpole himself was very much opposed to the Stamp Act and supportive of the Americans' fight for fair treatment by the British government (see box on p. 465).

In 1742 Sir Robert Walpole, Horace's father, resigned from his post as first lord of the treasury and British Prime Minister. He was then made Earl of Orford. On March 23, 1742, Walpole gave his first speech in the House of Commons, the lower house of Parliament, in defense of his father, who was being attacked by his political enemies. Robert Walpole died in March 1745.

Develops Strawberry Hill

In 1747 Horace Walpole leased a building at Strawberry Hill, Twickenham. The property, ten miles west of London, was a forerunner of the kinds of suburbs that are common near London today. He bought the building two years later.

Strawberry Hill was a pioneer achievement for Walpole. He remodeled it in an architectural style that later became known as Victorian Gothic; the style became popular in Europe and the United States. Walpole's house featured towers, arches, painted glass, a chapel, a library, and a notched roof. Its interior featured collections of pictures, furniture, and decorative "curiosities," as well as books of all sorts. Strawberry Hill is also noteworthy because it contained the first printing press located in an English private house.

Creates art catalogue, begins memoirs

In 1747 Walpole wrote *Aedes Walpolianae: or A Description of the Collection of Pictures at Houghton Hall in Norfolk*. This catalogue of the outstanding collection of pictures at Robert Walpole's home was the first catalogue of its kind in England and served as Horace Walpole's memorial to his father. The book also contained Walpole's "Sermon on Painting," in which he discussed the merits of various styles of painting.

Walpole began writing his political memoirs as a record of happenings based on his personal observations and knowledge in 1751. From February to September 1753, he sent nine written contributions to a publication called *The World*. They were satires on such diverse subjects as landscape gardening, letter writing, and the politeness shown by the robbers who stole money from him, among other topics.

Walpole described himself in a March 1775 letter to Richard Bentley as an alert but detached spectator. He wrote, "In short, the true definition of me is that I am a dancing senator—not that I do dance, or do anything by being a senator; but I go to balls and to the House of Commons—to look on: and you will believe when I tell you that I really think the former the more serious occupation of the two: at least the performers are more in earnest." This passage is typical of Walpole's type of wit and occasional sarcasm.

Literary critic Martin Kallich warned readers about this passage; in it Walpole gave an impression of himself as an amateur who only dabbled in politics or art. Kallich pointed out in his biography of Walpole that "he was really very deeply committed to these areas of activity, as his history and memoirs ... and his literary and art criticism ... conclusively demonstrates."

Protests injustice of British government

From 1754 to 1757 Walpole was a Member of Parliament, first for Castle Rising, Norfolk, then for another area in England called King's Lynn. During this time, he made an effort to save the life of a man named Admiral Byng. Byng had been given a military trial and was scheduled to be executed for the wartime loss to the French of the Mediterranean island of Minorca.

Walpole was unable to save Byng's life, so in May 1757 wrote *A Letter for Xo Ho,* a serious satire on the cruelty of the British government for executing the man. Walpole always showed sympathy for the underdog and tried to protect individuals from being the targets of unfair acts of power by superior forces. Walpole thought the punishment given Byng was unjust and that the man had been used as a scapegoat for the mistakes of the British government.

Prints collections of his writings, an art history, a Gothic novel

In April 1758 Walpole printed *A Catalogue of the Royal and Noble Authors of England.* The book lists the works of various royal and noble authors and gives accounts of interesting and curious events in their lives. Later that year, *Fugitive Pieces in Verse and Prose* appeared. It is a collection of a number of Walpole's earlier poems along with various articles on political subjects and other never-before printed essays.

In 1762 Walpole began writing *Anecdotes of Painting in England,* but it was not completed until 1771. The book provides a history of English art, including painting, architecture, sculpture, engraving, and other forms, from the earliest times to the mid-1700s.

Walpole's *Castle of Otranto,* which is recognized as the first Gothic novel, appeared in 1764. It portrays everyday characters caught up in incidents that have supernatural elements. About the writing of this novel Walpole commented that he "had a dream, of which all I could recover was that I had thought myself in an ancient castle ... and that on the uppermost bannister of a great staircase I saw a gigantic hand in armour. In the evening I sat down, and began to write, without knowing in the least what I intended to ... relate."

Travels to France, writes historical work and tragedy

Walpole enjoyed traveling in continental Europe, and in the summer of 1765 he went to France. In Paris he met Madame du Deffand, who was blind. Deffand had been part of the dazzling court life of France in the early eighteenth century. In 1750, after the death of her husband, she had moved to Paris and was at the center of a large and distinguished group of socialites and thinkers that had begun to diminish by the 1760s. Walpole loved Paris and made four more visits to see Deffand, the last in 1775. The two grew to share a closeness and affection that lasted for many years.

The last year Walpole served in Parliament was 1768. In February of that year he wrote *Historic Doubts on the Life and Reign of King Richard III.* The book sought to justify the life of the British king despite the many crimes he was accused of. That same year Walpole completed *The Mysterious Mother,* which was printed at Strawberry Hill. The tragic drama tells the story of a woman's deliberate violation of the taboo against incest (sexual contact between closely related blood relatives).

Walpole Champions Cause of American Revolutionaries

Throughout the American Revolution (1775–83), Horace Walpole was a strong supporter of the rights of Americans (he was unusual in Great Britain for calling them Americans, not "colonists"). He opposed British government attempts to force the colonists to pay taxes while having no say in the way they were governed.

Beginning in 1774, after news of the Boston Tea Party reached England, Walpole's letters reflected an intense interest in American affairs. The Boston Tea Party was an act of protest against British taxation in which Americans threw hundreds of chests of tea into the Boston, Massachusetts Harbor.

In a letter to American educator Horace Mann in August 1775, Walpole wrote, "If England prevails [in forcing the Americans to pay taxes], English and American liberty is at an end!" Walpole always hated war, and believed that the British government had unjustly provoked the Revolutionary War. According to Bernhard Knollenberg: "The ground for Walpole's fear that British victory would destroy liberty in America is self-evident [it requires no proof or explanation]. Once Parliament, by force of arms, established its asserted authority to tax the colonies as it pleased, what was to prevent it from exploiting the colonies as ruthlessly as the East India Company ... with the [approval] of Parliament, [was] exploiting India?—a development which Walpole had followed with horrified attention."

Many historians agree that even before the signing of the Declaration of Independence in 1776, a great many Englishmen, perhaps even the majority, opposed England's efforts to force the colonists to pay what Americans viewed as unjust taxes. After France had entered into the Revolutionary War, the war's expense increased for the British and the likelihood of their winning decreased. By that point, most British people likely favored peace, even if it meant that America would gain its independence. Knollenberg pointed out, however, that "for about two years between the middle of 1776 and the middle of 1778, Walpole must have felt himself pretty much a 'loner,' and whatever may be thought of the rightness of his position, deserving of admiration for his [courage] in outspokenly maintaining it through thick and thin."

Historian Mark Boatner said that certain of Walpole's works are of special interest to those studying the American Revolution. They are edited by various authorities, and appear under the titles *Memoirs of the Last Ten Years of the Reign of George II* (1846), *Memoirs of the Reign of King George III* (4 volumes, 1845; re-edited in 1894), and *Journal of the Reign of George III from 1771 to 1783* (2 volumes, 1859, re-edited in 1909).

Books on gardening and architecture

Walpole was an expert gardener and interior decorator, and he enjoyed writing about those subjects. *The History of the Modern Taste in Gardening,* which he wrote some time before 1770, revealed the change in the popular attitude toward nature, particularly landscape gardening, that took place in the mid-1700s. During that time the popular, old-fashioned symmetrical gardens gave way to the more irregular types of gardens in the landscaping of English parks.

The author's *A Description of the Villa of Horace Walpole at Strawberry Hill* appeared in 1774. It was enlarged in 1784, then again in 1786. The book describes Walpole's unique and rather whimsical house; he wrote in the preface, "It was built to please my own taste, and in some degree to realize my own visions." The next year Walpole printed *Hieroglyphic Tales.* (Hieroglyphic means hard to understand.) The book is a collection of six stories of fantasy written to amuse the children of his friends.

Declining years

In 1791, upon the death of his nephew, seventy-four-year-old Walpole became the fourth Lord Orford. By then he was troubled by various ailments common to the elderly. His final years were saddened by the violent deaths of many of his friends in France who were killed by angry revolutionaries during the French Revolution (1789–99).

Walpole spent much of his time entertaining and playing cards. As a very old man he developed a close friendship with the Berry sisters, two young women in their twenties named Mary and Agnes. They were intelligent, pretty, well-bred, charming, and interested in his stories of the past. Walpole called them his "twin wives" or his "dear both," and gave them a cottage on his property to live in. The never-married elderly man spent many happy hours in their company.

At the age of eighty Walpole fell ill and died on March 2, 1797. He was buried at Houghton in Norfolk, England. In his will he left the cottage on his property to its inhabitants, the Berry sisters.

Becomes a controversial figure

Walpole became a controversial figure after his death. Thomas Macaulay, a nineteenth-century English historian and politician, wrote a negative summation of Walpole's character. According to Kallich, Macaulay found Walpole "incapable of sincerity; odd and incompetent; a poor judge of character who 'sneered at everybody' and whose opinions about men and things, 'wild, absurd, and ever-changing' were almost worthless." Macaulay's observations on Walpole were once widely quoted and even widely believed. But in more recent times, historians have called Macaulay's writings about Walpole unfair and distorted. Today Walpole is looked upon as a more direct, consistent, kinder, and wiser man than the people in the nineteenth century believed him to be; his achievements are also more highly valued.

The famous British novelist Virginia Wolfe once observed about Walpole: "Somehow he was not only the wittiest of men, but the most observant and not the least kindly; and among the writers of English prose he wears forever and with a peculiar grace a [crown] of his own earning."

For More Information

Boatner, Mark M., III. "Walpole, Horatio or Horace." *Encyclopedia of the American Revolution.* Mechanicsburg, PA: Stackpole Books, 1994, pp. 1160-61.

Kallich, Martin. *Horace Walpole.* New York: Twayne Publishers, Inc., 1971.

Ketton-Creme, R. W. *Horace Walpole: A Biography.* Ithaca, NY: Cornell University Press, 1964.

Knollenberg, Bernhard. "Walpole: Pro-American." *Horace Walpole: Writer, Politician, and Connoisseur.* New Haven, CT: Yale University Press, 1967, pp. 85-90.

Walpole, Horace. *Selected Letters of Horace Walpole.* Introduction by W. S. Lewis. New Haven, CT: Yale University Press, 1973, pp. xi-xix.

Web Sites

"Horace Walpole." Richmond Upon Thames Local Studies Collection. [Online] Available http:www.richmond.gov.uk/leisure/libraries/wal.html (accessed on 10/13/99).

Mercy Otis Warren

Born September 25, 1728
Barnstable, Massachusetts
Died October 13, 1814
Plymouth, Massachusetts

Playwright, historian

"I look with rapture at the distant dawn, And view the glories of the opening morn; When justice holds his sceptre o'er the land, and rescues freedom from a tyrant's hand."

Portrait: Mercy Otis Warren. *Reproduced by permission of Archive Photos, Inc.*

Mercy Otis Warren produced both prose and poetry while running a home and parenting five sons. She wrote plays making fun of Americans who stayed loyal to Great Britain during the American Revolution (1775–83), as well as patriotic poems and a history of the Revolution. This intelligent woman also exchanged letters and engaged in political discussions with such well-known patriots of her day as **Samuel Adams, John Adams,** and **Abigail Adams** (see entries).

Mercy Otis Warren was the daughter of James Otis, a farmer, merchant, and politician, and Mary Allyne Otis, a descendent of the Pilgrims. The Otises, who lived in Barnstable, Massachusetts, had thirteen children in their strict but loving home. Six of them died before reaching adulthood.

Warren's mother helped her servants with milking cows, building fires, cooking meals, making clothes, washing, and producing household items. Because her mother was so often tired, pregnant, or recovering from childbirth, Warren took on many of the family chores at a young age. But her heart was in reading and studying. The Otises stressed the importance of education and received many newspapers.

Their home served as a center for patriotic discussions in which their children were welcomed to participate.

Warren was very close to her favorite brother, James Otis, three years her senior. In 1743 he left home to attend what is now Harvard University in Cambridge, Massachusetts. James shared with his sister many of the ideas he learned there. With his encouragement, Mercy Warren read books of philosophy, literature, history, and religion.

Marriage and children

James Otis opened a law office in Plymouth, Massachusetts, in 1748, while also working for his father's import business. He later became one of the leaders of the American revolutionary movement. It is likely that Otis introduced his sister Mercy to his friend, James Warren, the son of a well-known Plymouth lawyer. In 1754, when Mercy Otis was age twenty-six, she and James Warren began their long and happy marriage. Her husband would become a successful businessman, lawyer, and politician.

In 1757 Warren gave birth to the couple's first son; between 1759 and 1767 four more followed. During the late 1750s and 1760s, most of Warren's time and attention was spent raising her children. Warren believed women needed to be educated in order to help their children become good citizens. Although Warren enjoyed her intellectual pursuits, she believed that a woman should put her domestic and wifely duties ahead of any pastimes. She squeezed her reading and writing into periods throughout the day when she had no immediate chores.

Colonists protest taxes

Like many of the colonists, over time Warren moved from supporting Great Britain to opposing what she believed was the mother country's unfair policies of rule and taxation. Warren's brother James was one of those who led the protests against the Stamp Act of 1765, which he saw as a move by Great Britain to tax the colonists against their will so the British government could raise money to pay off its war debts. The Stamp Act forced the colonists to buy specially stamped paper for legal documents; documents written on any other paper were not considered legal. At that stage, neither of the Warrens was in favor of a violent revolution by Americans.

In time the British government withdrew the Stamp Act because the colonists had reacted against it so strongly. However, the British government was not deterred, and in 1767 Parliament passed the Townshend Acts. With the Townshend Acts in place, England could tax the colonists for imported paper, lead, glass, paint, and tea. Eventually protests by the colonists succeeded in getting all the taxes lifted except the tax on tea, an item that was widely used in America.

The tragic life of James Otis

James Otis, who corresponded frequently with his sister, became physically and emotionally ill in the late 1760s, and by the early 1770s he was no longer able to remain active in Massachusetts politics. British historian Catharine Macauley had written to James Otis in 1768 to support his defense of colonial rights. Warren wrote back, explaining to Macauley that, because of his poor health, James was no longer able to write. A correspondence began between the two women, and Macauley provided Warren with a female role model. Warren soon started writing poems and plays that ridiculed the pro-British men who held public office and she encouraged American patriots to continue their fight for American rights.

The Tea Act inspires a poem

In the early 1770s Great Britain passed the Tea Act, which permitted the British East India Company to sell its tea at a deep discount in America, but it also charged taxes on the tea. Angry at the Tea Act, colonists joined together to protest ships carrying English tea landing on American shores. Patriot leaders feared that Americans might be tempted by the cheap tea and would give up their opposition to British taxation policies that they considered unfair. The fear was unfounded; cut-price tea could not lure Americans away from their quest for independence.

In late 1773 three British ships bearing tea landed in Boston Harbor. A group of American patriots stationed themselves at the dock to prevent the tea from being unloaded. On December 16, members of Samuel Adams's patriotic group the Sons of Liberty disguised themselves as Native Americans, boarded the three anchored British ships, and threw about 340

John Adams Attacks Mercy Otis Warren's *History*

Many historians believe that Mercy Otis Warren's description of John Adams in her *History* was fair and perceptive, but her old friend was unhappy with the portrayal. Beginning in July 1807, he sent Warren a series of letters in which he called the work fiction and insulted her family. His letters became angrier and crueler.

Warren wrote several letters in response, expressing her shock, hurt, and anger at his opinions. She reminded him that the book described him as being an upstanding citizen and complimented his genius and integrity. But she had challenged some of his political opinions. She observed that he had "pride of talents and much ambition" and that in his later years he may have "forgotten the principles of the American Revolution" and "discovered a partiality in favor of" governments ruled by royalty.

Adams's attacks grew more intense with each letter. At one point Warren replied: "Though I am fatigued [tired out] with your repetition of abuse, I am not intimidated," and she continued to defend herself. Unfortunately, Adams saw Warren's criticisms as a personal betrayal because he had encouraged her to write such a history. Many of the friends they shared believed that Warren had written as objectively as possible and that Adams's complaints lacked merit. In time Adams's anger cooled down somewhat, but their relationship never returned to its former closeness.

crates of tea into Boston Harbor. In her later writings about the American Revolution, Warren noted that "The American war may be dated from the hostile parade of this day," when the tea was thrown into the harbor.

Future president John Adams wrote to the Warrens and encouraged Mercy to write about the Boston Tea Party. Warren's 1774 poem hailed the promise of her new nation and encouraged American women to refuse to buy any products that were imported, including jewelry, lace, fabrics, ribbons, and especially tea.

Warren home center of patriotic activity

In the early 1770s the Warrens became firm supporters of the American cause. Mercy Warren was a witness to the

In many of her plays, Mercy Otis Warren made fun of Americans who stayed loyal to Great Britain during the American Revolution. *Reproduced courtesy of the Library of Congress.*

protests planned by the patriots against the royal government. According to Warren's diaries, the patriotic organization called the Committee of Correspondence was founded at her house in 1772. This letter-writing network joined towns and villages throughout the colonies in an effort to further the cause of colonial rights.

In 1776, after the United States declared its independence from Great Britain, James Warren was made Second Major General of the Massachusetts militia (an army made up of citizens rather than professional soldiers). In 1777, he became a member of a three-man group that purchased supplies and helped organize the American navy. As a result of his involvement in the war effort, James Warren was forced to neglect family affairs.

Mercy Warren missed her husband terribly when he was gone and she managed the family's business affairs on her own. Fortunately, she received constant moral support from the wives of fellow patriots, including Abigail Adams and Martha Washington. Like many women of her time, Warren traveled about Massachusetts to visit her husband while he served in the military.

Warren's writing career

Shortly after her marriage in 1754, Warren had begun her writing career with poems. In some of them, she complained about the frequent separations that took place when her husband was engaged in the "endless strife" of politics. At the time that Warren wrote, women were generally shut out of politics. They were not allowed to vote and were not welcomed into political discussions. Throughout her lifetime Warren experienced a tension between her desire to write and share her opinions and the need to remain a proper lady.

Warren's male relatives were very supportive of her opinions as an educated woman. Other male patriots encouraged her in her writings because they felt her outstanding ability with words could be used to further the patriotic cause. But that did not mean they necessarily believed in equality for women. Patriots Samuel Adams, John Adams, and Abigail Adams were frequent visitors at the Warren home, and Mercy Warren established a lifelong friendship with Abigail Adams. Both women participated in discussions with the male patriots in which their opinions were both solicited and respected.

Writes patriotic plays

Warren wrote plays to actively promote the revolutionary cause. In them she ridiculed the Loyalists, American colonists who stayed loyal to Great Britain. During the mid- to late-eighteenth century, many Americans thought it was not respectable to attend plays, and even though she authored many plays, Warren never attended a play during her lifetime. It was not until years later that the public presentation of plays became acceptable. Many of the characters in Warren's plays were obviously based on patriots of the period, including her own husband, and they were portrayed as mythical figures of ancient stories.

In Warren's first play, *The Adulateur,* written in 1773, she warned her fellow citizens that they might soon have to take up arms to defend their liberty. Warren's second play, *The Defeat,* also written in 1773, poked fun at greedy men who turned against their countrymen for personal gain.

Warren's finest piece of work may have been her play *The Group,* a comedy written in 1775. The play featured Loyalists who sat around playing cards, drinking, and stating their opinions in ways that made the patriots who read it laugh loudly. The play convinced some of the people of Boston to take part in active resistance against Great Britain.

As for politics, Warren viewed the much-discussed proposed Constitution of the United States to be an evil plot to replace individual rights by the rule of the wealthy, whose concerns were far removed from those of the common people. Some of Warren's poems from 1779 and 1780 reflect her fear that people were no longer being motivated by patriotism but by the desire to accumulate goods.

The Warrens' lives after the revolution

James Warren returned home after the Americans defeated the British in the Revolutionary War (1775–83). He served as Speaker of the Massachusetts House of Representatives in 1787 but was defeated in his bid to become lieutenant (pronounced lew-TEN-uhnt) governor and retired to his home to manage his farm.

In the decade following the American Revolution, Warren faced the mental breakdown of her college-age son and her own health problems, including exhaustion, depression, and bad headaches. She took comfort in the beauty of her family's large, tree-shaded house in Plymouth, Massachusetts, where she lived for the rest of her life.

Loss and its aftermath; later writings

Three of Mercy and James Warren's sons died during the couple's lifetime. Woodrow, an adventurer, was killed in an Indian ambush, and Charles and George died of illnesses. The oldest Warren son, James, became a teacher and postmaster and helped his mother complete research for a book she wrote on the history of the American Revolution. Another son, Henry, became a farmer. Warren and her sons remained close as they grew older and wrote frequently when they were apart. Sadly, Mercy Warren's troubled brother James died in 1783 after being struck by lightning.

In 1780 Warren had begun publishing pamphlets, short booklets on political subjects. In her 1788 pamphlet entitled *Observations on the New Constitution and on the Federal and State Conventions,* she stated her opposition to the new Constitution of the United States because of its lack of a bill of rights.

At that time a public debate was raging over the issue. While some patriots, such as John Adams and **Alexander Hamilton** (see entry), were in favor of a strong central government, others like the Warrens wanted a weaker central government. They believed a bill of rights would protect the weaker from the more powerful. In time the Bill of Rights was added to the Constitution.

Final plays

In 1790 Warren published all of her poems along with two early plays under her own name. Revolutionary-era patriots had usually published their works without author names or using pen names (made-up names) that protected their identities from revenge by the pro-British. With her name now appearing on her writings for the first time, Warren received public praise for her work from such people as **George Washington**, the Adamses, and **Thomas Jefferson**, among others (see entries). John Adams later came to criticize her when their political ideas differed (see box).

Also, in 1790 Warren wrote *The Ladies of Castile,* which contained a pro-revolutionary message. The play focused on the uprising of a group of people in Spain, and in it Warren featured women characters for the first time.

Warren's historical play, *The Sack of Rome* appeared the next year. It portrayed the invasion of the city of Rome by a destructive enemy tribe in ancient times. The play contained vigorous language and violent action. By then, Massachusetts society had begun to attend plays. Warren hoped to see her plays performed on stage, but they never were.

Writes history of the revolution

Warren's three-volume work, *The History of the Rise, Progress and Termination of the American Revolution,* written over many years, was published in installments (one chapter at a time) in 1805. The book covered American history from the Stamp Act of 1765 to the end of the eighteenth century. It provided an eyewitness account of the political, military, and economic events that took place both in America and abroad.

Warren's *History* described British policies and American responses to them; the process that led Americans to seek independence from Great Britain; the difficult progress of the war and the victory of the Continental (American) army at Yorktown, Pennsylvania; the process of the writing of major American documents, including the U.S. Constitution; and offered a look at the presidencies of George Washington and John Adams. A major purpose of the book was to remind new generations of the importance of liberty and the type of government in which the supreme power rests with all the people entitled to vote.

Warren's manuscript may have sat on the shelf unread were it not for the efforts of a Protestant minister who arranged to have it published in 1805. By that time Warren was nearly blind, and her son James had to help her edit the book.

Most of the factual information in her history was correct, and she even used footnotes, a rarity at that time. However, the work caused a serious rift in her friendship with former President John Adams, who felt it treated him unfairly (see box).

Warren's final years

Warren's son Henry had married in 1781, and she enjoyed the years of the early 1800s being a grandmother to his eight children. As time passed, she grieved the loss of many friends and her husband James, who died in 1808, after fifty-four years of marriage.

Mercy Otis Warren fell ill and died on October 13, 1814, at age eighty-six. She was a woman who had learned to live within the established roles granted to women of the eighteenth century, yet she indirectly challenged them through her writings. She had found a way to combine her writing talent and political beliefs to become the first female historian of America.

For More Information

Anthony, Katharine. *First Lady of the Revolution.* Garden City, NY: Doubleday, 1958.

Brown, Alice. *Mercy Warren.* New York: Scribners, 1896, reprint, Spartanburg, SC: Reprint Co., 1968.

Fritz, Jean. *Cast for a Revolution: Some American Friends and Enemies 1728–1814.* Boston: Houghton Mifflin, 1972.

Laska, Vera O. *Remember the Ladies: Outstanding Women of the American Revolution: A Commonwealth of Massachusetts Bicentennial Commission Publication.* Boston: Thomas Todd Publishers, 1976.

Levin, Phyllis Lee. *Abigail Adams.* New York: St. Martin's Press, 1987.

Meyer, Edith Patterson. *Petticoat Patriots of the American Revolution.* New York: The Vanguard Press, 1976.

Warren, Mercy Owen. *History of the Rise, Progress and Termination of the American Revolution.* 3 vols. Indianapolis. Reprinted by Liberty Fund, Inc., 1989.

Withey, Lynne. *Dearest Friend: A Life of Abigail Adams.* New York: The Free Press, 1981.

Zagarri, Rosemarie, Alan M. Kraut, and Jon L. Wakelyn, eds. *A Woman's Dilemma: Mercy Otis Warren and the American Revolution.* Wheeling, IL: Harlan Davidson, 1995.

George Washington

Born February 22, 1732
Pope's Creek Plantation, Virginia
Died December 14, 1799
Mount Vernon, Virginia

First president of the United States, military leader, farmer, surveyor

"I beg it may be remembered by every Gentleman in the room, that I this day declare with the utmost sincerity, I do not think myself equal to the Command I am honoured with."

Portrait: George Washington. *Reproduced by permission of AP/Wide World Photos.*

George Washington is one of the greatest soldier-statesmen the United States has ever produced. He led his country to victory in the American Revolution, helped draft the U.S. Constitution, served as first president of the new nation, and established a lasting reputation for honesty, heroism, dedication, and service.

George Washington was born at Pope Creek Plantation in northeastern Virginia on February 22, 1732. His parents were Augustine Washington and his second wife, Mary Ball. Washington had two older half-brothers, Lawrence and Augustine, and five younger brothers and sisters: Betty, Samuel, John Augustine, Charles, and Mildred (who died as a baby).

When Washington was three, his family moved to a farm called Little Hunting Creek, and then to Ferry Farm. Washington's boyhood included much time spent outside in the fields and woods, a love that stayed with him all his life.

Washington's father died when the boy was only eleven, and the family had to manage their money carefully. Like many farm boys of the time, it is likely that Washington was taught at home before he entered the small school in Fredericksburg, Virginia, which was across the river from Ferry Farm. This was the only formal education Washington ever had, and it was limited. He learned math, reading, history, and geography, but not foreign languages, literature, or the arts. His education reinforced Washington's natural inclination to be methodical and detail oriented. At the same time, he was learning to manage a plantation (a large farm) that produced tobacco, fruit, vegetables, and grain.

His older brother, Lawrence, encouraged George to read to fill in the blanks in his education. Washington did so throughout his life, researching and reading about every new situation he faced, from military tactics to politics to farming. "I conceive that a knowledge of books is the basis on which all other knowledge rests," he would later write to a friend. As a youth, Washington spent a great deal of time at his brother Lawrence's home, Little Hunting Creek, which would later be called Mount Vernon. His days there opened a new world to George, including foxhunting, theater, dancing, and the art of conversation. At Mount Vernon, George met and mingled with the families of upper-class Virginia plantation owners, learning to mimic their way of talking, dressing, and acting. Before Lawrence died in 1752, he arranged that eventually Mount Vernon would belong to George.

When he was about fifteen, Washington's school days ended. He took a job as a surveyor, a person who measured land plots so they could be sold, to help support his mother and younger brothers and sisters. In 1748 Washington's work as a surveyor took him into western Virginia, near what was then the American frontier. In 1749 the young Washington was appointed surveyor for Culpeper County in Virginia. This position gave him a steady income and a chance to purchase land. Eventually these purchases would make Washington one of the largest landowners in all of Virginia.

Washington's journeys and his brother Lawrence's war stories (he had served in a British unit in a brief war against the French) made the young Washington think about a military career. In colonial America, the British military protected the people in the more populated areas while American-born officers and soldiers called militia helped guard farms and communities on the edge of the frontier. Washington decided that he would apply to the governor of Virginia for a militia command, and in 1752 he was appointed a major of an American regiment in southern Virginia.

In the fall of 1753, when the governor needed a volunteer to carry a message to the French in Ohio, Washington volunteered. The governor wanted French soldiers to remove themselves from the Ohio River Valley, which he considered to be part of Virginia. After a difficult trip, Washington delivered the message. When the French commander refused to leave, Washington carried this news back to Virginia. Upon Washington's recommendation, Fort Prince George was built at what is now Pittsburgh, Pennsylvania, a signal to the French that the Americans would not give up this rich fur-trading territory.

French and Indian War

After this mission, Washington was promoted to lieutenant colonel and he set about recruiting men to man Fort Prince George. He learned that American soldiers were not paid as much as British soldiers, his first taste of the inequity that would continue to trouble the Americans. The fort fell to the French in the spring of 1754, and they renamed it Fort Duquesne (pronounced doo-KANE). Washington's men built another, named Fort Necessity, which was lost to the stronger French force in July 1754. Washington's engagement with the French was the first skirmish in what became the French and Indian War (1756–63).

Neither the British military nor the American colonial government held Washington's lack of success against him. Instead, they praised his fearlessness in battle and his good leadership style. However, Washington resigned from the militia when he learned that his rank would be reduced so that British officers could always have a higher rank than the colonial officers.

Washington had another chance to learn about military life and the conduct of war. He volunteered to be an aide to General Edward Braddock, who had come from England to fight the French. Braddock, who might have learned something from Washington, chose to disregard the advice of this soldier who had fought the Indians on their home ground. Braddock and most of his soldiers were wiped out in an assault in 1755 on Fort

Washington inherited the Virginia estate Mount Vernon in 1761 and retired there in 1796 to live the remaining years of his life.
Reproduced by permission of the Detroit Photographic Company.

Duquesne (it was rebuilt as Fort Pitt after the French burned it in 1758). Washington brought the surviving men to Virginia. By the time he retired from the French and Indian War, Washington was the American colonies' first real hero. He was also the American most acquainted with soldiering.

Life as a Virginia planter

Washington hung up his sword and settled down to run Mount Vernon, which he inherited in 1761. At the age of twenty-seven, he married a pretty widow named Martha Dandridge Custis. Martha had two children, John "Jackie" Custis and Martha "Patsy" Custis. Washington's main focus for the next fourteen years was on being a loving husband and stepfather, a farmer who experimented with crops and raising animals, a local judge, and a member of the House of Burgesses (the local Virginia government, which met in Williamsburg, Virginia).

As a member of colonial government, Washington grew familiar with the democratic process first hand. He also met and grew to know many of the men who would lead the American Revolution, including **Thomas Jefferson** and **Patrick Henry** (see entries).

Trouble with Britain

At the end of the French and Indian War in 1763, Great Britain won huge tracts of land in Canada and the United States. Now burdened with heavy war debts, the British thought it only fair to tax the Americans to help pay for managing the new lands. Unfortunately, the tax laws were passed in London, where the British government met. The Americans were not consulted and they bitterly resented this.

By this time, the thirty-one-year-old Washington was an imposing figure. His uniforms were tailored to fit a man who was six feet, three inches tall, and who weighed about 200 pounds. His hair was dark brown, his eyes light blue-gray. He walked with the grace of a natural outdoorsman and rider. He carried himself with dignity and authority, as was proper for a wealthy landowner, political leader, and military commander. Although his many portraits show a man of thoughtful, even stern expression, his friends knew that Washington could unbend in company and enjoyed a good laugh.

Washington was one of the first colonials to suggest that the Americans resist British taxes. He proposed boycotting (not buying) British goods. His idea grew in popularity until the British governor of Virginia decided it was time to punish the leaders of the tax rebellion. In 1769 the House of Burgesses was closed, and the legislators were told to go home.

Instead, Washington began meeting with some of his friends in a Williamsburg tavern. The Americans' need to make decisions on their own would result in the creation of another, larger governmental body, called the Continental Congress. In April 1775, the tense situation came to a head when the British marched on Concord, Massachusetts, to seize American war supplies stored there. This was the first battle of the American Revolutionary War. At the Second Continental Congress in June 1775, Washington began attending sessions in his Virginia militia uniform to show that he was ready to take military action against the British.

Accepts generalship of American army

After the battle at Concord, the American soldiers pursued the fleeing British all the way back to their Boston headquarters and surrounded the city. The Second Continental Congress asked the colonies' best known soldier, George Washington, to take charge of the American forces. On June 16, Washington accepted the position of commander-in-chief of the Continental army. It was a job that would last through eight years of war, through the British surrender at Yorktown, Virginia, in 1781, and the Treaty of Paris ending the war in 1783.

Washington had the right characteristics to make him a successful leader of the rebelling American colonies. As an experienced soldier, he was not afraid to take up arms to defend his rights. As the foremost colonial soldier, he saw it as his responsibility to teach his officers the art of war and how to conduct themselves as gentlemen. Realizing that his formal education was inadequate, he was open to other sources of information in new situations. For instance, during the bitter winter encampment at Valley Forge, Pennsylvania, in 1777–78, Washington welcomed Baron Frederick von Steuben, a professional Prussian (German) officer who drilled the American army into a skilled fighting unit. With von Steuben's help, Washington completed the work he had begun outside Boston, when he worked to shape the individual state militia units into a single Continental army. Washington also became close friends with the **Marquis de Lafayette** (see entry), a young French aristocrat who joined Washington's staff early in the war. Washington was also a wonderful organizer, and could make the most of limited resources.

Most historians agree that Washington's real genius was in fighting a defensive rather than an offensive war. That is, Washington did not wage a fierce campaign to wipe out the British army (which he knew he could not do with his smaller, ill-equipped army). Instead, he kept the British generals from cornering, capturing, and defeating his army. He camped around Boston to force the British retreat from there in March 1776, thereby keeping hope of an American victory alive. He then anticipated the British move to New York, and moved the American army there to tie up the British forces. When the British marched on Philadelphia, Pennsylvania, in September 1777, they found the Continental army blocking their path at

While Washington Was President

George Washington served as President of the United States for two terms, 1789 to 1796. His presidency was a time of great political, geographical, financial, and social change. Among the events that occurred or began during Washington's terms were:

1789

- George Washington elected first President of United States of America
- The French Revolution begins
- North Carolina admitted to the Union
- Postmaster General named, and a national postal system is established
- U.S. Supreme Court begins its first session

1790

- First U.S. Census conducted (population is approximately 4 million people)
- Rhode Island admitted to the Union

1791

- Bill of Rights, the first 10 amendments to the U.S. Constitution, adopted
- Vermont admitted to the Union
- Congress charters the First National Bank
- Site on the Potomac River selected for national capital

1792

- George Washington elected to a second term as President
- Kentucky admitted to the Union
- New York Stock exchange opened
- Political parties established in the United States
- U.S. Mint opened in Philadelphia, and a standard system of coinage was adopted
- Washington exercised the first presidential veto, showing how the balance of power works among the three branches of government

1793

- Eli Whitney invented the cotton gin (short for "engine"), making cotton a more profitable cash crop for the American South
- Washington refused to side with France in its war with Britain (Neutrality Proclamation)
- First official Cabinet Meeting showed the president could be open to advice
- Fugitive Slave Act passed, allowing owners to hunt down escaped slaves across state boundaries

1794

- Whiskey Rebellion put down, first test of the new federal government and its army
- Ohio Valley opened for settlement by white pioneers following defeat of Indians at Fallen Timbers
- Jay's Treaty settled the question of commerce with Great Britain

1795

- First major turnpike completed, linking Philadelphia with Lancaster, Pennsylvania

1796

- Tennessee admitted to the Union

Brandywine Creek. Washington did not always win his encounters with the British, but he did make sure that the British paid heavily in men and equipment for any gain they made.

Eventually, Washington moved his small army southward to Virginia, met up with General Lafayette's army, and confronted the British at Yorktown, Pennsylvania. With their backs to the sea, the British found that their navy could not rescue them. America's French allies and their twenty-four battleships had blocked the British access to the shore. On October 19, 1781, British General Lord Charles Cornwallis surrendered his army of more than 7,000 men to Washington, effectively ending the American Revolutionary War. For the next two years, Washington held his small army together until a peace treaty was signed. When Congress was slow to pay the American soldiers, one of Washington's officers suggested he become king and take over the new American nation. Washington reacted quickly and harshly, once and for all saying that America would be a democracy, not a monarchy.

Then in 1783, word came that the Treaty of Paris had been signed. Britain had publicly declared its loss of the American colonies. "Having now finished the work assigned me, I retire from the great theater of action, and bidding an affectionate farewell to this August [honored] body, under whose orders I have so long acted, I here offer my commission, and take leave of all the employment of public life," he said to the Continental Congress. Then, at the age of fifty-one, Washington said good-bye to his officers and once again returned home to run his plantation.

Retires; recalled to Constitutional Convention

Washington seemed content to retire from public life and concentrate on being a gentleman farmer at Mount Vernon. He experimented with breeding mules, hunted foxes, entertained his plantation friends, and wrote letters to many of the leaders of the new nation.

Before long, it became clear that the new nation would again need Washington's leadership. The Articles of Confederation, the document that held the states together during the Revolutionary War, was failing to hold the country together after it. In May 1787 Washington became one of the delegates to the Constitutional Convention in Philadelphia. The goal of the meeting was to draft a new document with rules for how the national government was to be run. The delegates unanimously elected Washington president of this convention.

By that summer, a new U.S. Constitution was drawn up and sent to the states for ratification (approval). It called for election of a president by the people, and provided for a method of making and changing laws through bills passed in a Congress that had two parts (the Senate and the House of Representatives). The Constitution also made sure there was a balance of power in government by having three branches with equal power, the presidency (executive branch), the Congress (legislative branch), and the Supreme Court (judicial branch). During the debate, Washington argued for the need for a strong federal government and suggested a larger House of Representatives, so more people could be involved in passing laws. By July 1788, the Constitution had been ratified, and a presidential election was held.

Elected first President of the United States

Not surprisingly, Washington was Congress's choice as first president of the United States of America (today, everyone votes in presidential elections). Washington took the oath of office on April 30, 1789, at Federal Hall in New York City, then the capital of the United States.

Washington's presidency was an uncharted course. "I walk, as it were, on untrodden ground," he said. Everything he did was without precedent (a previous example), and he could to a large extent define his job. He did so with deliberation and thoughtfulness, the way he approached every task in his life. "We are a young Nation, and have a character [reputation] to establish. It behooves us [we should] therefore to set out right for the first impressions will be lasting, indeed are all in all."

Washington tackled four major problems during his first term of office: 1) organizing the new government, 2) improving its relations with Great Britain, 3) getting its finances in order, and 4) making peace with the Indians, so westward expansion of the country could continue.

To help him organize the government, Washington quickly named a group of advisors that would become the first cabinet and included leaders such as **Alexander Hamilton** (see entry) as secretary of the treasury and General Henry Knox as secretary of war. Washington's goal was to stay out of the constant European wars, although this proved difficult because of the aid France had given America during the Revolutionary War. Under Washington, however, the United States did maintain neutrality (not taking sides) and this helped improve relations with Great Britain. Washington knew that the country could not grow financially until it had settled its war debts, so the federal government took on the debts the states had incurred during the war. He also encouraged establishment of a national bank and common system of money. And he tried to make peace with the Indians on the western frontier (Pennsylvania and Ohio). This was done first through trade treaties and later through the Indians' final defeat in fighting at Fallen Timbers near Toledo, Ohio, in 1794. At the end of his four-year term, Washington again believed his public service to be done and made plans to return home.

Reelected unanimously

Instead, Washington was reelected unanimously to a second term as president in 1792. In his second term of office, Washington encountered criticism, which hurt him deeply. He had given much of his life to defending and defining the new nation, and was unused to public criticism. But Washington had helped set up a nation in which public debate was encouraged, and differences of opinion were bound to flourish. One such difference arose between the Federalists (like Washington and Hamilton), who supported a strong federal government, and the Democratic-Republicans (or anti-Federalists, like Jefferson), who believed that the states should have more power in making decisions. This argument was the reason that political parties were formed. In fact, Washington was the only president who did not belong to a political party when elected.

Two highlights of Washington's second term dealt with presidential and governmental authority. In 1792 he used the first presidential veto to turn down a law proposed by Congress. Washington felt that the law would create more seats in government for the northern states. When the legislation was made more fair, Washington did sign it into law. In 1794 Washington demonstrated that the federal government was here to stay when he called up an army to defeat the Whiskey Rebellion in western Pennsylvania, where citizens were protesting the new federal tax on whiskey.

Washington once again set precedent in 1796, when he refused to accept a third term as president. After giving his famous "Farewell Address" in March 1797, Washington returned home to Mount Vernon and his life as a farmer.

Retires to Mount Vernon

Washington's last years were lived peacefully at Mount Vernon in the company of his wife and friends. While riding over his estate in December 1799, he caught cold during a snowstorm. The cold worsened into a throat infection and he became severely ill. At the age of sixty-seven, George Washington died at home on December 14, 1799, and was buried at Mount Vernon. One of his friends gave him this epitaph: "First in war, first in peace, and first in the hearts of his countrymen, he was second to none." Washington is also known as the "Father of the Country."

Today we see much evidence of Washington's impact on the United States. A state is named for him, as is the national capital, Washington, D.C. He has universities, towns, counties, and even a national holiday named after him. The Washington monument on the Potomac River is the tallest all-stone structure in the world. Washington's face is also pictured on the dollar bill, the quarter, and numerous stamps.

For More Information

Chase, Philander D. "George Washington." *The American Revolution 1775-1783: An Encyclopedia.* Vol. II: M-Z. Edited by Richard L. Blanco. New York: Garland Publishing, 1993, pp. 1733-49.

Fleming, Thomas. "The World Turned Upside Down: The American Revolution, Fighting for Independence, Pt. 3." *Boys' Life,* December 1997, pp. 22-26.

Meltzer, Milton. *George Washington and the Birth of Our Nation.* New York: Franklin Watts, 1986.

Wayne, Bennett, ed. "George Washington: Father of Freedom." *The Founding Fathers.* Champaign, IL: Garrard Publishing, 1975, pp. 57-103.

Whitney, David C., and Robin Vaughn Whitney. "George Washington: The First President of the United States." *The American Presidents.* 8th ed. Pleasantville, NY: Reader's Digest Association, 1996, pp. 1-16.

Phillis Wheatley

Born c. 1753
West Africa
Died December 5, 1784
Boston, Massachusetts

Slave, poet

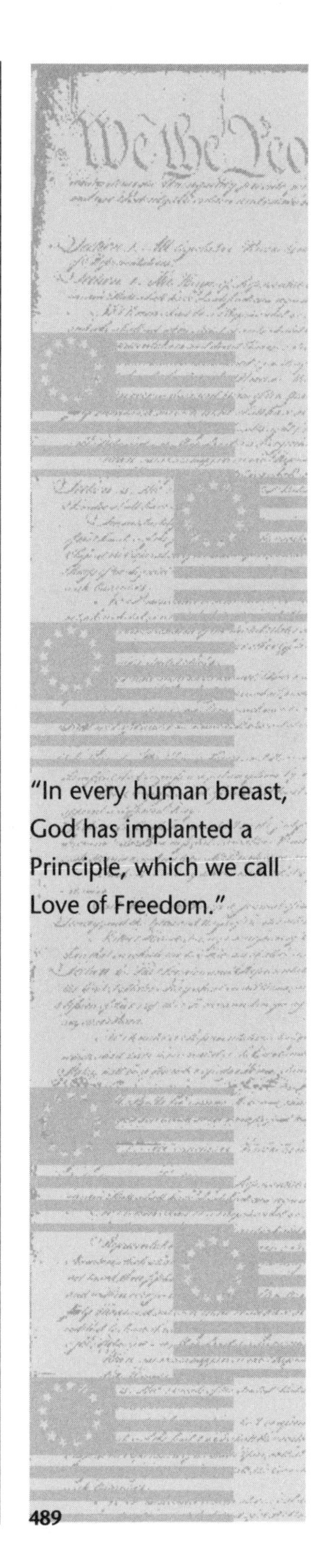

"In every human breast, God has implanted a Principle, which we call Love of Freedom."

Phillis Wheatley, who spent her childhood as a slave, has been called the "Mother of Black Literature." The young girl became a sensation in Boston in the 1760s when her well-crafted poems made her famous. Wheatley's writing abilities and intelligence were an impressive example to English and American audiences of how a person can triumph over the circumstances of oppression.

In the mid-eighteenth century, slave trading played a large role in America's economy. Ships would leave the American East Coast for the West Indies in the Caribbean Sea with products to trade there for rum. They then traveled on to Africa, where they traded the rum for men, women, and children, who were transported back to America to be sold as slaves. During the trip across the seas from Africa, people were jammed together in unsanitary conditions, and many died from sickness or starvation. Young Phillis was kidnapped from West Africa and brought across the Atlantic Ocean on the slave ship *Phillis,* which landed in Massachusetts's Boston Harbor on July 11, 1761.

Phillis Wheatley wrote her first poems at about age thirteen. Many of her early works were tributes written in praise of someone who had died. *Reproduced courtesy of the Library of Congress.*

Sold as a slave; becomes educated

After the *Phillis* arrived in Boston in 1761, the captain placed a notice in the newspaper that he had slaves for sale. Susanna Wheatley, the wife of John Wheatley, a wealthy Boston tailor, went aboard the *Phillis* to find a young girl to serve as her personal servant. A thin child with attractive features aroused her sympathy, and Susanna was able to purchase the young girl for a small sum from the captain. The captain was eager to sell Phillis, as he was afraid the thin child might die soon and he would lose his investment in her.

The Wheatleys lived with their twin children, Mary and Nathaniel, in a house with many slaves. They named the new slave Phillis after the ship on which she had sailed from Africa. Because of her size, and the fact that she was losing her front teeth, the Wheatleys thought Phillis to be about seven years of age. In time her health improved, but she remained a small and delicate person who suffered from the breathing ailment asthma for the rest of her life.

Young Phillis proved to be very intelligent, and Susanna Wheatley allowed her time off from her chores to be given lessons by the Wheatley's teenage daughter, Mary. Unlike the other slaves, Phillis was permitted to eat most of her meals with the family, except when they had company. After learning to read and write, she went on to study astronomy, ancient and modern geography, and ancient history, as well as English literature, Latin, the Bible, and poetry.

Phillis's dearest friend was a young woman named Obour Tanner, who lived in Newport, Rhode Island, as the slave of James Tanner. The two young women probably met when the Wheatleys visited in Newport. Though the two young women rarely saw one another, they sent letters back and forth for many years.

Early poems

Phillis wrote her first poems at about age thirteen. In the poem *On Being Brought from Africa to America,* she challenged members of white society who saw African people as less than human. Many of Phillis's early poems were tributes, written in praise of the achievements and character of someone who had died. Her poem *On the Death of the Rev. Dr. Sewell when Sick, 1765* was widely read in New England.

During the 1700s, many in New England spoke of the evils of slavery, and in May 1766, several citizens of Boston requested that slavery be completely done away with. But the lawmakers took no action. Phillis herself seldom wrote about the issue of slavery.

One of Phillis's most famous poems, *To the University of Cambridge,* was written in 1767. The poem addressed the students of what is now Harvard University in Cambridge, Massachusetts. Phillis had learned that the students, who had a reputation for being loud and unruly, were protesting because they had been served stale butter. Phillis, with the disadvantages of being black, a slave, and female, could only imagine what it would be like to receive a fine education. She thought it silly that they would waste their energies worrying about something so minor as stale butter and encouraged them to be grateful for their opportunities:

> Students, to you 'tis given to scan the heights
> Above, ...
> And mark the systems of revolving worlds, ...
> Improve your privileges while they stay,
> Ye pupils, ...
> Let sin, that baneful evil to the soul,
> by you be shun'd ...
> An Ebonite [African] tells you 'tis your greatest foe.

Gains fame locally for her poetry

It was not long before it became fashionable for upper class Bostonians to invite "Mrs. Wheatley's Phillis" to come to their homes and read her poetry. It seems that Phillis was aware of her unusual status in colonial society, in which many people believed that whites were superior to non-whites and acted accordingly. When Phillis was invited to the homes of wealthy whites, she always refused the seat offered her at their dining tables and asked that a small, simple side-table be set for her to have dinner apart from the rest of the company.

Phillis did light chores around the Wheatley house, but could ignore them when she felt ready to write her poems. Unlike the other slaves, she was granted her own room with both heat and light. She was given paper and pencils to keep near her bed in case she awoke with ideas to jot down. Despite the special attention she received, Phillis managed to remain friendly with the other slaves.

When she was doing housework, Phillis paid attention to events going on around her. Once two gentlemen named Hussey and Coffin came to the Wheatley house and told a tale of how they had narrowly escaped being washed overboard on a sailboat during a storm on Cape Cod, Massachusetts. She remembered this story and incorporated it into a poem entitled *On Messrs. Hussey and Coffin.* Critics praised Phillis's poem about their adventure for its intensity of emotion, well-crafted images, and spirituality.

Poems become known internationally

In her 1768 poem *To the King's Most Excellent Majesty* Phillis praised King **George III** of England (see entry) for ending a tax called the Stamp Act of 1765, which was hated by the colonists. In 1770, Phillis wrote a poem in honor of a minister named George Whitefield who died from an asthma attack. Although Whitefield was a generous man who raised money to help homeless people, he had defended the practice of slavery using verses from the Bible. Still, Phillis had admired him.

In the mid-eighteenth century, it was customary to advertise poems for sale in the newspaper. The printing of Phillis's poem *On the Death of the Rev. Mr. George Whitefield, 1770* may have been paid for by Susanna Wheatley or the printer himself who thought it would sell. The poem was distributed throughout New England. Susanna sent a copy to Great Britain to the Countess of Huntington, a close friend of both her and the deceased clergyman. The countess arranged to have the poem published in London and Phillis soon gained an international reputation.

In 1771, Phillis's long-time tutor, Mary Wheatley, married John Lothrop, pastor of the Second Congregational Church of Boston. Mary left the Wheatley house to set up a new home with him. That same year, John Wheatley retired.

During the winter of 1772, Phillis was troubled with asthma and tuberculosis, a serious lung disease. Still, she and Susanna chose twenty-eight poems and had them advertised in a Boston newspaper. But not enough people ordered the book to pay for its being printed. Susanna had Phillis write to the Countess of Huntington and ask for her support in getting the book printed in London. The countess admired the poems and promised to see that they would be printed.

Travels to Great Britain

In 1773, the Wheatleys' doctor suggested that Phillis take a trip to London, thinking that the sea air would help her regain her health. Susanna Wheatley arranged for the trip. Plans were then underway for the British publication of Phillis's collected poems in a single volume. Susanna wrote to the Countess of Huntington in gratitude for allowing the young poet to dedicate the book to the countess. Before her departure, Phillis wrote the poem *Farewell to America,* in which she revealed her sorrow at leaving Susanna.

During Phillis's stay in Great Britain, she met many important people who were impressed with her conversational skills and writing talents. She was given presents and books by several royal admirers and was delighted to possess her very own books for the first time.

Phillis's poems appeared in popular magazines in America and in Great Britain. With the help of the Countess of Huntington, a volume of thirty-nine of Phillis's poems, entitled *Poems on Various Subjects, Religious and Moral,* was published in Great Britain in 1773. It featured the poems for which she is most honored and remembered. The book was favorably received by critics and readers alike and has been reprinted many times. That year also saw the printing in Boston of several of Phillis's other poems in praise of people who had died.

Shortly before Phillis was to have the honor of being presented to King George III of England, she learned that Susanna Wheatley was very ill. She immediately left for Boston, though she herself was still in poor health. She arrived there in October 1773. In March 1774, Susanna Wheatley died.

Slavery in the Americas

The shameful practice of slavery has existed in the world since ancient times. A slave is a person who functions as a servant to another and is considered a form of property. A slave can be bought or sold.

After their discovery of the New World in the fifteenth century, Europeans began kidnapping people from the coast of West Africa and sending them on ships to perform labor in North and South America. The process of acquiring Africans for the transatlantic slave trade was known as the Middle Passage. It included organizing the voyages to Europe and the Americas, capturing individuals from various African nations, building holding areas for the slaves, transporting them across the seas to the Americas, and distributing them there once they arrived.

An estimated 8 to 80 million Africans were enslaved and sent to work in the Americas from the sixteenth to the nineteenth centuries. Arriving at an accurate figure is impossible because of the inaccuracy of shipping records of that time. Most slaves were captured in West Africa or West Central Africa. The majority of those enslaved and transported to the Americas were males between the ages of fourteen and twenty-five, but the ships also carried a small percentage of women and children to America's shores.

In North America, although some slaves worked in towns or cities in the North and South, most lived on large farms in the southern part of the United States, where they toiled as servants and fieldworkers. How the slaves were treated depended largely on the type of work they did. House servants, such as Phillis Wheatley, generally had a much more comfortable existence than did the field slaves, who usually lived under terrible conditions. Slave families were often torn apart and children were separated from their parents and sold to the highest bidder.

Some historians believe that slavery was instituted in America by landowners because it was the only way to profitably raise large-scale crops on the vast areas of free, American land. Native Americans originally inhabited these open plots of land until the Europeans used force to seize the land from them. Because of the huge amounts of available and cheap land, most free laborers would not work for someone else when they could have their own land to work for themselves.

In the late eighteenth and early nineteenth centuries, European nations began to outlaw the slave trade. In the United States, the slaves were freed only after decades of political battles that ended in the bloody American Civil War (1861-65).

Phillis wrote to her friend Obour Tanner: "I was treated more like a child by her than her servant." She also informed Tanner that John Wheatley had granted her freedom from slavery shortly after her return from England.

Phillis made the acquaintance of some of the best known political figures of her time. When **George Washington** (see entry) was appointed head of the Continental army that fought to free America from Great Britain, Phillis sent the general a letter along with a poem she had written about him. The 1775 poem was entitled *To His Excellency General Washington.* A grateful Washington wrote back and invited her to come and visit his headquarters. In March 1776, Phillis made the trip to Cambridge, Massachusetts, to see him. It is interesting to note that during this same period, Washington continued to own black slaves.

Hard times begin

After Susanna's death, Phillis occasionally stayed at the Wheatley house and sometimes at the homes of Wheatley relatives. In 1778 John Wheatley died, leaving no money for Phillis in his will. Her friend and teacher, Mary Wheatley Lothrop, who died the same year, also failed to provide for her.

For the first time, Phillis had to find a way to take care of herself. With money tight and food scarce and expensive because of wartime shortages, she was unable to sell enough books to make ends meet. During the time of upheaval throughout the Revolutionary War (1775–83), she sewed for a living, earning just enough money to rent a little apartment.

Marries and has children

In 1778 in Philadelphia, Pennsylvania, Phillis married a young, free black man named John Peters, whom she had met some years before. Phillis's biographers have portrayed her husband in different ways. One painted him as a handsome, respectable grocery store owner, with good manners, who ran into trouble with his business. Another described him as an intelligent man, and good speaker. He and Wheatley soon fled from Boston, where the Revolution was raging, to the village of Wilmington, Massachusetts. They lived there in poverty for several years.

In 1778 Wheatley wrote a poem to honor the memory of an American general. In the poem, the young woman spoke about freedom for America and freedom for the African slaves who lived there. She questioned how Americans could long for their own freedom and, at the same time, "hold in bondage Afric[a]'s blameless race."

In 1779 Phillis Wheatley had hoped to put together a book of thirty-three poems and thirteen letters. She advertised for buyers in the newspapers of Boston. **Benjamin Franklin** (see entry) tried to help her get them published. But even with his help, hard times caused by the war prevented her from getting enough buyers.

According to most accounts, Wheatley had three children with John Peters, and all suffered from ill health. Her first child, a son, was born in June 1779. That same year Wheatley's family moved back to Boston. For a time John may have held a job sailing on a seagoing ship. The couple lived for a while with the niece of Susanna Wheatley, but finally ended up in a boarding house in the slums of Boston, Massachusetts, where Wheatley did chores to earn money for food.

Hard times for Phillis and her family

After the signing of the 1783 Treaty of Paris that ended the Revolutionary War, Phillis wrote the poem *Liberty and Peace,* in which she rejoiced in her country's independence. That April the last of John and Susanna's children, Nathaniel Wheatley, died; no mention was made of Phillis in the wealthy man's will. That same year Phillis gave birth to a little girl, but lost her son to a stomach ailment.

Although they were still in grief over the death of their son, the family tried to look to the future. John Peters decided to try running a business again, and opened a bookstore in Boston. Unfortunately, the business did not succeed, and Peters soon went broke. Unable to pay his debts, he ended up in prison. Phillis barely scraped by, taking in other people's laundry to support her family.

A tragic end

When relatives of the Wheatleys sought out Phillis in the fall of 1784, they found her living under horrible circumstances. By that time, two of Phillis's children were already dead. After observing the ailing Phillis and her dying third child in a filthy apartment, one of the Wheatley relatives wrote: "The woman who had stood honored and respected in the presence of the wise and good of that country which was hers by adoption ... was numbering the last hours of life in a state of [terrible] misery."

Phillis Wheatley and her last child died in Boston on December 5, 1784. She was only thirty-one years old. Several local newspapers reported her death, but the names of the friends and family who attended her funeral went unreported. At the time of her death, Phillis's husband was probably still in prison. The burial places of Phillis and her children are unknown.

Some time after the death of his wife, John Peters reportedly visited the daughter of the Wheatley relative who had cared for Phillis and her child just before their deaths. He demanded and received the unpublished manuscript of the second edition of Phillis's poetry. He was said to have already sold the books she had received as gifts during her trip to London. Peters eventually moved to the South. No one knows what happened to the second volume of Phillis's poetry; it was never found and never published.

For More Information

Mason, Julian D., Jr. *The Poems of Phillis Wheatley.* Chapel Hill: University of North Carolina Press, 1966.

Robinson, William H. *Phillis Wheatley and Her Writings.* New York: Garland, 1984.

Robinson, William H. *Phillis Wheatley in the Black American Beginnings.* Detroit: Broadside Press, 1975.

Sherrow, Victoria. *Phillis Wheatley.* Broomall, PA: Chelsea House Publishers, 1993.

Shields, John C., ed. *Phillis Wheatley: A Bio-Bibliography.* New York: Oxford University Press, 1988.

Weidt, Maryann N. *Revolutionary Poet: A Story about Phillis Wheatley.* Minneapolis: Carolrhoda Books, 1997.

Wheatley, Phillis. *Poems of Phillis Wheatley: A Native African and a Slave.* Bedford, MA: Applewood Books, 1995.

Web Sites

Liberty! Chronicle of the Revolution. Diversity. [Online] Available http://www.pbs.org/ktca/liberty/chronicle/diversity-phillisw.html (accessed on 4/5/99).

The Middle Passage. [Online] Available http://3mill.bitshop.com/middlePassage/mphome.htm (accessed on 4/5/99).

John Wilkes

Born October 17, 1725
London, England
Died December 26, 1797
London, England

Political leader, writer, publisher

"The government [of Great Britain] have sent the spirit of discord through the land, and I will prophesy, that it will never be extinguished, but by the extinction of their power."

Portrait: John Wilkes.
Reproduced courtesy of the Library of Congress.

John Wilkes was a London radical who favored revolutionary changes in England's political structure. His newspaper articles irritated King **George III** (see entry) and British lawmakers (Parliament) so much that he was several times expelled from his seat in Parliament. The public was outraged over this treatment, and the important question was raised—whether Parliament could ignore the will of voters. Wilkes became known as a champion of the common people and a crusader for freedom of the press and the reform of Parliament. American colonists made a hero out of him because of his support for the American Revolution (1775–83).

John Wilkes was the second son and one of five children born to Israel Wilkes, a London malt distiller (a maker of alcoholic beverages), and Sarah Heaton Wilkes. The distillery provided a good income, and Israel Wilkes was rich enough to afford his own coach, six horses, and a fine London home. He supported the official Church of England, but his wife was a dissenter, one who did not like the form of worship used by the official church and who opposed government-controlled religion. Israel Wilkes was a tolerant man who respected his wife's dissenting views. The couple frequently entertained educated people in their home.

Israel Wilkes had planned that his son John would get only a basic education in reading and writing, but he changed his mind when he saw how bright the boy was. John was then sent to be educated in the classics by a Presbyterian minister (the classics are the art and literature of ancient Greece and Rome). London had a large number of well-educated churchmen, and being tutored by one was a common first step before going on to a university. Wilkes's teacher emphasized the importance of expressing oneself freely, a lesson Wilkes took to heart.

In 1744 Wilkes went to Leyden University in Holland, where he met **Charles Townshend** (see entry) and other rich young Englishmen. During his two years abroad, Wilkes did not study very hard, but he took advantage of every opportunity to travel throughout Europe. He returned home with the reputation of an educated man. In 1749 Wilkes was elected a member of the Royal Society, an exclusive group of rich, educated men who met to discuss scientific and other topics; members also wrote and published papers.

Early marriage; unsavory habits

In 1749, at his father's urging, Wilkes married Mary Mead, heiress of a wealthy grocer; she was ten years older than he was. In 1750, Mary Wilkes gave birth to a daughter, Mary (called Polly). The couple separated soon after the child's birth, and Wilkes kept custody of the child (it was common in those days for fathers to control their children). It was arranged that Wilkes would receive enough of his wife's property to allow him to live comfortably without working. In 1758, Mary Wilkes had to go to court to stop her husband from pestering her for more money.

For several years after his separation from his wife, Wilkes associated with a rich crowd of lazy young men. He did little that was useful, instead indulging in frequent affairs with women, gambling, and playing mean tricks on both his friends and his enemies. Wilkes belonged to a secret organization called the Hell-Fire Club, whose members met occasionally in the ruins of an old church to perform Black Masses (they celebrated the devil in a mockery of the Roman Catholic mass). At one such mass, Wilkes terrified his companions by suddenly releasing a baboon disguised as the devil.

Wilkes is described by biographers as extremely unattractive, with an odd squint that gave him an evil appearance. However, he could be charming and witty, and he had a talent for writing. By 1757, he seemed to have grown bored with his life. He embarked on a path that embraced both journalism and politics. However, he did not do it in a quiet way.

Enters public life

In 1757 Wilkes was elected to Parliament from the district of Aylesbury where, thanks to his wife, he had possession of a large estate. In Parliament, he was a strong supporter of the politician **William Pitt** (see entry). He hoped that Pitt would use his influence to get him a position as ambassador to Constantinople (Turkey) or governor of Quebec (Canada). When neither position was forthcoming, Wilkes blamed Lord Bute (pronounced BOOT), another politician and the special favorite of King George III. He was so angry that he began to attack both Bute and King George in print.

Wilkes's nasty articles greatly offended the king and his advisers, but the public was delighted. In 1762 Wilkes and a friend founded their own newspaper, *The North Briton* (a Briton is a native of Great Britain). Wilkes now had a whole newspaper in which to attack and poke fun at King George and Lord Bute; he didn't stop with them, but made targets of old friends, other politicians, and even children he knew.

With the edition of the paper printed on April 23, 1763, Wilkes went too far. In an anonymous article, the king's advisers were attacked as "tools of despotism and corruption." (Despotism is rule by absolute power, not by law.) The article hinted that a peace treaty recently signed with France was dishonorable and dishonest, and the king knew it. As a result of Wilkes's article, the king became very angry.

Tossed into Tower of London

King George's secretary of state issued a warrant (a legal document) commanding that the authors, printers, and publishers of *The North Briton,* issue number 45, be arrested.

As a result, nearly fifty people were arrested and jailed, including John Wilkes. Wilkes protested that the warrant was illegal, because it did not mention any names. He also claimed that he had special privileges against being arrested, because he was a Member of Parliament. In spite of his protests, Wilkes was imprisoned in the Tower of London and charged with seditious libel. This was a very serious charge; libel is any written, printed, or pictorial statement that damages a person by attacking his good name or exposing him to ridicule, and sedition is conduct or language intended to incite rebellion against the authority of the state.

In prison, Wilkes was not allowed to speak to anyone. His house was thoroughly and messily searched, and even his personal papers were seized. At a court hearing, the judge ruled that as a Member of Parliament, Wilkes could not be arrested for libel and was let go. Wilkes was hailed as the hero of the common people of London. Some time later, Wilkes's success led to reforms that protected other people from similar treatment by the government.

Wilkes went back to attacking the king and his advisers in print. On November 16, 1763, Wilkes was shot in the stomach by a supporter of King George. The man had challenged Wilkes to a duel, a move that many people believed was a government plot to get rid of Wilkes. The following week, Parliament voted that a member could indeed be arrested for publishing seditious libel. Wilkes fled to Paris, France, rather than be arrested. While he was away, Parliament expelled him for having previously published an "obscene libel" entitled *Essay on Woman,* and Wilkes was declared an outlaw.

Exiled; returns to fight for free press

Wilkes had a fine time in Europe. After he recovered from his wound, he took a mistress and traveled through Italy. He began work on a book, *History of England,* which he never finished. His mistress deserted him and he returned to Paris, but he felt uncomfortable there. His lifestyle was costly, his daughter's education was expensive, his writing earned little money, and he was running out of funds.

In early 1768, Wilkes returned to London, hoping to restore his good name and his government position. He wrote to ask for the king's pardon but was ignored. Londoners had not forgotten him, however, and in March 1768, a huge majority elected him a Member of Parliament for the district of Middlesex. Wilkes was still considered an outlaw; after his election he surrendered and was imprisoned. A mob tried to rescue him as he went from court to jail, but he escaped the mob and returned to jail. From his cell he wrote a passionate letter to his supporters, who continued to surround the jail. By May 10, 1768, a crowd of 15,000 had gathered outside the prison, shouting "Wilkes and Liberty," "No Liberty, No King," and "Damn the King! Damn the Government! Damn the Justices!" ("Justice" is another word for judge). British soldiers tried to break up the mob, and seven people were killed.

Wilkes was sentenced to a jail term and a fine, and he was again expelled from Parliament. Elections for his Middlesex seat were held in February, March, and April 1769; each time Wilkes was re-elected, and each time, Parliament overturned the elections. Wilkes declared war on the government, publishing letters attacking the government for its unfair and illegal treatment of him and blaming them for what he called the "massacre" outside the jail.

In April 1770 Wilkes was released from prison. He was banned from Parliament, but he could still write articles for the newspapers. He continued to attack what he believed to be a corrupt government. (**Benjamin Franklin** [see entry], who was living in London as a representative of the American colonies, agreed with Wilkes that Parliament was corrupt). When Parliament tried to prevent London newspapers from publishing reports of government debates, Wilkes challenged the decision. Faced with the opposition of Wilkes and a huge crowd outside their doors, Parliament gave up their attempt to suppress the news. Wilkes had struck a blow for freedom of the press.

Darling of London mobs, American revolutionaries

In 1771 Wilkes was elected sheriff of London and Middlesex. In a time when Great Britain operated under a harsh system of treating prisoners, Wilkes courted popularity by stopping the practice of holding a prisoner in chains during the prisoner's trial. He passed a measure that forbade soldiers to attend executions. Witnessing executions was a form of entertainment in those days, and soldiers were stationed to keep the crowds in order. Without crowd control, the common people loved him; however, people high up in Parliament dismissed him as the darling of the mobs.

In 1774 Wilkes was elected Lord Mayor of London and a Member of Parliament from Middlesex. He was obviously a very popular man, and this time, no one opposed his taking his seat in Parliament. Wilkes was just in time to voice his opinion on the Intolerable Acts, the measures adopted by Parliament to punish the city of Boston, Massachusetts, for the Boston Tea Party.

For more than ten years, anger had been building in the American colonies over taxes and other measures imposed on them by Parliament. The matter reached a head with the dumping of 342 chests of British tea in Boston Harbor on December 16, 1773. Relations between England and America went downhill from there, and the first shots of the American Revolution rang out at Lexington and Concord, Massachusetts, on April 19, 1775. Just nine days before, John Wilkes had presented to King George a protest over British treatment of the colonies.

Throughout the American Revolution, Wilkes continued to speak out against his government's conduct, in the process becoming the man King George most disliked. At the same time, he pressed for "just and equal representation of the people of England in parliament." His protests came at a time when industrial cities in England were growing quickly but had fewer representatives in Parliament than older, smaller districts, whose representatives jealously guarded their power. It would be another fifty years before Wilkes's ideal of fair representation was realized. Wilkes's phrase "the rights of Englishmen" was adopted by American rebels as they pleaded

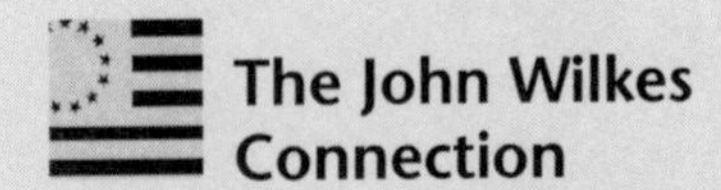

The John Wilkes Connection

Some interesting people are connected in one way or another to John Wilkes. Another British politician who lived at the same time as Wilkes, a man named Isaac Barré, also became famous in America as a champion of freedom. It was Barré who coined the term "sons of liberty" to describe the American rebels; the name was taken up by a radical group formed by **Samuel Adams** (see entry). Today, the town of Wilkes-Barre, Pennsylvania, pays homage to Wilkes and Barré.

John Wilkes's older brother Israel had a son, Charles Wilkes, who discovered Antarctica in 1840 and later became a hero during the American Civil War (1861–65). A distant relative of John Wilkes, John Wilkes Booth, will always be remembered as the man who assassinated President Abraham Lincoln in 1865.

their cause to King George and Parliament. To American patriots, Wilkes became a hero.

Gordon Riots

Wilkes was involved in another ugly mob incident in 1780 called the Gordon riots. English Catholics had been persecuted for hundreds of years, and beginning in 1778, some of the punishing laws against them were lifted. In 1780, Catholic-hating mobs reacted angrily to these changes in the laws. Wilkes played a courageous role in the event, reminding the mob of the authority of the law.

Wilkes kept his seat in Parliament until 1790. Wilkes was more interested in French and Italian literature and painting than in politics. He continued writing essays, translated some ancient poems from Latin, and wrote some of his own poetry, which he dedicated to his beloved daughter.

Last days

Wilkes divided his time during the last seven years of his life among his three homes, one on the Isle of Wight and two in London. He died nearly penniless in one of his London homes on the day after Christmas, 1797. He was buried in a London chapel with only a wall tablet to mark the burial spot. It read: "The Remains of John Wilkes, a friend to liberty." He left behind his daughter Mary, who died unmarried in 1802. He also had a son and a daughter by someone other than his wife.

Wilkes is summed up in *The Dictionary of National Biography* this way: "Wilkes had fine manners and an inexhaustible fund of wit and humour which made his society acceptable even to those who ... thoroughly distrusted him. In his vices he was by no means [unusual]; and his tender affection for his daughter and the constancy of his friendship ... are redeeming traits in his character."

For More Information

Boatner, Mark M., III. "Wilkes, John." *Encyclopedia of the American Revolution.* Mechanicsburg, PA: Stackpole Books, 1994, pp. 1203-05.

Churchhill, Winston S. *A History of the English-Speaking Peoples.* Volume 3: *The Age of Revolution.* New York: Dodd, Mead, 1983, pp. 163-99.

Web Sites

"Wilkes, John." [Online] Available http://www.spartacus.schoolnet.co.uk/PRwilkes.htm (accessed on October 13, 1999).

Index

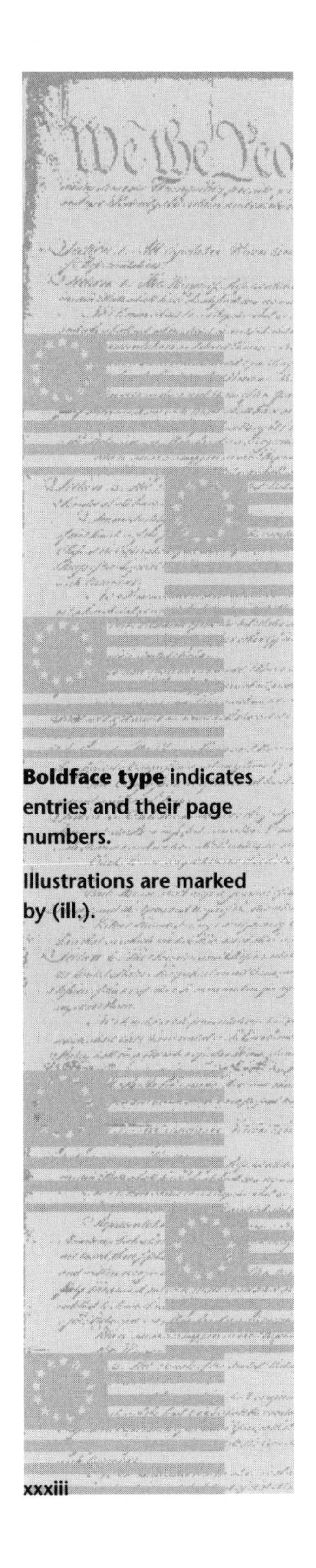
We the Peo
Boldface type indicates entries and their page numbers.
Illustrations are marked by (ill.).

B

C

D

E

F

G

H

I

M

N

O

P

Q

R

S

T

U

V

W

X

Y

Z

REFERENCE